NO HEROES, NO MONSTERS

ANNA ARDIN

NO HEROES, NO MONSTERS

What I Learned Being
the Most Hated Woman
on the Internet

www.bod.se
info@bod.se

© 2024 Anna Ardin
Coverphoto: Joel Nilsson
ISBN: 978-91-8057-611-6
Original title: Iskuggan av Assange, 2021

Förlag: BoD – Books on Demand, Stockholm, Sverige
Tryck: BoD – Books on Demand, Norderstedt, Tyskland

For the feminists, every single one of you

> **A wise woman wishes to be no one's enemy; a wise woman refuses to be anyone's victim.**
>
> Maya Angelou

I am one of the two women who, in 2010, told the police that Julian Assange had sexually assaulted us. WikiLeaks fans worldwide—certainly myself very much included—probably wish I'd had no reason to make my report, but I did. Of course, I didn't know the legal terminology for what had happened, but to me, it was an assault, and I will continue to call it that.

For his work with WikiLeaks, however, Julian Assange was accused of something else entirely: espionage. These accusations are unjust and have more to do with truth, transparency, and freedom of speech. On the other hand, the sexual assault accusations are not related to espionage or free speech but rather to his personal behavior. That behavior and the debate following the police report ultimately concern women's rights. Should popular and powerful men be allowed to behave however they want toward women or not?

These are two separate accusations that have nothing to do with each other. I am not accusing WikiLeaks of assault, and WikiLeaks' work is hardly furthered by allowing its representatives to behave however they please.

I was convinced that WikiLeaks was doing important work for peace and openness. That was why I worked to have Julian Assange come to Stockholm and speak, and that was why I let him stay in my apartment. He assaulted me in that context. Only a few days later, he spent the night at the place of another woman who later testified he did something similar to her. It was a coincidence that we happened to get in touch with each other, but I didn't want to leave her defenseless. So, I went with her to the police and gave a statement about how he had behaved toward me. It sounds dull, but that was the limited extent of my involvement in the case.

During these years, two tribunals have been held to settle the question of guilt and investigate the truth in our accusations of sexual offenses: one official legal tribunal via the police and the courts and another via discussion forums on the internet and in the press. This experience is precisely what this book is about—the official legal process Julian refused to participate in and the media frenzy Julian was active in, which I did everything I could to avoid for ten years.

I haven't had the least involvement in what the various prosecutors, defense attorneys, governments, and PR agencies have done. I have waited and listened. I cooperated when the police and prosecutors asked questions. I testified on a few occasions about the harassment that followed the report, but to avoid influencing the legal process, I have not spoken publicly for all these years about the actual events.

We will never know if Julian is legally an offender, but I can describe the events as I experienced them. Instead of testifying in the trial that never took place, I would like to tell my version here, like this. Perhaps this case will illustrate the dialogue we must all keep open about gray areas and assault. I am just one of the millions of women who have not been respected. This is a book about what it was like to be behind the headlines during a decade-long media frenzy and how the hate online affected me after reporting my experiences of an assault. This is an account without angels or monsters, where heroes can be villains and where truths may be hidden somewhere in the nuances between black and white.

My goal is to be completely honest and transparent with this book. I have double-checked my memories with the help of journal entries and other previously unpublished texts, as well as interviews, conversations with other people who were there, newspaper articles, and by searching various online forums. I have done my best to reproduce the sequence of events and their order correctly. At the same time, of course, it is a fact that most of this happened many years ago. What day a specific thing occurred or the wording of an exchange may not be exact, but it is as close as I can ever get. All of the quotes from anonymous trolls are authentic and illustrate the hatred and threats directed at me during various periods.

Still, these comments may have ended up under a different date in this book than on which they were initially written.

Thank you for reading.

Anna Ardin

2010

Tuesday, August 10, 2010

"The founder of WikiLeaks wants to come to Sweden. Do you want to invite him and arrange a seminar?"

This question comes from a journalist named Donald and is put to the Religious Social Democrats of Sweden, an organization that is both my job and fills my spare time. We have had several interactions with Donald thanks to our shared commitment to human rights in Palestine, but his connection to WikiLeaks is news to us.

WikiLeaks is an organization that contributed to two leaks that attracted a great deal of attention during the spring and summer. Collateral Murder was published in April. It is a shaky film from a military helicopter in which American soldiers film each other shooting at Iraqi civilians and kill 15 people, two of whom are Reuters reporters. At the end of July, WikiLeaks contributed to "Afghanistan Leaks," a large number of classified military documents about U.S. warfare in Afghanistan, released simultaneously in *The Guardian*, *The New York Times*, and other media outlets worldwide.

It is not a coincidence that Donald calls us specifically, asking whether we want to hold a seminar with WikiLeaks. After 80 years of agitating for peace, the Religious Social Democrats of Sweden have demonstrated and protested against the wars in Afghanistan and Iraq. They have been called the Brotherhood Movement, named after *Brotherhood*, a newspaper first published in 1927, and have worked for human dignity and respect of God's creation since then. Therefore, they are an obvious ally in work against war crimes.

The footage and documents that WikiLeaks leaked this year are even more unacceptable to us but have become substantial proof of the immorality of the U.S. during the war. Mercenary soldiers financed by the U.S. government have committed serious human rights abuses. The number of civilian casualties in Iraq is probably many times higher than reported, and espionage and kickbacks clearly play a crucial role in international diplomacy. These are problems that need to be brought to daylight to be solved and issues that are now being discussed broadly, thanks to WikiLeaks.

But these things are essential not only to the Religious Social Democrats but also to me personally. I am pro-liberty and a Social Democrat. I dislike the authorities and hate imperialism and wars of aggression. I condemn jailing people for their political views and not giving dissidents fair trials. I abhor that the West clothes its plundering wars regarding development, fighting terrorism, and promoting women's rights—even though the effects sooner increase terrorism and set women's rights back. And in all of this, equitable peace in the Middle East has felt particularly important since recently seeing, in person and with my own eyes, the misery and hopelessness inside the world's largest outdoor prison, the utterly bombed-out Gaza. WikiLeaks seems to stand for the same things and wants to expose the abuses of power that underlie the wars in Afghanistan and Iraq, regardless of the terms they are couched in.

However, I've never heard of Julian Assange, and I don't understand what it means to be the founder of

WikiLeaks. For example, where's the secretary-general, the director, or the chairperson? But regardless, it's evidently something cool. The footage from the Apache helicopter is enough of an argument.

My boss says yes to Donald's query, and we decide to call the seminar "The Truth Is the First Casualty of War," as British women's suffrage activist Ethel Annakin Snowden memorably put it in 1915 when she criticized the use of women's rights to argue for war during World War I.[1] Waging war requires lies—mythmaking and propaganda about the enemy being different, an eviler sort of people who threaten us—and the censorship of information regarding the war's actual consequences. The truth is rarely simple, obvious, or absolute, but striving for it is always a precondition for peace and justice.

I arrange Julian Assange's trip from London to Stockholm with the help of Donald, our organization's chairperson Peter, the president of our youth wing, Victor, and a Swedish-Israeli journalist, Johannes, WikiLeaks' contact person in England. I also arrange for us to borrow the Swedish Trade Union Confederation Hall for the seminar, send out the press release, and invite people. Everything happens very quickly. Both time and financial resources are tight.

Assange's plane ticket costs more than we can afford, but we decide it is worth prioritizing this. The visit will draw attention to issues of international solidarity, ending the war, and possibly placing all the troops in Afghanistan under UN command. Among the more knowledgeable people in our circles—peace activists and people who work for truth and transparency—many are familiar with WikiLeaks and view it as a symbol of righteous resistance.

We also find out that WikiLeaks is interested in starting the publication of an online newspaper in Swedish in order to benefit from Sweden's strong protections for freedom of expression and freedom of the press. So, we begin discussing the options for supporting WikiLeaks as it establishes itself in Sweden as an organization and publication.

The seminar we are arranging is scheduled for the morning of August 14. Julian Assange will arrive on Thursday, August 12, and we are responsible for his accommodations for two nights in connection with the seminar, i.e., August 12 and 13. He would prefer not to stay at a hotel, he informs us, but rather live as secretly as possible. Since I will be away working at a festival those nights anyway, I offer to loan out my studio apartment in central Stockholm. The price is right for our financially strained organization, and it will be secret—the way Julian wants it—while also giving me some status. I will get to be in the thick of things and know the people being discussed. It will be a status marker more valuable in my circles than earning a large salary, owning an environmentally friendly car, or any of the other usual indicators.

Wednesday, August 11, 2010

There is an enormous amount of interest in the seminar. In the press release, we write that journalists have priority, but so many journalists sign up there's almost no room for anyone else. I need to turn away hundreds of people.

Maria, a young woman who reads about the seminar on Twitter, gets in touch. In her message, she writes she can volunteer and help with whatever might be needed if it means she can attend. Her help feels very welcome amid the stress of organizing everything. I reply that we don't currently have any volunteer assignments, but something might suddenly come up. If she can be there well in advance and stand by just in case, then she is welcome to attend.

Thursday, August 12, 2010

A Christian youth festival called Free Zone (Swedish *Frizon*) is being held in Kumla, a couple of hours west of Stockholm, which I am attending as a representative of the Young Christian Left (*Ung kristen vänster*). I staff our information tent along with a few other people. We talk to young people interested in international solidarity, religious freedom, how all people are equally valuable, and caring for all creation. In a talk on stage about Christianity, politics, faith and solidarity, Christian anarchists rebuke me for not being radical enough. But out among the festival attendees, we're also forced to debate teenage Creationists (who say things like "you may have monkeys in your family, but I don't"), opponents of abortion, and people triggered by our very presence there—primarily because the Christian Social Democrats, in particular, were instrumental in convincing the Church of Sweden to allow same-sex marriages just over a year earlier. But worst of all, I meet young people who seem to have been trained to divide the world between them and us, using religion as an argument.

While we're there, the WikiLeaks spokesperson picks up an envelope with the key to my apartment, which I had left at a local shop on the intersection between Götgatan and Blekingegatan in Stockholm.

Friday, August 13, 2010

I was supposed to stay in Kumla until Saturday morning and then go directly to the Swedish Trade Union Confederation's LO Castle building, where the seminar was going to be held. But the pressure leading up to the seminar, both from people who want to attend and journalists who wish to write about it, is so great that everything that needs to be looked after can't be done remotely. I am needed in Stockholm and feel like I've had my fill of homophobic Christian Rights people who lack solidarity.

I contact Donald and receive confirmation that Julian Assange thinks sharing my apartment is totally fine. So, I meet Julian for the first time at the door to my apartment.

"I've been looking through your underwear drawer," he says, holding up a bra. "I saw the size of this and thought, *she's someone I'd like to meet.*"

He seems partly serious, and I don't know how to respond. It's quiet for a second. It feels uncomfortable. Then I laugh it off.

We decide to go out to eat at a small, local restaurant near my apartment. "They're watching me," Julian says.

"Hmm," I reply.

"They're watching me," he repeats with a lowered voice.

Four floors down on the other side of the building, cars are parked on both sides of the street. Julian walks around to look in the windows but doesn't see anyone inside. None of the cars have tinted windows. None of the cars looks suspicious. He looks for a little longer. I stand there watching him. It's hard to decide whether he's serious or kidding, but at any rate, he feels ready to proceed after a while, and we continue walking.

It's a pleasant evening on Blekingegatan, the street Greta Garbo lived on as a child. We get Thai food and mineral water, and Julian monitors the flow on Twitter so intently that he doesn't even hear the waitress when she tries to ask him if he wants more rice. He reads aloud from a British tabloid article about his hair and mentions with joy and pride that the paparazzi chased him in England. But here in Stockholm, no one seems to have recognized him yet, and those parked cars sit there, perfidiously empty of observers. It strikes me several times that he seems like a person who needs someone to take care of him.

It is fun to chat with him. He seems bright and friendly. We have many similar values and a structural analysis based on the same goal of human liberation. I don't need to explain why I think equality is important or have all the arguments about the inherent value of a peaceful world. We agree with and build on each other's views, as I do with my best friends, even though we have only spent a couple of hours with each other. We look at human rights issues in the same way, but feminism and equal rights for women seem to be an exception to this for him.

"But that's a very strange inconsistency, Julian," I say.

He laughs apologetically and responds, "The feminists caused the war in Afghanistan."

I laugh. There is no reasonable way that the man who, literally speaking, epitomizes the helicopter perspective on global politics right now can be so stupid that he seriously believes women's rights caused the most recent in a series of the great powers' abuses against Afghanistan, merely because it fits his purposes to get Western opinion on his side. But with a smile, he insists that feminism and demands for gender equality bear responsibility for the war. I continue laughing and decide to believe he is joking. I don't know how else to deal with him.

The waitress is still waiting to hear if he wants more rice. I take him by the shoulder and give him a little shake as if to try to wake him up, and he responds that yes, he would like more rice.

After dinner, we walk back to my place and continue our discussion of global politics and the next day's seminar. I have a mattress under my bed, which I get out for him to sleep on.

I have made my own bed and set out sheets for Julian's mattress, but it's as if he does not understand that he should make it himself. He just looks neutrally from me to the sheets.

When I hand him a teacup, he suddenly caresses my hand with his thumb. I am a little surprised and think, *oh, where did that come from?* It was like a bolt out of the blue since we hadn't flirted at all during the evening. I pretend not to notice it and go out into the kitchen, where I stand for a moment. The realization sinks in that Julian Assange wants to make out.

I think about Andreas' acidic comment when he discovered that the WikiLeaks founder would stay in my apartment.

"Oh, so you're going to score with Assange?"

"No," I replied. "I'm not going be staying there."

Andreas and I became a couple many years ago when I moved to Uppsala to study, and only six months later, we took a trip to Cuba together. At a market in Madrid, during a layover, we bought rings that cost seven euros and got engaged.

He had just started studying for his Ph.D. in data communications, and we called ourselves each other's "orange halves" from the Spanish for soul mates. We fought all our political battles together, arranged big parties, had the same friends, and loved each other very intensely. We were convinced that the constant stress, which made him irritable and preoccupied, would disappear once he had finished his dreadful dissertation. And with that, all our problems as a couple would go away.

But nothing improved after he defended his dissertation. He began a management job for an organization and became even more stressed and distracted. We postponed our plans to have kids from as soon as we finished our studies to some unspecified time in the future. When I hugged him, he stood with his arms straight down until I asked him to hug me back. He accepted my love but gave me almost nothing in return. Despite this, we remained a couple; I couldn't imagine anything else.

He needed an assistant, he said. He couldn't keep up with all his administrative tasks, and his receipts were in utter chaos. I asked around among my friends for tips and found a woman who seemed great. She started working, and they got along well.

Six months later, we were sitting in his little studio apartment on Kungsholmen, and he handed me a letter. He sat across from me while I read it. He wrote that he couldn't say what he wanted to express. My heart was pounding so loudly it was interfering with my thoughts, my pulse racing and throbbing in my temples because I had a feeling about what I was going to read. He had started a new relationship with the woman we had recruited together.

We continued to hold onto the tatters of our relationship for over a year. He wanted to cultivate his other relationship and hold onto me at the same time. And there I was, humiliated, off in one corner of the boxing ring of his life. He broke up with me several times, but he came back crying after each and said that this time, it would all be different. Despite all this, he continually settled on wanting me to accept his wishes for an "open relationship".

It hurt so much, like being stabbed in the heart. Sometimes I haven't been able to get out of bed. Whole nights have been spent in sleepless tears. But the most serious consequence of my relationship with Andreas may have been the destructive relationship I developed with myself.

After talking to a couple's counselor, I finally ended the relationship, and I have officially been single since the spring, although we still see each other.

Before and after I broke up with him, I dated many very fine men. Some I dumped brutally and immediately, and others I clung to or pushed away. Some I was downright mean to. And my heart has remained with Andreas the whole time.

One of the many ways I used to numb the pain and cope with the breakup was translating "7 Steps to Legal Revenge,"[2] which I had found on a message board earlier in the year, into Swedish. I placed a link to it on my blog, and Andreas was hurt. He resented my even thinking about revenge at all.

After living in various sublet and sub-sublet apartments with short contracts and big water leaks, I finally bought my first little apartment all of my own on Tjurbergsgatan in Stockholm's Södermalm neighborhood, and that's where I'm living now. It is here I stand on the balcony, looking out over the inner courtyard and the windows of my 200 neighbors. I'm still not feeling great, but I'm on the mend. It might be a pretty fun thing—and no big deal—to "score with Julian Assange."

A semi-famous Australian. A jealous ex-fiancé vaguely impressed by celebrities.

So why not? I think.

Everyone I have talked to about the seminar over the last few days seems to agree about how exciting it is that the WikiLeaks founder is staying at my place. A few days ago, a crowd of fans stood screaming as if at a rock concert when Julian spoke. Their screaming reinforced Julian's image of a person considered so cool in certain circles that you yourself become cool simply by having a mask with his face on it in front of your own. If that's what they think, then he must really be cool.

During my long on-again-off-again period with Andreas, my selection criteria for whom I'll make out with has grown lax. It's been fun, too, and has worked out well many times.

So, you're going to score with Julian Assange, Andreas says again in my head.

Yeah, maybe, I think.

Then I walk back into the room and over to Julian, where we make out a little and chat. He falls asleep in his clothes on my short, uncomfortable sofa. He's completely exhausted, and I think it's cute that he can sleep just like that. I take a picture with my phone. *The great Assange sleeping like a kid on my little sofa*, I think, and upload that restful prelude to tomorrow's seminar onto Facebook. I instantly receive many likes and impressed comments in my feed from relatives and childhood friends as well as coworkers and even a gender studies researcher.

"You should be president or something," the researcher writes.

It's kind of nice that he fell asleep, and that we decided not to make out anymore. I change into my nightgown, brush my teeth, and am just about to go to bed. But when I turn off the overhead light, Julian wakes up. He strokes the outside of my thigh, stands up, kisses me, and pulls up my nightgown. I'm not willing and don't like it, so I try to pull the nightgown down instead. He tugs several times, harder and harder. The seams start creaking as though they'll tear. He starts pulling my panties off, too. Then, to keep the clothes from ripping, I let him take everything off. I don't want to spoil the mood.

It feels bad. It's going too fast. It feels like I started something I shouldn't and can't stop it. The most unpleasant thing of all is that I notice the change in the way he's treating me. He stops chatting with me. He stops listening to my body language and what I'm saying. I no longer feel like the political and intellectual equal I was just moments ago. It's as if he's swapped out my whole raison d'être. I get a very strong sense that he thinks I owe him something he has already paid for. It's as though since I agreed to A, I have therefore renounced my right to stop B.

If I were permitted complete freedom to choose, I would cut this short and go to bed now. But I don't feel free. I feel I'm facing a clear demand to continue. It feels bad, but not bad enough to make a fuss, not bad enough to risk anything worse.

We lie on the bed, him on top and me underneath. It's pleasant for a while.

We roll around, and when he takes off his pants, I notice a distinct smell—sperm. Evidently, he hasn't showered off some old bodily fluids. From there, my discomfort escalates. He holds my arms over my head and presses his shoulder hard against my throat. I'm forced to gather all my strength to press my chin toward my chest to get air and make sure my voice box isn't injured. I try to move and twist around, but he pushes his shoulder so hard into my throat that my silver necklace bites into my skin.

He's holding my arms at the wrists, his chest lies heavily over mine, and he's using one knee to try and push mine apart. I can't concentrate on anything other than getting air against the pressure on my throat, making me passive. I think that is his intention.

With my arms pinned over my head and my nightgown having been torn off, I understand very well what's expected of me and what I've agreed to by not speaking up, not articulating the words, and not using the feminist self-defense I had learned. Because while I want to stop, I don't want to be weird or difficult. I don't want to dramatize the situation or exaggerate the fact that I no longer feel like it.

Men usually pick up on these kinds of things, anyway. They understand if I don't want to and will lie down; I'll get a hug, and we'll go to sleep. Maybe we'll pick up where we left off another day when it feels like more fun. That's what my experiences with these types of situations have looked like. Julian doesn't react that way at all. It's more like he's demanding his right and demanding I should continue. Oddly enough, inside, I feel the same thing he is signaling, that I've promised him something and have set out on a path leading in this direction. I've bought the tickets, and now it's time to ride.

Even though I'd rather stop, I accept continuing but on one condition, which is absolute—protection. For a long time, Julian tries wordlessly to negotiate his way out of this.

He tries to hold onto me by force so he can proceed without a condom, and I resist, trying to shift my lower body away. Julian doesn't make the least effort to let go or ask what I want. He keeps pressing.

When I move, he moves after me; when I repeatedly pinch my legs together, and he stops me as I reach for the nightstand, it's clear I don't count. It's like a wrestling match without an audience or referee where I'm at a total disadvantage. To him, I'm probably not even there anymore. It is only my body—my forcibly undressed body—that is there. Repressed sobs build behind the lump in my throat. I feel on the verge of tears and completely powerless.

I pull as much as I can to get my arms free and curl into a fetal position beneath him. This way, I succeed in locking my legs to the side so that he can't push them apart.

This is when I scream. Not literally, but when I realize I'm not going to be able to win with physical strength, I do something that feels just like screaming. I break the silence.

"What are you doing?" I say.

"*What are* YOU *doing*," he snaps angrily as if accusing me.

"Why are you holding me down? I want to use a condom," I tell him. He releases me and lets me move.

According to the "rules" for what's considered to be a "real assault," I shouldn't compromise here. I should say no. I should say no, no, no. I should say that word, the only thing that counts. I should scream so loudly the neighbors can testify. I should try to get up and run out of the apartment. I should, in other words, humiliate myself in front of my neighbors and be held responsible for my mistake of letting it go this far. I should leave him with his rage and horniness—if he'll even let me leave the room—run out, call the police, and ask them to arrest him. Or I should take the chance that a "no" gets him to let go of me, then pack his bag and throw him out here and now.

But the coldness in his eyes, our shared knowledge that he's stronger than me, my experience of his completely ignoring what I want, and my being convinced he's planning to have sex with me no matter what I say makes me assess the situation differently to how I will assess it later during rational reconstructions of the event. What settles it, maybe more than anything else, is the thought I should not make a scene. The feeling is driven by the primaevally strong norm to not exaggerate.

If I say the word "no" now, it will very likely be effective. A no is potentially as definitive as kicking him between the legs and screaming for the neighbors. That is precisely why I do not say it. It would be an overreaction; surely, it will be better now. I see myself as a reasonable person, not a drama queen.

So, I give him the condom and wait for him to put it on. But he doesn't do it. He holds the condom in his hand and tries to proceed without it. I think, *He has to give in now anyway; it's impossible to misunderstand what I want.* It's clear enough to give someone a condom and sit and wait without it needing anything to be said. Although a small act of resistance, I still think it's too much. I remind him.

Finally, he puts it on, and I end up underneath him again. He's not holding my arms anymore but instead lying with his full weight on my chest. He enters me and presses down so hard against my neck that I feel like I'm suffocating. I'm still trapped beneath him but struggle so I can get my chin between us and push him up a little bit, away from my throat. My struggle to find ways out continues, but less intensely. I try to gain control of the situation and cool it down a little, to resist, close my eyes, and convince myself that it's OK or could be OK. One strategy I try is attempting to enjoy it.

Maybe that's what allows me to pull free. He releases the pressure from my chest and neck, and I can finally get some proper air and take a deep breath. He gives me permission to move around so that I'm on top and, for a second, I have a sense of control.

Again and again, though, he enforces that *he* makes the decisions and that *he* is stronger than me. He does this by holding onto me a little too long or grabbing parts of my body roughly. He doesn't use force; he indicates it. All possible compromises seem to be based on my acceptance and continuance. *If I make a fuss*, I think, *then there probably won't be any compromise.* That's how I understand it. So, I try to avoid making too much fuss.

Julian has his shirt on. It seemed important to him that I should be naked as quickly as possible but that he should wear as much clothing as he could. That difference—me naked, he dressed—makes me think he doesn't consider it worth undressing. There's no trace of tenderness, no desire for more bodily contact than necessary.

I want to take off his shirt, not because I want more bodily contact, but to show I'm an active participant, that I'm not just an object he can use. Julian doesn't want to take it off. This is foggy, but I think I get it off him in the end.

Being active, trying to take control, and even succeeding in gaining control, diminishes my degradation. Maybe I'm legitimizing his behavior, but in this situation, it's a way of saving myself. I even succeed in having a micro-orgasm, which makes us a little more equal; it's more reciprocal and less of an assault and power display.

Then he's pressing down on my neck again. I feel like I'm suffocating, and his lack of care and total self-focus frustrates me.

After a little while, he firmly grips my hands again, but only with one, and suddenly pulls out. Simultaneously, I hear a clear snapping sound, like a balloon popping, and I'm convinced he has taken off the condom, considering his resistance to wearing one. I manage to get one hand free and feel to check. No, it's still on.

That I was able to get him to use a condom and keep it on is an enormous relief. The feeling I have can be described as a worm that has escaped from a hook. I push my anxiety about the sound aside, and I let him continue, even though my body is still trapped.

After maybe fifteen minutes, he's done.

He does something odd after his orgasm; he attempts to make me come. The gesture is confusing after the last thirty minutes of cold indifference.

Again and again, I have wondered how to describe the assault and my own actions. I know many people expect a black-or-white truth. To accept what happened and call it an assault, people expect a monster to have violated an angel. But how do I avoid pleasing them? How do I avoid the stereotype of the monster to get closer to the leaden, gray truth? How do I avoid making myself look better than I am, and how do I deal with the inconsistencies in my actions? In real assault stories, there's almost never a monster violating an angel but rather one human being violating another.

Reviews of this book from Julian's network of supporters will upgrade an orgasm or two into watertight evidence that no assault took place. All of the victim's human inconsistencies become ammunition for those who want to prove a sex offender is innocent. Victims of crime know this. But the truth is often right there, in what is perhaps more human than inconsistent, in the gray areas.

There's a big wet spot on the bed. "What's this?" I ask.

How could his semen have gotten into me and then run out? "You were very wet," he replies.

"No, Julian. I wasn't," I say.

Because I really wasn't. It's obvious that it's from him; that snapping sound was the condom breaking. This is pretty important since a broken condom does not serve any purpose against disease or unwanted pregnancy. But he says nothing about the condom breaking, pretending nothing happened. His right thumbnail is long and sharp, and his lie, *you were wet*, puts a heavy lid on my question.

We say no more about it.

I don't know the word yet, but what Julian is doing is gaslighting me, a form of manipulation in which information is distorted, misrepresented, or omitted, or where information is presented with the aim of making the victim doubt their own memories, their own experience of reality, and their own mental health. It's appallingly effective.

He says something that both he and I know isn't true at all, but through a sort of mutual theater in which we both pretend we believe the illusion; reality then starts to blend with his conscious—and to me, obvious—lie. After a little while, I'm unsure where the line is between truth and lie.

I find my broken necklace next to me on the bed and set it on the nightstand. Then, I go to sleep.

Saturday, August 14, 2010

When I wake up in the morning, I find the empty condom on the floor and throw it in the trash.

I write a short note to Julian.

> *Hi Julian, it wasn't pleasant at all for me to sleep with you, so you and I won't be doing that again, but I want to give you a checklist with a few suggestions for the sake of your future partners:*

—Don't break people's necklaces.
—Don't press your shoulder against their throats so that they almost suffocate.
—Don't ejaculate inside people if they don't want that.
—Shower.

I set the note in a folder he uses to gather notes from fans, records of various scholarships and donations he's received, and groupies' phone numbers. If he sits down and checks it, he'll find the note from me too. I feel like I've faced the conflict but also escaped it by defending myself this way.

When Julian wakes up, we both act as if nothing has happened. His WikiLeaks coworker Johannes, whom I arranged Julian's travel with, is going to pick him up in a taxi. Julian thinks I should go with them, but I leave alone and take the metro.

We set things up and try to connect Julian's computer to the projector in the LO Castle building. We need an adapter, so when Maria, the volunteer, arrives, we immediately send her to buy the necessary cord.

Journalists pour in, take their seats, and Julian gives his presentation about WikiLeaks and the importance of truth and transparency in putting a stop to war crimes. I have a long list of journalists in line for interviews afterward. The seminar resembles a press conference rather than a public lecture.

One of the few non-journalists at the seminar is a young woman representing Sweden's Pirate Party.

"Can I have your autograph?" she says to Julian when she manages to push her way to the front after the presentation.

"No," he says. "I don't give autographs as a matter of principle." "But you don't understand," she replies. "You're my Brad Pitt!" They talk for a while, but a moment later, she's gone from the hall.

"Damn," Julian says to me. "I should have gotten her phone number."

The first interviews take place indoors with public television, radio, and evening news programs. Afterward, we need to leave the hall and move outside into the sun. I keep track of the time on a bench by a statue of August Palm. The journalists ask questions, and Julian answers patiently.

For some reason, he wants to sit right in the broiling sun. It's roasting, and the heat makes his TV makeup run. Sweat mixed with makeup drips down onto his clothes, and his shirt grows wet, as each newspaper, magazine, and channel get its promised minutes.

While Julian is busy with interviews, I chat with Maria and the journalists who are waiting.

"Look at his finger," I say to Maria. "Do you see that engagement ring he's spinning?" Julian found my ring from my broken engagement with Andreas at my place and, without asking, has brought it along and put it on. He makes a show of twisting the ring around in front of the journalists. I say that he probably wants to start some sort of speculation. I smile as I speak, but it does not feel OK at all.

The papers *Arbetaren* (*The Worker*) and *Computer Sweden* are the last two to get to ask questions.

"I should have gotten her number," he says again as the stream of questions subsides. He's referring to the young Pirate Party representative. Then, he repeats her declaration that he has entered the Brad Pitt league of sexiness.

I have never met Brad and don't want to contribute to creating new myths; however, I find it extremely difficult to see the similarities between him and the man sitting here with his unbrushed teeth and goopy TV makeup pretending to be engaged. I ask for my ring back and get it, feeling a little unwell in the heat.

It's afternoon, and everyone is hungry. My organization invites its staff and participants to lunch at Bistro Bohème on Drottninggatan. Maria is invited by our chairman Peter as a thank you for her assistance in getting the cord; she ends up sitting next to Julian at the table. They flirt. He feeds her crisp bread, and they seem to like each other.

"What are you doing this afternoon, Julian?" I ask.

"I don't really know," he replies.

"I can take you to a museum," Maria says. They leave together after lunch.

Nice for him, I think. It feels good not to need to be responsible for him. Instead, I have time to arrange a crayfish party at Donald's request. He reports that Julian has heard of this Swedish August phenomenon and is eager to try it.

I search through my event invitations and ask around. When I don't find a pre-planned crayfish party he can attend, I instead buy crayfish and invite a few people over to my place for a potluck party.

Julian has slept in my apartment for two nights now, which is what we agreed on from the beginning, but he still has not moved out. I don't want him here. During the day, I get in touch with a friend in the Pirate Party who finds a couple willing to host him. The couple can't or don't want to come to the party, but they live nearby and promise to pick Julian up later.

On my way home, I spot a person I recognize from the seminar at the subway station and say hi. We start talking and I invite him to the crayfish party. He doesn't have time to come tonight but says he can help me get some Schnapps for the party. He's cute in an innocent way and smiles the whole time. I feel like there's an amorous look in his eyes when he looks at me. I go with him to his apartment to get the Schnapps, and he says we should get together sometime. *Absolutely*, I say, *that would be fun!*

One of my closest friends, Petra, comes over to my place to help. We met for the first time in the Uppsala student union, where she, just like me, was working on gender equality issues. She's currently working on a Ph.D. in statistics and has represented Sweden in international chess competitions. I usually describe Petra as the only genius I know. She's also an extremely sharp feminist analyst.

"It was awful. Actually, the worst lay ever," I say.

My own voice sounds skeptical and bewildered as I tell her what happened the previous night. I realize that the snapping sound wasn't the condom breaking but rather *being* broken. Even though he only used one hand, he broke it quickly and skillfully, as if he had done it many times before.

"He broke the condom on purpose?" I say as if I don't believe it myself.

"What? Super weird," Petra says. "Why would he do that?"

I have no answer to that. Even though it happened and I heard the sound when it broke—a second before I felt him enter me—he managed to make me believe it didn't happen. If there's no answer to why someone would do that, then it's illogical to think it happened. I'm forced to choose between logic and fact. The story fits together better if I choose to ignore reality. It's a paradox I cannot resolve.

Saturday, August 14, 2010, Evening

Evening arrives. It's a beautiful and warm Swedish late summer evening. My friends, Julian's friends, and I have drinks in the kitchen. Julian doesn't show up at seven, as we had said. Nor at eight. He doesn't come until just after nine. There are crayfish left, and the party continues in the lovely outdoor common space owned by HSB, the cooperative housing association.

Julian is a terrific person in many ways. Incredibly quick-thinking, funny, with a knack for constantly coming up with unexpected angles. The party attendees volley banter back and forth like table tennis balls over a net, and we laugh a lot. It's the type of environment where I'm at my happiest.

The Julian who attends the crayfish party is a completely different one than the Julian who humiliated and used me the night before—I decide not to see the horrible Julian anymore, just the nice one. And it appears as though I can make that choice. In the conversation tonight, I am once again an equal, someone worth listening and responding to.

I write on Twitter about how wonderful it is to hang out with some of the smartest and most fun people—people like Kajsa and Johannes, whom I talk to most.

How warm the weather is and how light the evening is. How privileged I am.

I have marks on my neck from the snapped necklace, a nagging worry about HIV, a broken heart, and the desire to show an ex I'm going to be fine without him. But I don't display that openly. Just as all people do, I choose to show a portion of myself and my feelings, a portion of the truth, not its whole. The entirety wouldn't fit into Twitter's 140 characters. There's rarely room in the light for the entirety with all its nuances.

Since Julian was so late, he has only been here for an hour or two before the couple from the Pirate Party come to pick him up. He ignores them while they sit there dutifully, obviously uncomfortable. It's starting to get late when Julian whispers he's not planning on going with them.

"Maybe Julian can follow along later if you go on

ahead," I suggest.

"Sure," they say.

"No! Look at them," Julian whispers to me. He thinks they're boring and lame.

He makes it clear that he won't go with them without causing a scene and that he's not planning on going there later, either. But at the same time, he understands that I don't want him to stay with me, so he tries to find another place. Among other things, he tries to accompany my friend Kajsa home. He tries asking straight out, but I have told her what happened yesterday, both about the ruined condom and how he held me. Kajsa has taken my warning seriously, sidesteps the question, and slips away from the party instead. As the conversation around the table continues, Julian instead tries to get ahold of a personal contact.

"Ah, the woman from the seminar," I say. But Julian smiles secretively and refuses to confirm.

"Whatever," I laugh.

During questioning, I later say that I'm relieved he wants to leave, but at the same time, I'm worried for the girl's sake. I want to warn her somehow, but I don't really know what for. It also feels impossible to do that without it being interpreted as my being jealous that Julian, the star, has chosen a new place to stay. Instead, I try to help him find transportation to Enköping, where he says he wants to go. The last busses and trains seem to have already left for the night, and Johannes is very clear that he does not want to bring Julian home with him.

Julian hasn't packed. He doesn't want to give back

my key and seems to take it for granted that my home is his home. After everything that's happened—not least how he treated the friendly Pirate Party folks who tried to offer him their guest room—I'm on the verge of just going upstairs and packing his bag for him. The others will back me up if I demand my key back. However, it feels even more embarrassing to make a fuss now.

How do I explain that it was OK that he stayed with me one night when I was also there but that it has become important today that he leaves? I don't want to risk being questioned about what happened; it's too hard to answer without risking entanglement. I feel ashamed.

Shame is perhaps the most social of emotions. Regardless of who or what gave rise to it, it floats around in search of a host. Once it attaches to its host, shame becomes like an autoimmune disease and breaks the resistance of anyone too attentive to society and its norms.

And so, I absorb the shame that Julian should feel. I cover the whole thing up and decide that it's OK. He has behaved well tonight, and it has felt like reparations for being treated as an equal and friend. So, I cover for him: I contact the couple who offered him a place to sleep, thank them on Julian's behalf, and make excuses for why he can't come. He can stay with me. He's created a situation where the only responsible thing to do is what he wants. Once again, I take on this responsibility.

I liked Julian at dinner yesterday and when we went back to my place, and he was lying there cutely on my sofa. I liked him at the seminar today and tonight at the crayfish party. But in bed yesterday, I could have been a doll or an animal; I could've looked like anything and been anything. I could have participated—better, maybe, simpler for him—but the point is that it didn't matter. He switched on his program and did his thing. I was disconnected. He had his objective, and I was the means. Maybe I could have put a few sticks in the wheel, a few obstacles in the way, but he was going to go where he wanted to go. And wherever he wanted to go, I had to go along.

Tonight, I think, *I'm not going to permit him to switch on his program.* I think I have figured out what I need to do to avoid that.

When we go to bed to sleep, I'm wearing a nightgown, and he's wearing his clothing and TV makeup. Julian wants to be in the bed, despite the mattress I made up on the floor for him. We're tired and drunk, and I accept him lying where he wants. I even ask him to spoon me. In a way, this behavior is completely wrong. There's an obvious risk of him misunderstanding the signals or, once again, transgressing my limits. However, at the same time, I feel like *I'm* using *him* if anything. I don't want to have sex, I want to have closeness, and I pretend that Julian is Andreas. It's fine; Julian doesn't say or do anything stupid.

Sunday, August 15, 2010

Julian has a meeting with Donald and Johannes, and they decide to meet at my place. I make lunch. It's nice, like we're at a restaurant or at Julian's house and I'm the staff. The guests thank both Julian and me and then become engrossed in important conversations. They leave the dirty dishes on the table.

I decide that I'm now doing this out of duty. It isn't Anna the private citizen who cleans, washes the dishes, airs the place out, and makes coffee, but rather the official one. Julian doesn't notice what I do; he just takes it for granted. My home is his free hotel, his assisted living facility. But I also exploit the fact he is here. So, when a journalist for my movement's paper, now called *Tro & Politik* (*Faith & Politics*), sends a few questions, I put them to Julian. He sits on the sofa, and I lie in bed and interview him. Julian says his last name is Korean, Ah Sang. Yesterday he said it was French. He explains WikiLeaks and discusses risks and projects. I take the opportunity to ask a few extra questions, but he does not want to answer how many children he has.

"I've heard it's four."

"Who said that?"

I don't respond but instead read an email some girl has sent: "Hi, I've heard that you're in touch with Julian Assange; tell him that he's the most beautiful man there is and that he looks like an elf in *The Lord of the Rings*."

"Ask her to send a photo," Julian replies.

Then, he asks me when I'm supposed to get my period. I respond that I don't know.

Later he is going to dinner with the head of the Pirate Party to talk about some servers.

Neither Donald nor Johannes can go with him, so Donald asks whether I can go as a representative of WikiLeaks in Sweden to show him the way and help with press contacts. *Cool*, I think.

I've already hinted at it, but a while before we leave my apartment, I ask, "You're still wearing your TV makeup, and you smell. Aren't you going to take a shower before we go?"

"No, I don't need to," he replies.

The restaurant in Stockholm's old town, Gamla Stan, is only a few kilometers from my place in Södermalm, so we decide to walk.

I was hardly the only one who had never heard of Julian Assange a week ago. Collateral Murder has, of course, hit the western world like a bomb, and during the summer, WikiLeaks became famous. But up to this point, WikiLeaks has been an organization, not a person. Thanks to yesterday's seminar, however, Julian has been on TV and in all the papers. We walk along Götgatan and around Slussen, a place with a high concentration of people interested in international and political news. On the way to dinner, we run into strangers who pat him on the back and say, "You should get the Nobel Peace Prize," and send appreciative glances in our direction. We run into a friend of mine who gasps in admiration—at least, that's my interpretation of it. All the cries of "keep up the good work" are directed at me as well. An incredible, positive mood surrounds him. Someone makes the same mistake that many people I've been in

[34] Compare with Schyman, 2002
[35] Kjöller, 2011
[36] Domscheit-Berg, 2011
[37] Agenda, 2011
[38] Kolmisoppi, 2012
[39] Gibney, 2013
[40] Bennett, 2010.
[41] O'Hagan, 2014
[42] The site is now shut down, and the content has been erased.
[43] Polisen.se, 2020
[44] Jonasson, 2010
[45] Nilsson, 2010
[46] SKL, 2010
[47] Michael & Satter, 2016
[48] Pink & Forward, 2019
[49] A reference to the Islamic State, daesh.
[50] Ny, 2017
[51] Wennstam, 2004
[52] Wennstam, 2004
[53] Jeffner, 1998
[54] Hattenstone, 2017
[55] Poitras, 2017
[56] Satter, 2018
[57] TT, 2019
[58] Freeman, 2019
[59] Sverker, 2010
[60] X & Haley, 2002
[61] Pettersson, 2010
[62] Stewart et al., 2019
[63] Domscheit-Berg, 2011
[64] Shakespeare, 1806
[65] Cantwell, 2019
[66] Rönngren, 2020
[67] Ardin, 2011, January 5.
[68] Davoise, 2019

Notes

[1] P1, Swedish Radio, 2020
[2] An anonymous contribution at the site eHow.com (The original post has since been removed.)
[3] Ardin, 2010, August 20
[4] Karlsten, 2010
[5] Balksjö, 2010
[6] Magnusson, 2010
[7] Ölander, 2010
[8] Ardin, 2010, September 6
[9] Guillou, 2011
[10] Brown, 2010
[11] Original Huffington Post version is unavailable. Exact wording may differ.
[12] Vargese, 2010. This post quotes Wolf's original article that was later changed.
[13] Wolf, 2010
[14] This page has since been deleted
[15] Koljonen, 2010
[16] Bennett, 2010
[17] Somaiya & Burns, 2010
[18] Bennett, 2010
[19] Lindberg, 2010
[20] Amnesty, 2008
[21] Ardin, 2011, Januari 5
[22] Pilkington, 2011
[23] Ardin, 2011, January 25
[24] Schultz, 2011
[25] Swedish Criminal Code, chapter six, first paragraph.
[26] Schultz, 2011
[27] Quinn, 2011
[28] Jonasson, 2010; Nilsson, 2010; SKL, 2010
[29] Guillou, 2011
[30] Guillou, 2011
[31] SVT, 2010
[32] Dagens Nyheter, 2010
[33] Dagens Nyheter, 2010

Anna Ardin's book is very important because she courageously shows the gray spectrum of violence and the extent to which the invisibility of this form of violence can harm the victims and the common human values at the same time.

Our MeToo movement has also experienced how a narrative violence causes great harm to women who speaks up against abuse. Since much of sexual violence is committed by men with social prestige from leading circles of the society, the victims of these criminals are once again abused - by mental manipulation saying that perpetrators can only belong to the colonial and the right-wing. The intellectual left-wing man who has access to analysis tools thus becomes so supported and powerful that even some feminist movements cannot resist.

For MeToo in Iran, Anna describes something important, that has been suppressed in Iran's freedom movement, and this suppression continues to this day.

#MeToo Iran

Anna Ardin, like so many women who defend themselves against assaults by influential men, is turned from victim to abuser. Anna Ardin writes a plea for women's rights and encourages them not to give up. With No Heroes, No Monsters, she gives voice not only to herself, but to all other women who are not believed.

Joanna Piekarska, Aviva Berlin, Germany

Straight to the point, without embellishment or paraphrases, No Heroes, No Monsters recounts the summer 2010 events in Stockholm involving Julian Assange. It is also a story about the rise and fall of Wikileaks, witch hunts, media frenzies, threats that affect women who tell their stories of power abuse and the complexities of being human.

Sofia Mirjamsdotter, journalist and winner of the Swedish "big journalist award"

This is an incredibly important book. Although I do not know Anna Ardin, I am proud and impressed by her courage and strength. I love that her personal life and all of her doubts are included. Her story provides hope of a positive development of work of the police and the Swedish justice system. I hope that the book vindicates all those who were never believed, never reported or never had their case tried in court.

Cecilia Bödker Pedersen, the Big Sister Association, Sweden

Through her honest story, Anna Ardin helps us understand that the world is not black and white. She also shows that women, still and all too often, are not equally trusted and prioritized - regardless of which space or level of society we are talking about.

Farida Al-Abani, Feminist Initiative, Sweden

Anna talks about the intersection of gender and politics, about heroes being unquestionable even in progressive movements, about the value of women in politics, about the value of women's narratives and how little they seem to weigh compared to the heroes' value. Anna honestly praises the hero but also makes him accountable. This is a responsible thing to do and it takes huge amounts of courage to tell such an honest story. For women like me, who are fighting on several fronts, every protest against harassment, assault and violation by male heroes has always been met with the statement "You are destroying the movement". This way of dealing with the issue of sexual violence under the guise of defending the movement only distances the movement from its truth and original values. Anna shows us this very well. She shows us how the right-wing movement and the extreme right align, and empathize with the left-wing movement in silencing women who narrate. Anna confronts us to ask ourselves during and after reading the book: how much can a movement deny the truth before it leads to self-destruction?

Katayoun Keshavarzi, Café 60 Media, translator and publisher of No Heroes, No Monsters (سایه ی آسانژ، من شهادت) in Farsi

Ardin's book makes the conversation about sexual violence less rabid. Anna Ardin reported Julian Assange and got the whole world's comment fields against her. Eleven years later, she tells her side of the story, reminding us that even people with good qualities can abuse others.

Rebecka Kärde, Dagens Nyheter, Sweden

The whistleblower site Wikileaks reveals abuses by US forces in Afghanistan and Iraq. One of its founders, Julian Assange, is globally celebrated. But when he visits Sweden, two women report him to the police for sexual assault. In the book No Heroes, No Monsters, Anna Ardin talks openly about how the abuse happened, how it made her feel and the frenzy that lasted for almost ten years. A hero does not rape. Popular men don't rape. Assange is the hero and Ardin the villain, a whore who wants to destroy Wikileaks. If Assange dies, it will be her fault. A distorted image of Ardin runs amok across the world, while friends and like-minded people turn away. Even equal rights activists who are considered to have seen through the social structures are confused. Everyone wants to protect Assange. The hatred for and threats to Ardin are sometimes so strong that the police assess that Ardin needs personal protection. As a reader, it's hard not to be engulfed, and sometimes I get downright nauseous. Eventually, the public image of Assange begins to crack, and Ardin receives support from many. No Heroes, No monsters is a story without pretentiousness. The book is well written and thought out; Ardin, neither victim nor avenger, skillfully balances integrity, insight and perspective. No Heroes, No Monsters exposes structures on several levels and opens up many important discussions.

BTJ, Swedish Library Service

Quotes

Anna Ardin has written a sincere book about life in the shadow of a hero; a report that we can place side by side with Klubben, Catch and Kill *and* She said *in the category of reparations.*

Expressen, Sweden

Factual in detail and in a perfectly comprehensible manner, Ardin reports, in diary form, of the incriminating and years-long media hunt. Sadly, Ardin's ultimate statement from 2020 is that the criminal complaint was probably important, but that it would have been better for herself if she had kept quiet – a realization she shares with many victims of abuse. A recommended reading!

Bianca Mertin, EKZ Bibliotheksservice, Germany

10/12/some-shit-im-sick-of-hearing-regarding-rape-and-assange.html
Wassgren, Linda. (2010). Police Report Anna Ardin Reg. no. 0201-K246336-10.
Wennstam, Katarina. (2004). *En riktig våldtäktsman : en bok om samhällets syn på våldtäkt.* [A real rapist: a book about society's view of rape.] Bonnier.
Wolf, N. (2010). December 7. *Julian Assange Captured by World's Dating Police.* Huffington Post. From https://www.huffpost.com/entry/interpol-the-worlds-datin_b_793033
Sidan redigerades och delar av texten ströks den 25 maj 2011.
X, Malcolm, & Haley, Alex. (2002). *Malcolm X Självbiografi.* [*Malcolm X Autobiography*] Ordfront.
Ölander, Micke. (2010). *Här är förhöret med Assange - ord för ord.* [Here is the interrogation of Assange - word by word.] https://www.expressen.se/nyheter/har-ar-forhoret-med-assange---ord-for-ord/

Several of the references I cite or refer to have been removed or changed between the time I began writing this book, until now. This is due, among other things, to companies and blogs going out of business, or to parts of the content being considered controversial, therefore I sometimes refer to secondary sources that cite the original source.

Shakespeare, William. (1806). *The Tempest.*
SKL. (2010). *Analysresultat SKL Slutredovisning.* [Analysis results SKL Final report.]
Somaiya, Ravi, & Burns, John F. (2010). *Under 'High-Tech House Arrest,' WikiLeaks Founder Takes the Offensive.*
https://www.nytimes.com/2010/12/23/world/23wikileaks-assange.html
Stewart, James B, Goldstein, Matthew, & Silver-Greenberg, Jessica. (2019). *Jeffrey Epstein Hoped to Seed Human Race With His DNA.*
https://www.nytimes.com/2019/07/31/business/jeffrey-epstein-eugenics.html
Sveland, M. (2013). *Hatet: en bok om antifeminism.* [*The Hate: A Book of Antifeminism.*] Stockholm: Leopard.
Sverker, Jonatan. (2010). *Nya FBI-uppgifter om Martin Luther King chockerar.* [*New FBI information about Martin Luther King shocks.*]
https://www.dagen.se/nyheter/1.1530491
SVT. (2010). Den andra våldtäkten. [The Second Rape. Movie.]
TT. (2019). *Julian Assange döms till 50 veckors fängelse.* [Julian Assange is sentenced to 50 weeks in prison.]
https://www.aftonbladet.se/nyheter/a/MRAQ9r/julian-assange-doms-till-50-veckors-fangelse
Varghese, R. (2010). December 17. *Some Shit I'm Sick Of Hearing Regarding Rape And Assange.* Hämtat från 3 Quarks Daily:
https://www.3quarksdaily.com/3quarksdaily/20

regler/gripen-anhallen-eller-haktad/
Quinn, Ben. (2011). *Julian Assange 'Jewish conspiracy' comments spark row.* https://www.theguardian.com/media/2011/mar/01/julian-assange-jewish-conspiracy-comments

Riddle, H. (Februar 24, 2011). The judicial authority in Sweden -v- Julian Paul Assange. From https://www.aklagare.se/contentassets/cc904ed99288454586d8608b5fb9b133/judaut-sweden-v-assange-judgment.pdf?fbclid=IwAR2rBufo9Nic2Oo9l_fIcLoyyviyEkaESxrEF2fiiGVe32DmPhzwU7p8nXc

Rönngren, Jenny. (2020). March 6. UN support for conspiracy theory on Assange rape case. *Feministiskt perspektiv.* https://feministisktperspektiv.se/2020/03/06/un-support-conspiracy-theory-about-rape-case-against-assange/

Satter, Raphael. (2018). *Aided by Holocaust denier, Julian Assange sought Russian visa in 2010.* https://www.timesofisrael.com/aided-by-holocaust-denier-julian-assange-sought-russian-visa-in-2010/

Schultz, Mårten. (2011). *Våldtäkt är ingen gummiparagraf.* http://magasinetneo.se/artiklar/valdtakt-ar-ingen-gummiparagraf/

Schyman, Gudrun (2002) "The Taliban Speech" from the left party congress in. Available at http://www.svenskatal.se/20020118-gudrun-schyman-talibantalet-tal-pa-vansterpartiets-kongress-2002/

against Assange is closed.]
https://www.aklagare.se/nyheter-press/pressmeddelanden/2017/maj/utredninge
n-mot-assange-laggs-ned2/
O'Hagan, Andrew. (2014). *Ghosting*.
https://www.lrb.co.uk/the-paper/v36/n05/andrew-o-hagan/ghosting
P1, Radio Sweden. (2020). October 31. Krigets första offer är sanningen. [The first casualty of war is the truth.]
https://sverigesradio.se/avsnitt/1603783
Pettersson, Mattias. (2010). *Tala är guld*. [Talk is golden.] From the Swedish proverb Speech is silver, but silence is golden
https://www.aftonbladet.se/kultur/a/P35WE7/tala-ar-guld
Pilkington, Ed. (2011). Januari 13. WikiLeaks delivers contribution to Bradley Manning defence fund. *the Guardian*. From
https://www.theguardian.com/world/2011/jan/13/wikileaks-bradley-manning-defence-fund
Pink, Aiden, & Forward, The. (2019). *Julian Assange's Long History of Alleged anti-Semitism*.
https://www.haaretz.com/amp/world-news/europe/julian-assange-s-long-history-of-alleged-anti-semitism-1.7119313
Poitras, Laura. (2017). *Risk. [Movie.]*
Polisen.se. (2020). *Gripen, anhållen eller häktad. Regler om frihetsberövande och beslag under en brottsutredning.* [Arrested, arrested or detained. Rules on detention and seizure during a criminal investigation.] https://polisen.se/lagar-och-

https://www.dn.se/ledare/signerat/trasig-eller-forstord/.
Koljonen, J. (2010). Dags att prata om det. December 18. From Dagens Nyheter: https://www.dn.se/kultur-noje/kulturdebatt/dags-att-prata-om-det/
Kolmisoppi, Mats. (2012). *Det läckande förtroendet. Mats Kolmisoppi läser Julian Assanges memoarer.* [*The leaking trust. Mats Kolmisoppi reads Julian Assange's memoirs.*] Februari 29. https://www.hd.se/2012-02-29/det-lackande-fortroendet
Lindberg, Camilla. (2010). *Vad är en sprucken kondom?? [What is a cracked condom??]* http://camilla-lindberg.blogspot.com/2010/12/vad-ar-en-sprucken-kondom.html
Magnusson, Lisa. (2010). *Med Assange blottas vår sorgliga syn på sexualitet. [With Assange, our sad view of sexuality is laid bare.]* https://www.aftonbladet.se/debatt/a/ka8zWa/med-assange-blottas-var-sorgliga-syn-pa-sexualitet
Michael, Maggie, & Satter, Raphael. (2016). *As WikiLeaks Spills High-profile Secrets, Privacy of Vulnerable at Risk.* https://www.haaretz.com/world-news/privacy-of-vulnerable-at-risk-as-wikileaks-spills-secrets-1.5428593
Nilsson, Anders. (2010). Samtal med forensiker på SKL. [Conversation with forensics officer at SKL.] Dnr 0201-K246336-10.
Ny, Marianne. (2017). *Pressmeddelande: Utredningen mot Assange läggs ned.* [Press release: The investigation

Freeman, Hadley. (2019). *Pamela Anderson's Assange blanket conceals the truth of his detention.* https://www.theguardian.com/fashion/2019/may/08/pamela-anderson-julian-assange-blanket-wikileaks-belmarsh?utm_source=headtopics&utm_medium=news&utm_campaign=2019-05-08

Gibney, Alex. (2013). *We Steal Secrets* [Movie.]

Guillou, Jan. (2011). *Julian Assange – ett litet äckel utan principer. [Julian Assange – a repulsive little chap without principles.]* https://www.aftonbladet.se/nyheter/kolumnister/janguillou/article12926443.ab

Hattenstone, Simon. (2017). *Laura Poitras on her WikiLeaks film Risk: 'I knew Julian Assange was going to be furious'.* https://www.theguardian.com/film/2017/jun/29/laura-poitras-wikileaks-film-risk-julian-assange

Jeffner, Stina. (1998). *Liksom våldtäkt, typ: om ungdomars förståelse av våldtäkt. [Like rape, kind of: about young people's understanding of rape.]* Brevskolan.

Jonasson, Lennart. (2010). Analysresultat SKL delrapport 1. Sakkunnigutlåtande. [Analysis results SKL interim report 1. Expert opinion.] dnr 2010012311.

Karlsten, Emanuel. (2010). *Konspirationsteorierna kommer att flöda. [The conspiracy theories will flow.]* https://www.expressen.se/nyheter/emanuel-karlsten-konspirationsteorierna-kommer-att-floda/

Kjöller, Hanne. (2011). *Ledare: Trasig eller förstörd. [Editorial: Broken or destroyed]* October 6.

Bennett, Catherine. (2010). *So, Mr Assange, why won't you go back to Sweden now?* https://www.theguardian.com/commentisfree/2010/dec/19/julian-assange-wikileaks-sex-offences

Brown, R. (den 9 december 2010). *Assange didn't order cyber war: lawyer.* From The Australian: https://www.abc.net.au/news/2010-12-10/assange-didnt-order-cyber-war-lawyer/2369838

Cantwell, Oisin. (2019). *Någon borde lyssna på Julian Assanges pappa. [Someone should listen to Julian Assange's father.]* https://www.aftonbladet.se/nyheter/kolumnister/a/0n02o2/nagon-borde-lyssna-pa-julian-assanges-pappa

Davoise, Marie. (2019). *Open letter in response to UN Special Rapporteur's op-ed on Julian Assange.* https://medium.com/@mariedavoise/response-to-un-special-rapporteurs-op-ed-on-julian-assange-e911e0684182

Dagens Nyheter. (March 27, 2010). *Fel signaler kan ha påverkat pojkens beteende. [Wrong signals may have influenced the boy's behavior.]* From dn.se: http://www.dn.se/nyheter/sverige/fel-signaler-kan-ha-paverkat-pojkens-beteende

Domscheit-Berg, Daniel. (2011). WikiLeaks : historien bakom sajten som förändrade en hel värld. [*Inside WikiLeaks My Time with Julian Assange at the World's Most Dangerous Website.*] Stockholm: Bokförlaget Forum.

Sources

Agenda. (2011). Interview with Birgitta Jónsdóttir.
Amnesty. (2008). *SVERIGE: Bristande rättstrygghet för våldtagna kvinnor.* [*SWEDEN: Lack of legal certainty for raped women.*]
https://www.mynewsdesk.com/se/amnesty_int ernational__svenska_sektionen/pressreleases/sv erige-bristande-raettstrygghet-foer-vaaldtagna- kvinnor-237847
Ardin, A. *Police report* (August 20, 2010). Dnr 0201- K246336-10. (L. Wassgren, interviewer)
Ardin, A. (August 21, 2010). Dnr 0201-K246336-10. [Interview]
(S. Wennerblom, interviewer)
Ardin, Anna. (September 6, 2010). *Dnr 0201-K246336- 10.* [Interview]. (E. Olofsson, interviewer)
Ardin, A. (Januari 5, 2011). Förhör. Dnr 0201- K246336-10. [Interview]
(M. Gehlin, interviewer)
Ardin, Anna. (Januari 25, 2011). *Interrogation. Dnr 0201- K246336-10.* [Interview]. (M. Gehlin, interviewer)
Balksjö, Jessika. (2010). *30-åriga kvinnan: Jag utsattes för övergrepp.* [*30-year-old woman: I was abused*]
https://www.aftonbladet.se/nyheter/a/qnJwX1 /30-ariga-kvinnan-jag-utsattes-for-overgrepp

And, of course, to my incredibly committed publisher Anders and everyone else at *Bazar publishing*, who supported and guided me in everything from structure, language, and source references to law, politics, and common sense for the original Swedish version. Thank you for giving me this chance to tell my story completely on my terms.

Thanks to Henrik and our children, who came into my life and changed everything to become so much more wonderful. Thanks also for the support and motivation to write this.

And finally, the very biggest thanks to Maria. Thank you for sisterhood and support during these years, where we have shared experiences in many ways; thank you for your invaluable help in reading and fact-checking my script. Above all, however, I want to thank you for making me realize the seriousness and daring to stand up for the truth about the "hero." What he did to me was not a one-time occurrence, and what he did to us—and what many other men have done and are doing—cannot continue to go on as if nothing happened. If we don't set the limit, who will?

Thank you to Nicke and Hasse and your team at Uppdrag granskning for doing the report on Bjästa. It has helped me a lot. Thank you also for getting in touch, listening, working on reviewing, and carefully following up on the case and all the harassment in its wake.

Thank you, Alex and Alexis. I'm glad I let you convince me to participate in your HBO documentary, *We steal secrets*. I am grateful that you managed to separate the issue of openness and transparency from the issue of sexual abuse so clearly that you conveyed the message that it's possible to support WikiLeaks' cause without allowing its representatives to get away with behaving badly.

To Anna-Klara and Jenny at *Feministiskt perspektiv* and all other journalists who worked to seek truth and transparency for real.

To Jenny at Tenenbaum publishing for all the support and involvement in the writing and thinking during the early years and right up to the end.

To Caitlin and Rowan who helped me checking the English version, to Katayoun who translated and published in Farsi and made the book available for readers in Iran and Afghanistan, to Antje who translated the book into German, everyone at Elster & Salis who published in Switzerland, Austria and Germany, to Sasha and Agnes who helped me produce the audiobook in English.

ten years, one of my most important people, my bedrock, who stood firm and matter of fact during frenzy after frenzy in the media and who continued to work on the case long after he stopped getting paid. He has been my safe embrace who listened carefully and understood my perspective, my trashcan where I could send all journalists who wanted statements, my guide who gave me the right advice, and my moral backbone who explained that it does matter even when everything felt pointless. He thought it was only right to donate my royalties to Diakonia's work for women's rights globally, that it was alarming that women's sexual and reproductive rights were being reduced again, and he supported my writing. We had planned to close the case with a dinner after this book was finished. I wish I had shown him what I wrote before it was too late. This world will be a little less wise, a little less righteous, and quite a bit lonelier in the shitstorms without him.

Thanks also to Pia, who worked on the case at Borgström's law firm, who methodically stood up to keep calm, not prejudge the process, and not speaking out despite Julian and his long lines of lawyers and PR consultants' tricks, lies, insane offers, and ugly campaigns.

Peter, the police officers who were given responsibility for my personal protection and who did not comment a word that I continued to participate in public contexts but just showed up and sat in the audience.

Thanks to Sofia, Gustav, Maria, Agnes, Sonja, Johanna, and all the other writers and journalists who raised and addressed issues of abuse, gray areas, and online hate in #talkaboutit, even though the recommendation in 2010 was extremely strong: keep quiet about it. Otherwise, it will get worse. And to everyone who continued sharing and analyzing during #metoo. To Tara, Marie, and everyone else who supported us and who demanded the defense of women's rights within the UN system. To those of you who still wanted to nuance the discussion about victims and perpetrators to find the delicate balance between neither diminishing nor magnifying.

Thanks to Abdulkader, Hanna, and Göran, who hired me during the period when it was at its worst. You saw who I am and what I can do, and that I am someone else than what the trolls tried to claim about me.

Thanks also to Andreas, who actually stood up when it mattered—sorry I linked to that revenge list; it was stupid. I never intended to hit back for what you did anyway, although I'm still angry.

During all these years, it has been more than clear how correct my choice of lawyer was. Claes was, for exactly

> *Show me the woman who thought it was worth reporting a sex crime because she got good money and attention or shut up and listen to the women who dare to tell. Today is International Women's Day. A day when we stop being ashamed.*

March 9, 2020

I get a picture of a Tweet where WikiLeaks writes that they have a new income plan through suing the *Guardian* for all the "fake news" they wrote about the organization. I feel like talking to David Leigh, Julian's former friend and collaborator, regarding the release of the Collateral Murder video, among other things. He's also gotten a lot of hate from Julian's fans over the years, and I want to ask him for some advice. He answers my email in less than two minutes, and a moment later, we're talking in a video conference.

He's incredibly sympathetic and says he's really encouraged by the fact that I'm now planning to tell my story. And then we talk about forgiveness. He has previously written that he thinks Julian should apologize to us and that perhaps we can forgive him; he believes Julian has already been locked up for so many years. Friends of mine have been upset with Leigh for talking about forgiveness, and they've said it's typical to tell women to settle for an apology. But I understand what he means and agree with him. Julian has a right to forgiveness—if he wants it.

Julian's stay at the embassy meant 24/7 access for visitors, full service, and free Internet, and it was essentially voluntary, so I find it hard to see it as punishment. But for me, punishment is completely irrelevant. I would have been just as satisfied if he hadn't had to spend a single day in jail and hadn't been fined a single pound. I'd have forgiven him gladly. I can see myself at the front of the demonstration train shouting, "enough is enough; let him have another chance!" but I cannot create reconciliation myself. Demanding that he be excused and redressed without the slightest expression of remorse, admitting that he hurt people, or even trying to be part of some sort of solution does nothing but excuse and justify his sex crimes. I will never do that.

Thanks

Thanks to my group 8, Laboremistas, the girls in the Social Democratic Students in Uppsala. And to Sara, Mattias, and everyone else from Rebella and Faith and Solidarity. Thank you for study circles, breakfast meetings, wine, song, and debate about patriarchy, feminism, abuse, hierarchies, subordination, intersectionality, and the fight for equality. Several of you have also been there during this horrible time of the legal process with reading, texts, analysis, food, rooms, and cheer. Without you, I would never have been able to be so strong and convinced in this process; you laid much of the foundation for how I came to see events such as those I experienced.

Thanks to Mom, Dad, Alexandra, and all the friends, acquaintances, and colleagues who supported me. Thanks to Somar, who came with me when the police sent me to Spain, to Petra and Pontus, who hid me in Stockholm. When job, partner, and home were taken away, the opportunity to live with you was absolutely crucial for both my body and my mind. Thanks also to Marta, who put her soul into cleaning social media, to Ida, who, with the help of Eva and Simon, among others, managed to defund the web magazine that was the first to expose me by writing to their advertisers, and to all the tweeters, lawyers, feminists, debaters, and blogger who contributed insightful analysis. Thanks to the teachers and classmates at Bromma community college who, in connection with my training to become a deacon, supported me in sorting things out with God and within myself and made sure I resumed writing this book.

Thank you to all the strangers who believed me and sent encouraging greetings even when lies, exaggerations, and misogyny were spread all the way to the newspapers when left-wing men came out and used their weight to say they knew something about what happened that night and when right-wing people and anti-feminists used the opportunity to prove their own political points. To all of you who helped me collect quotes from them for this book so that I did not have to be that exposed to them.

Thanks to Thomas and the Social Democrats in the city of Stockholm, who supported me and chose to wholeheartedly stand by my side, even though the outbreak happened right in the final sprint before the election.

Thanks to Linda, the police officer who met me at Klara police station. I wish that all of you around the world who go into police stations and report abuse are immediately believed and supported. That even if the perpetrator is not convicted, you have an absolute and unlimited power to decide over your own body. Those who don't respect it have de facto screwed up, and that's not OK, as Linda told me. Thanks also to the police officer MG, Mats, who then became responsible for the investigation in the family department, for your commitment, and to Anna and incredible," says Claes.

"No," I say. "I am done hoping for court trials and responses from Julian, I will submit my testimony to the media tribunal instead."

I'm not the least bit interested in compensation, and I don't want to listen to him anymore. The only thing I want now is to be allowed to be heard out just once.

March 8, 2020

On my shelf is a stack of papers I requested from the prosecutor and the police. It's been there for a while. Several weeks. After working intensively with Melzer's letter and realizing that over 300 lawyers for human rights have signed a joint petition[68] in which they believe that Melzer acted wrongly and demand that he back down, I suddenly have enough strength to go through reading the entire preliminary investigation.

I take a photo of the page in the interrogation where I answer the question of what I earned from reporting and if I received any money. I answered, "nothing," but the police needed almost a whole page to transcribe my answer when I explain what I had lost. It just pours out of me. Line after line after line is about the consequences for me, my family, my safety, my finances, my housing situation, and my social life. I call it baroque that I should've gone to the police with the motive of earning money and attention because, in reality, I couldn't even work, as I had to spend all my waking hours escaping attention. I post the photo on Facebook and write:

extradition trial. She claims that the prosecutor did not "bother" to question Julian before he had to leave the country. She claims that Julian himself contacted prosecutors but that he could not wait any longer and "was forced" to leave on September 27. Thus, it's the same fallacy that Melzer uses to say that the prosecutor violated her office. The same information that was disproved in court and the same misleading that *her own association* issued a warning to a lawyer for. I email her and comment on the blog post that she might want to correct this since it has been very credibly proven to be false information. But she neither answers nor corrects. What could be proven as lies in the legal process has become fact in the media tribunal. Even in the eyes of well-educated lawyers.

But having investigated this as much as I possibly can, with my limited expertise, it seems like there were, in fact, no serious errors in the legal process at all. The police and the prosecutors seem to have done what they could. On several occasions, they have also made great extra efforts to find solutions. But it has been in vain due to the obstruction of Julian and his friends. Claiming that the justice system broke down, in this case, is based on a party submission from a suspected rapist, which does not match reality in crucial parts.

Claes thinks I should demand compensation from Julian. He believes that we have a good chance of winning if we lift the abuse civilly and that I have the right to remuneration for the damage Julian caused me with the abuse.

"He has also defamed you deliberately; there is plenty of evidence for that. It's absolutely responsibility for Julian (again) and sign demands for him to be pardoned. The British verdict on the breach of bail, Sweden's suspicions of sex crimes, and the U.S.'s suspicions of data breaches are still mixed up. This happens despite the fact that the sentence for the breach of bail has been served, the trial for sex crimes has been closed, and I have nothing to add regarding the suspicions against him regarding espionage. I don't even understand how a pardon would work, and I don't understand whether they hope I'll be able to influence U.S. President Donald Trump in any way or if they rather want me to apologize for his sex crimes once again publicly. They keep threatening to hold me responsible for his death if I don't do as they say. Sometimes, it sounds to them like he was already dead, and I am the killer.

Julian's father says to the media that he thinks Julian should receive compensation from the Swedish state. If Julian applies for it, it might still be a process that will necessarily have to deal with sexual offenses as well. Then we get another chance to clarify the truth.

I would still, after all, like to see such a trial where we can actually go through the material and where the distortions can be sorted out in a systematic and impartial way. But I don't think that will ever happen.

February 25, 2020

Anne Ramberg was secretary general of the Bar Association when the Bar Association's disciplinary board issued a warning to Julian's lawyer Björn Hurtig for lying in court. Today, she blogs about the understood what it was going to be like. The utter absurdity of predicting what would happen. I feel an enormous urge to defend myself. The 40-year-old Anna wants to defend the 30-year-old Anna, who's sitting there crying in the interrogation.

I have to take a break from reading and visualize how I, my 40-year-old self, hold on to my 30-year-old self as I learned to in therapy. I tell her—me—that she did the right thing and that it was good of me to go to the police.

I'm taking a break from everything I'm doing to instead work on telling what really happened from my perspective. I will finally finish this book.

February 24, 2020

Today, a trial begins in London on the U.S.'s extradition request for Julian. The U.S. military considers U.S. war crimes to be secret, and whoever reveals them is consequently considered a spy. In addition, they think they have the right to pick up "spies" in all the countries of the world to punish them.

It's absolutely crazy, and the lawsuit has nothing to do with me, but the hate pours in, and I'm the scapegoat. Long lines of men add me on Instagram, comment on Facebook, Tweet, email and text, instant message, and sneer. The online tribunal carries on, with ever new hearsay witnesses and ever new attacks, with exactly the same invented sequence of events and conspiracy theories as always, although, of course, they now also have UN-stamped support.

People are calling and demanding that I take

steps. What 100,000 people have been discussing online for four or five months, people seem to think that I would have understood in the fifteen minutes I had to think about it."
"Yes."
"And it wasn't like that."
"So, you didn't even make such an estimate."
"No, I did not."
"No."
"And it's like this, yes, 'but you who work with the press, you damn well should have done that.' Well, yes. And if I had known, even one percent of all this that had happened, I would never have gone there. So, I will never recommend anyone to report rape any more... Because... And I've done that all my life, like [inaudible] trying to tell girls that you have to report because you have an obligation to other girls.

"But it's not worth it. That... Nothing good comes of reporting."
[crying]
"Mm. Let me know if you want a break."
"Yes [inaudible]."
"We're taking a break here, it's 20 minutes to 11."
(Break in the interrogation)[67]

I relive the feeling from the interrogation; how my voice stopped, and it was impossible to continue talking. I relive the overwhelming emotions that emerged when I just lifted the lid a tiny little bit when I sensed that the police thought I should have

"You are quite skilled in the context of the press, since you work as a press secretary."
"Mm."
"Could you see [how the case would be treated in the media] in front of you before? (...)"
"Not really, so it's completely..."
"(...) what effect would you expect from it becoming public?"
"Well, I thought my name would leak in connection with the trial. And I didn't think too much about when his name would come out, but I probably thought that, too, would be if we had a trial, or something like this, it will come out on Flashback before, probably. But not like that... Not that it would take on such enormous proportions. (...) But it is clear that I would have understood (...) that he would appear in the newspapers."
"Mm."
"Yes, but I don't know, it wasn't like that, I didn't include it in the calculation. I didn't even have... When [Maria] called, (...) then I had already thought that I wouldn't go there, that I wouldn't talk about it. But then it was like this, (...) I was in such a hurry that... Or like, I had to hurry as much as possible so that they wouldn't notice that I was away from work. (...) There have been a lot of discussions about this... In how many steps I have planned this. And like how I would have seen the logical chains both legally and journalistically and, and personally and everything like that. That I should have done impact analyzes in a thousand

I'm surprised by how incredibly difficult I find it to read. I was convinced that I had processed the sexual abuse. Convinced that it was a past chapter of my life and convinced that I remembered more or less what actually happened. I do, in fact, remember a lot, and I remember more details than what I told the police, and I am kind of reliving the events when I read, even though so much time has passed. Many times, I have thought and talked about the coercion and insemination, the belch in the face, and the feeling of being exploited in several different ways. But the incident was also rougher than I remember it. I didn't remember being close to crying during the abuse, but in my own story, I hear that I actually was. And the fact is that I had completely forgotten both that I visited the sexual health clinic and that I called the midwives as witnesses, forgot that I told them what happened, about the coercion, that I thought I had been infected against my will, and the strong discomfort. In the interrogation, I also tell a painful detail—that none of the midwives reacts to the fact that it's actually an abuse I describe. In the interrogation, I tell the police that the midwives don't say it might be illegal. None of them say anything at all about what he did is wrong. According to my retelling of the interrogation, they do not comment on this at all. And it hurts. If they'd said anything, it probably would've helped me realize the nature of the events sooner.

In the interrogation, the police also ask whether I should have been able to foresee the media's reactions:

expression. What we have done is to defend women's right to avoid abuse. A rule of law is able to defend both freedom of expression and the right of crime victims to have their case heard.

The situation for journalists and whistleblowers in the world is becoming increasingly strained. But too many of those who want to defend the ideals that Assange has so long claimed to stand for, instead spend time directly and indirectly slandering and campaigning against two individual women. They are victims of crime who, because of Assange's actions, never received a fair trial. Instead, they have been exposed to hatred, threats, and questioning for ten years. It has to end.

Claes Borgström
Lawyer, former plaintiff's attorney

Pia Engström-Lindgren
Former legal assistant at lawyer Claes Borgström, now lawyer

I have had lawyers who not only defended my interests in the legal process but also in public. Not only in court but also in the media, and not only until the statute of limitations but long after the mission has officially ended. It has been a blessing. I don't know how I would have managed without them.

February 22, 2020

Working with this book, I'm reading my own interrogation from January 5, 2011. It shocks me, and *district court, court of appeal, and the Supreme Court—have determined that Assange is suspected of the crimes he is accused of on probable grounds.*

It is noteworthy that a UN rapporteur demands that the Swedish government should have departed from the constitutionally protected principle of the sovereignty of the courts and given guarantees about future rulings on extradition to the United States. But when Melzer spreads conspiracy theories originating from a one-sided image that appears to have been provided by Assange's defense, he goes far beyond his mandate. No attempt appears to have been made to verify the factual information in the letter with other sources. This that the incorrect and one-sided information leads to serious and groundless accusations that people within the Swedish police and prosecutors in agreement with our client would have manipulated and withheld evidence and subjected the other plaintiff to pressure to change her testimony.

Melzer goes so far as to evaluate technical evidence, based on incorrect information he received from Assange's defense lawyers. The report also shows how Melzer personally believes "a real rape victim" should act, when evaluating the plaintiffs' alleged behavior after the alleged assaults. It is unreasonable that a UN rapporteur has such a poor understanding of how people can react to trauma.

Through his actions, Nils Melzer lowers the credibility and reputation of the entire UN when he singles out and suspects both the plaintiff and the Swedish authorities for deliberately and with political motives to damage freedom of country that does not extradite people to the United States if they are suspected of political crimes. He instead went to Great Britain—a country that has a very far-reaching extradition treaty with the United States—and appealed to the last instance not to be handed over to Sweden. This despite the fact that a transfer to Sweden and completion of the legal process surrounding the sexual crimes had made impossible extradition to the USA unless both Great Britain and Sweden granted this. It seems far more likely that Julian Assange did not want to appear in Sweden for fear of being convicted of sexual crimes.

Despite the fact that the suspected sexual abuse and the acts for which the US has charged Assange are not related, they have thus been linked in the debate. It was already years before any extradition request was received. Now this mix-up returns with renewed strength.

This is worrying in itself, but a more serious reason to react against this shift in the debate is that now even Nils Melzer, the UN special rapporteur on torture issues, seems to have chosen to join Assange's defenders. He has sent a letter to the Swedish government with, among other things, 50 statements which in various ways points to the conclusion that the Swedish state exposed Assange to torture. Most of these points are about impugning the plaintiff women or disputing the allegations they have leveled against Assange, as well as criticizing the police and prosecutors' handling of those allegations. Basically, all of the claims made in the 50 points are based on incorrect facts or interpretation. Melzer also completely ignores the fact that all of the legal bodies that have tried the matter—

In connection with the ongoing negotiations on whether the U.K. should approve the US request to extradite Julian Assange, the two Swedish women who accused Assange of sexual crimes have once again been subjected to a storm of threats, questioning and harassment. Not only do they have their stories discredited, but they are also accused of being part of a politically motivated conspiracy to silence Wikileaks and support the U.S.

A central part of the debate about the extradition is about claiming that the Swedish and British justice systems made mistakes in acting on the allegations of sexual abuse. All the consequences Assange "suffered," such as seven years in the Ecuadorian Embassy, are allegedly "punishment enough" or even grounds for Sweden to pay damages.

If Assange has suffered trauma due to the Swedish legal proceedings against him, that trauma is self-inflicted. Julian Assange has in the almost ten years that have passed since his initial refusal to cooperate on legitimate demands for HIV testing obstructed the sexual assault legal process by refusing to cooperate, refusing to appear for questioning, refusing to answer questions when questioning finally took place, and refusing DNA testing. In addition, he has hired at least one PR agency to smear the women who accused him.

Both Assange himself and his many defenders claim that his refusal to appear for questioning in Sweden was all about the fact that he does not want to risk being extradited to the United States. But when Assange left Sweden to avoid questioning about sexual abuse, he left a

That is simply what this is all about."

A large number of erroneous theories and claims that have circulated for years have now managed to find their way into one of our highest international human rights institutions. Julian's third defense strategy—that the accusations are a way for those in power to punish him for the WikiLeaks leaks—has, through an UN-labelled activist, become as close to an official truth as is possible for a lie. It's a way to officially try to exonerate Julian even though he never participated in the process that could have actually cleared him.

Claes is seriously ill, and the operations he's had for his back problems and the shunt he had operated on to regulate the fluid in his head have not helped as they should. He has to make an effort to get out of bed. It's clear when we talk on the phone that it's a struggle just to talk. But he wants Melzer's claims to be met publicly, and therefore we will write a debate article. He also tells me how important he thinks I am and that he's so happy that he got to work with me. I really feel the same way about him.

Together with Pia, Claes signs a response to Melzer. It takes time to publish the article and we decide to save it for the next time Melzer is in the media with the issue, which we expect will be soon. Unfortunately, Claes died of covid May 19, 2020, therefore I am instead publishing the article here, in this book:

many years. His business is to confront me with what I wrote to Melzer! Melzer has shared my emails with Julian's supporter network without my consent, and he's trying to refute me to defend Julian alongside them. In addition, they're working to ensure Julian does not have to be held accountable for any sexual crimes.

The Swedish government has responded to Melzer's letter. Among other things, they've explained how the independent Swedish judiciary works and that there's no basis for the accusations of political conspiracy. Melzer sends more letters to the government, and the state authority responds by referencing its first response. In the media, he continues to claim that the Swedish government "refuses to answer."

I talk to Pia and summarize it all to her:

> "Melzer believes that Sweden's institutions tortured Julian when they tried to hold him accountable for sex crimes. For real, a UN reporter claims that I, together with Thomas Bodström, an old minister whom I have never met, have directed a 10-year mass media drama, with the aim of sending a hero to death by torture in the U.S.A."

We fall silent for a moment and look at each other.

> "Once again," says Pia, "so-called representatives of human rights show that they do not think that women's rights are actually part of their work.

information but about details of how the police's electronic diary management works. Julian's defense also knows that there's no indication of any fabrication.

Yet this perfectly logical and technical micro-problem—and how the police solved it—has become the overwhelming evidence that there are no real charges against Julian at all.

But Melzer doesn't stop here in his conspiracy theory. He here adds that the police and I "share an agenda." There's no information on what this agenda would be, but what he does here insinuates I'm involved in the plot. He's not only saying that the police added things in the rewrite of the hearing but also that it's likely I had something to do with the hearing IK did with Maria and the transcript. I find this outrageous.

Since Melzer says that he himself has no right to double-check the factual information he receives from someone who claims to have been subjected to torture, I decide to help him. In a 23-page document, I show the logical explanations for this and all other inaccuracies and misunderstandings that Melzer relayed from Julian. He replies that he cannot take my statements as truth without investigating them further. Apparently, he *is* entitled to do his own investigation after all. But instead of investigating them, he starts using what I write against me.

Jesús Alcalá gets in touch. He's a retired journalist and a former controversial chairman of Amnesty in Sweden, whom I haven't heard anything about for preliminary investigation report (also leaked from Julian's lawyers) that explains what it's all about. Melzer states in his communication with me and in an interview with *Feministiskt perspektiv*[66] that he's prevented from seeking information himself. Because Julian's defense didn't share this memo with him, he hasn't seen it, even though the document is searchable online (scanned with fax numbers to Julian's defense attorneys and all). But even though Melzer doesn't want to hear this (as it proves there was no fabrication at all), I can explain what actually happened:

On the same Friday that we went to the police for the first time, IK made her first and only contribution to the long police investigation into the case, a questioning of Maria that ended close to seven o'clock in the evening. She took notes but didn't have time to finish before the weekend. On Monday morning, IK was no longer connected to the investigation and therefore did not have access to the document to finish transcribing the interrogation. She then asked MG, the police officer who had taken over responsibility for the case, what she should do. MG, who had access to the text, cut it out and emailed it to her. She created a new document that was not locked within the investigation, completed the cleanup, and saved the file. In the police system, documents are marked by the date they were created, not the date the interview was conducted. Both files are saved and can be compared, showing the issue is about editing a quickly written document, not about adding any new suspicion to it.

This is not a case of fabrication or new

He believes that it's compromising that Bodström is not only a social democrat but also a minister but fails to mention that Bodström left office four years before Julian's actions against Maria and me. He repeats the false information that there was no DNA on the condom I gave to the police, and he criticizes the prosecutor for taking an unreasonably long time despite the fact that Julian, according to Melzer, has done *everything he could* to cooperate.

I feel exhausted. Out of the 50 bullet points he presents in the letter most are completely wrong. Some are reasonably accurate but have been wildly interpreted, and several are downright offensive. He completely condemns the accusations against Julian and calls them an "unqualified 'rape suspect' narrative." So much for not taking a stand in the question of guilt.

Perhaps his strongest thesis is precisely what I heard the German media picked up: that the police fabricated evidence. According to Melzer, this fabrication consists of the police replacing the content of one of Maria's interrogations. He seems to think that this shows Maria was never subjected to any crime. The basis for his claim is an email exchange between two police officers.

In addition to the person referred to in the documents as IK, MG, a superior police officer, is also mentioned. In the email exchange, IK asks what she should do with an interrogation she cannot access. And MG replies that she should paste a text he sends her and then print and sign it with her own name. It may look fishy, but there's also a memo from the

February 21, 2020

A man named Nils Melzer answers my letter. He has a non-profit mission for OHCHR as Special Rapporteur against torture. But there is no report, he writes. It's instead about a letter that he, in his capacity as Special Rapporteur and as an official within OHCHR, has written to the Swedish government. He encloses the letter, and it turns out to be a mishmash of information he clearly received from Julian's defense. In this, he claims that Sweden has tortured Julian.

The letter begins with the reporter stating he has no views on the legal case and that he does not want to rule on the question of guilt. He writes further that his mission is solely about criticizing the states he believes are guilty of torture. But the whole letter, from the first to the last page, is about questioning Maria, me, our stories, the evidence, our behavior, and all the people who believed us and tried to push our cases forward. The letter states that a real victim would not have let an abuser stay in her apartment, would not have tweeted that the night after was nice and that a real victim would have warned Maria when she knew the abuser was about to have sex with her.

Furthermore, he believes that it's very suspicious that the police—who in the documents are called IK and do the first questioning of Maria—like me, belong to Sweden's largest party, the Social Democrats. He also falsely claims that the state "selected" Claes Borgström for us and suggests that it is because of his connections to the Social Democrats and mentions that Claes had his agency together with Thomas Bodström.

An official, legally legitimate court could have tried the case and acquitted Julian, but he refused to participate. Of course, he's legally innocent until proven guilty, but this seems like something that goes way beyond that. It seems to be about another landmark in the mob tribunal. I'm beginning to realize that there is some kind of UN document causing the increasing attacks on me. Something resembling an official judgment on the issue of guilt appears to have been published in the name of a major international body.

Before I have time to look it up further, I'm contacted by the magazine *Feministiskt perspektiv*, who asks if I know what this German TV channel means by "the accusations of sexual crimes have been fabricated."

This, too, must have something to do with the alleged UN report. If there is such a report, and it really says what people seem to believe, then that's bad, but it still seems highly unlikely. I start looking for the report to read for myself what it says. On the website of the Office of the UN High Commissioner for Human Rights, OHCHR, I can't find anything. I'm starting to wonder if it's a scam after all.

February 19, 2020

I'm sending a letter to OHCHR to alert them that a report spread in their name is causing a wave of disinformation and harming Maria and me. I say that I'm happy to help clear up any misconceptions but that I cannot find the report itself.

February 18, 2020

For a few years, I was mainly contacted by anti-feminists, fascists, incel men, and Trump and Putin supporters. But now I notice the attacks are once again coming from alleged human rights defenders and left-wing activists like the man from Karlskrona and his network.

    A friend who is a member of the EU Parliament calls and says that she's received a question about signing a protest list in favor of Julian Assange. According to several media, especially in Germany, it is now "clear" that he never committed any sexual abuse and that the accusations were made up. Based on this "false information," one of the German parliamentarians in the Social Democratic group has taken a stand and wants to get more people involved. My EU parliamentarian friend asks if she can pass my number over, and I say yes. The woman calls me, and I explain that it was actually abuse and that many courts have established suspicions on probable cause. She goes silent on the phone for a moment and then says:

"But then this UN report is not correct."

What UN report? The thing those querulant people discussed in the email thread may not be bullshit. It might be more serious than that. I say:

"No, I have not read it, but if some UN official suddenly takes the mandate to exonerate Assange from guilt, it seems extremely strange."

2020

November 22, 2019

A man in his 80s living outside Karlskrona who has contacted me many times writes yet another email. This time, he says something about the UN determining that the Swedish state subjected Julian to torture and wants me to comment on it.

I assume that what he's referring to is yet another juristic report, like the one he himself wrote, which gives the appearance of trying to take all sides of the matter into consideration. "All sides" includes mostly the worst bullies. In the report, he used, among other things, a picture of a fake front cover from *Time* that circulated a lot on the internet and where I was named "Slut of the year." His "report" contained numerous false statements, the same ones that Julian's defenders have been emphasizing all these years. Everything from claims about the manipulation of evidence to grand political theories about my motives for reporting. Once again, human rights are mixed up with men's rights, and once again, I'm made a symbol of the power to be fought. Julian's possible personal sexual criminality is defended as part of the fight for peace and freedom.

I estimate that this new report is something that few will take seriously and nothing that I need to put energy into. Instead, I get angry because he never quits and because there are still those who persist in sending me accusations and dodgy conspiracy theories. I ask him to stop and never to contact me again.

From an anonymous address, he forwards my email to some kind of list and accidentally includes me in further communication. I, therefore, realize that some of the anonymous emails I've received over the years came from him. His mistake also shows that he coordinates a supporter network for Julian, consisting of left-wing sympathizers and peace activists who run websites, leave comments in online forums, and organize meetings. They don't seem to have a problem with their activities happening at Maria's and my expense. On the contrary, they are another group of people who actively single us out as perpetrators. Maybe it was someone from this list I saw walking around with a wheeled shopping bag pasting photostatic copies with Julian's face on the association boards in the city center. I know for sure that I recognize the names of people who arranged and participated in the hobnob with Julian's father.

From the continued conversation, I understand that the people in this network are convinced that I, personally, am complicit in the torture of Julian. One of the women, a high-profile former politician and rumored mistress of Fidel Castro, states in one of the emails in the thread that I'm "responsible for Julian dying of mental torture in an English prison, denying the whole thing, and assuming the role of a martyr."

It is, of course, horrible to be accused time and time again of being someone who actively contributes to horrors. I believe that it is, and must be, possible to defend both women's right to get sex crimes tried and the right to leak socially important documents that show abuses in war simultaneously. And since it was out of the question for me to lie, I couldn't have done anything to mitigate anything of what hit Julian. But what upsets me the most is the lack of power analysis.

It's difficult to see how the fight to free Julian can succeed when their analysis concludes that I'm one of the most important people in power to be held accountable. This lack of analysis into who actually holds power here has also meant so many human rights defenders have failed to see how their fight was twisted into defending Julian's abuse of power against women rather than criticizing the U.S.'s abuse of power against whistleblowers. The fact that they spent their time fighting to free Julian from alleged sex crimes, causing smearing and belittling of sex crime victims, rather than fighting to free Manning, shows they haven't reflected enough on what the world actually looks like.

And I really wonder why they did this. They talk about bravery, but Julian has avoided the sex crime trial at any cost while Chelsea Manning de facto went on trial for leaking the same important documents that WikiLeaks then handed over to the *Guardian* and others for dissemination. And when Julian barricaded himself, Manning was locked up. Why, then, has the focus these ten years been Julian's fight rather than Manning's? Maybe because it's easier for many to identify with him than with her? Does he fit the image of the classic hero better than she does? Or is it even the case that the fight for freedom of speech for many is subordinate to the fight for men's rights? That the fight to defend Julian against "false" allegations of abuse is more important than defending whistleblowers against accusations of espionage?

December 9, 2019

A Swedish woman who was active during #metoo with her story is sentenced for defaming her perpetrator. The District Court writes that the information she provided about her perpetrator "referred to very serious criminality and were likely to cause [him] serious harm." They state that it was gross slander. Of course, it's sad that women aren't able to tell their stories about abuse, and for my own part, I'm a little worried about what might happen to me if I go ahead with this book I'm writing. At the same time, it feels like a sign that accusations of sexual crimes should not be decided in the media. And that's a good thing because that's exactly what became destructive to the #metoo movement.

Finally, hundreds of thousands of women dared to tell, but their common story about a social problem was gradually made invisible by celebrity gossip. Perhaps it was precisely the publication of names that made the campaign so large and so spectacular, but as the discussion was increasingly reduced to dealing with individual men, it lost much of its meaning. Instead of a broad movement to change the rules of the game, it resulted in the media chasing the players. Those who were named and exposed now seem to be returning one by one. They are excused and resurrected without expressing regret or willingness to change. And why would they? They were just following the rules.

evidence, such as the witnesses' memories, has weakened too much after so many years. Julian's tactic of delaying the process to avoid prosecution has succeeded.

The decision means that I'm no longer a witness and formally no longer—in *any* way—legally connected to the case. All possibilities to have the matter settled in court are now exhausted, and the tests that I, Maria, and the prosecutor wanted to have done will never be carried out. It's such an anticlimax. A deep sense of futility washes over me, like all these years have been for nothing. But I also feel relief. Now it will be obvious, I think, even to anonymous Christmas card writers, that whatever happens to Julian is beyond my control. Harassing me no longer has even the slightest chance of affecting Julian's situation, whether Mr. WikiLeaks or the sex offender Julian is the person you want to help.

November 20, 2019

Petra listened to the prosecutor's press conference yesterday and asks:

> "Who's that witness in Denmark?"
> "No clue!"

I smile at the amazing fact that more people were prepared to testify, even though it still means exposing themselves to risk. But also, that the police managed to keep the new witnesses so secret, even from me, that there was never any campaign against them.

It is also time to talk about what can happen to those who testify about abuse, about all non-punishable harassment, about openness and transparency, and about reconciliation.

November 14, 2019

A friend gets in touch and says that she was sitting on a train when she heard a young girl explain to her father that she *knew* the accusations against Julian were false. And with an impressive degree of detail, she explained many of the conspiracy theories and other fabrications that have flourished about the case. We note that these inventions have spread so widely and for so many years that they have become part of our folklore. That my loved ones respond to inaccuracies in a few occasional conversations that they happen to hear in public cannot change that.

It's time for me to tell my side. My friend, who's also writing a feminist book, suggests I get in touch with a small and newly started publishing house owned by businessman Petter Stordalen. I email the publisher and get in touch directly. After eight years of writing, thinking, and looking for the right publisher, I now think I have finally found the answer.

November 19, 2019

Prosecutor Eva-Marie Persson announces that today she's decided to drop Maria's case. During a press conference, she announces that Maria's statement is clear, long, and detailed and that she has left a credible and reliable story. She also says that the supporting

September 27, 2019

I'm at my publisher's booth at the Gothenburg book fair and see Jan Guillou. He's one of the people I was hoping to meet here to thank for his texts about my case. But he's pursued by a group of aggressive white men with television cameras filming very close to his face. It's a threatening situation, and there's no way to get to him. I know that he, too, is threatened by right-wing extremists.

November 13, 2019

I receive an envelope in the mail with proper handwriting on it. *It must be from a mean older lady*, I think. There are far too many mean aunties who send me anonymous letters, and this is probably another one. They usually include conspiracy theories, accusations, calls for shame, and an exaggerated confidence in my ability to influence the case.

Then I open and see a beautiful Christmas card from the Mouth and Foot Painting Artists' Association. I turn the card over and, yes, it's a nasty letter about me being a coward who won't tell the truth about the "rape." That's exactly what it says, with the rape in quotation marks. And it says URGENT, too, in capitals. She apparently thinks that there is a great hurry for me to tell *her* the truth. I'm genuinely disappointed that I was right.

But she *is* right in one way: it's time for me to tell the truth, *my* truth, about the crimes, regardless of the procedures of the courts.

September 26, 2019

Julian's father, John Shipton, has appeared in Stockholm. A friend has been invited to a "hobnob" with him and forwards the email. He asks if I have any questions.

I reply that I would really like to know where his father thinks Julian got his view of women from. I would also like to know what he thinks about Julian's view of his own genes and whether that view might have anything to do with his upbringing.

According to Julian's memoirs, he grew up with a single hippie and activist mother who, for several years, fled from town to town to escape a bizarre and authoritarian new-age sect. I can't help but wonder where his father was back then.

None of us go to this hobnob. But Oisín Cantwell does, and afterward, he comments in *Aftonbladet* on some of the questions that nobody in the room asked:

> *A bit over the top would probably be to prudently clear your throat and recall how CNN revealed in detail and well-substantiated this summer that Assange turned his room in the Ecuadorian Embassy into a command center, hosting Russian hackers just days before WikiLeaks published tens of thousands of stolen emails that came to affect the American presidential election in 2016. It would probably have been directly unpopular to ask questions about why Shipton allowed himself to be invited to Syria to rub shoulders with dictator Bashar al-Asad.*[65]

particular scene illustrates how Caliban tries to show himself and the world that he's strong and important. The rape attempt on the woman is not explained as sexual but as part of a long-term plan to create a kingdom of his own in the world, something important for the future.

Even though both the Swedish and British justice systems tried to give us redress—like Prospero, who protected Miranda—and take the case to trial, that, in fact, never happened. The media tribunal became, and still is, the arena where my case will (perhaps forever) continue to be processed along with so many other cases. The perpetrators' support troops come in all forms, as politicians, intellectuals, cultural figures, advocates of equality, ideological friends, or enemies worldwide. They argue differently, but perhaps there will always be those who push for us not to stop Caliban from populating the world.

September 9, 2019

The prosecutor says publicly that seven people were heard in the reopened investigation. I'm one of the five heard again, but there are also two new witnesses. I don't give much importance to it and don't get to know more than what people around me tell me they read in the newspapers.

people about all the places in the world where he was already a father. Many little Julians, one on each continent—he seemed to like that picture. Whether he then took care of the children, or whether they even existed, is another question.[63]

There seems to be a gray area in the legislation as to whether it's legal to attempt to reproduce with another human being against their will. But wanting to populate the world with one's own offspring by means of coercion and foul play is hardly anything new. I come to think about Shakespeare's 400-year-old play *The Tempest*, where Prospero saves his daughter Miranda who's about to be raped by the "monster" Caliban, with the words:

> Thou most lying slave,
> Whom stripes may move, not kindness: I have us'd
>   thee
> Filth as thou art, with human care; and lodg'd thee
> In my own cell, till thou didst seek to Violate
> The honour of my child.

Caliban replies:

> Oh ho, oh ho!—Wou'd it had been done!
> Thou didst prevent me; I had peopled else
> this isle with Calibans.[64]

Of course, *The Tempest* comments on Shakespeare's contemporaries much more deeply than that, but this power over the judiciary, it's too often both difficult and expensive to stop excusing abuses of power. The thing is though we must try if abuse is to cease to exist.

However, the article about Epstein is mainly about how he, with a very elaborate plan, hoped to "seed the human race" with his DNA by impregnating women on his large ranch in New Mexico.[62]

Epstein's many cases of abuse may have been partly rooted in a desire for sex and establishing hierarchical superiority, but an important reason also seems to have been geared toward reproduction. It's also a question of power, but of a different kind than that of the moment—the power over someone else's body beyond the present, the power to use another human's body to spread one's "superior genes." And it may not be unique to Jeffrey Epstein in particular.

August 1, 2019

I pick up Julian's former colleague Daniel Domscheit-Berg's book about WikiLeaks. My mother read it to me when it arrived, calling on the phone, and quoting different highlights as she read. But today, I feel like reading for myself what I heard he wrote about Julian's view of his genes.

> *We often talked about the theory of evolution. Not only is the stronger always superior, he would also be distinguished by the more vital offspring. His genes are especially worth spreading.*

> *I was there when he bragged in front of a large group of*

In internet circles that speak like this, Julian now seems to have quite a few ardent defenders.

July 31, 2019

Petra tells me of an article about Jeffrey Epstein, a financier with connections to Hollywood who's in custody for sexual abuse and human trafficking. Petra was the first person I told about the abuse, and she has followed the debate with me all these years. It's clear to both of us that the Epstein case shows how yet another famous and influential man is given room to commit further rapes when, through excuses and rationalizations (or even encouragement and direct calls for sexual violence), he receives support after the first ones. It happens in exactly the same way as when Michael Jackson, Harvey Weinstein, or the popular guy in Bjästa were allowed to continue, even though so many knew something was wrong.

Anyone who defends the abuse of important famous, popular, or influential people joins in and gives them the space they need to continue. Anyone who excuses and explains away an abuse is an accomplice to the next abuse. The people who support Julian by excusing and rationalizing the alleged abuse—or even encouraging him to commit abuse—have sometimes even received explicit social benefits. People who said they hope I get raped have been supported in their online forums, and my reports haven't led to a single investigation. It's been difficult and expensive for Maria and me to choose not to excuse or forget what happened. Even if the rule of law actually stands above patriarchy when it comes to burn in purgatory forever," and "Jesus is ashamed" mixed with outbursts about me being a lying whore. The far-right winds blowing in Europe are also felt in Sweden. The haters seem to feel they have a tailwind, and it gets to me.

The list of those among us who are considered disloyal to "the national values" that the far-right claims to protect can be made long: Muslims, Roma and Sami people, immigrants, refugees, Jews, homosexuals, journalists, trade unionists, and feminists. For the fascist fever dream of the "clean" society to take hold, we all need to disappear. They don't say it quite so openly yet, but I understand very well that they're referring to their violent fantasies about trials and death sentences against dissidents when they say, "we'll see you in Finspång," and that they mean we should be hanged when they talk about lampposts with our names.

In the small town of Finspång, extreme right-wing debaters believe that the "traitors of the people" should in the future be brought before military tribunals and answer for "all the misery they have caused the Swedish people." The threats are often more serious now but more covert. The increasing hatred, threats, and incitement also lower the threshold for direct physical violence against those who are labeled as "traitors" by the far-right. After all, Breivik meant that he only did what "everyone" was talking about, and he did not think that his mass murder was extreme but a necessary step from words to action. Hate is the foundation; incitement is the first step, and physical violence is the logical continuation.

seem to sympathize with WikiLeaks at all or with the original purpose of WikiLeaks. For them, WikiLeaks only serves as an argument to bring me down. In the same way that they look for anything that can lower the credibility of all those they perceive to be political opponents.

I am also used in various online forums as an argument for limiting women's suffrage and autonomy:

> *"One of the main arguments that women's suffrage was the biggest mistake ever is spelled Anna 'fucking whore' Ardin."*

Someone else writes:

> *"If she realized he wasn't going to use a condom, she could say no, right? She is the typical example of why women should not be considered to be adults in society. She is the living proof of why women cannot be considered equal to men."*

Regardless of whether I say something about the climate issue, migration policy, minorities, or women's rights, my person and my background are used as weapons against me. However, the Assange case is not the only line of attack. Nowadays, there are at least as many who use my deacon title and my faith as weapons in hate attacks against me. Statements such as: "You are the emissary of the devil," "you have forfeited your right to call yourself a Christian," "you do not deserve your office, you will end up in hell and children is, of course, disgusting and outrageous. But it's not, technically speaking, the same thing as celebrating the act. So, I have therefore apologized for my generalization. But the mob is completely unaffected. Established right wing tweeters, editorial writers, and even a major social democratic blogger are working as engines to target me in full force.

I've been subjected to hatred and threats at regular intervals since I became active in public debate. At first, it was limited to misogyny, anger at my criticism of the porn industry, or the rants of sexist bloggers. In 2010, it escalated into an unmanageable storm. I have always been convinced that the attacks against me will end, but they continue. Nowadays, they're not as big or as intense, but they seem to come more often. They have become something every-day rather than something extraordinary.

Without exception, Julian Assange is used as an argument against me in any debate. Of all the messages in my various inboxes today, at least 10–20 percent have been Assange-related. Someone concludes with, "how about Julian Assange, by the way," and someone else writes that it's "completely incomprehensible that someone wanted to fuck someone like you." Earlier campaigns against me become proof of my bad personality and low credibility: "The whole world knows you're a liar." Or my report against Julian is used as an argument for me to be silent in general: "Isn't what you did to Assange enough?"

Most of those who send these messages do not

June 6, 2019

My book on faith and politics is already sold out, and it's decided that a new edition will be printed.

The District Court announces that Julian is not to be detained. More interviews must be carried out with the witnesses, and Julian also needs to be questioned. Without this, the basis for detention becomes too weak. A European investigation warrant is issued to be able to question a witness abroad. I hope that this time the prosecutor will be able to carry out the necessary tests or that Sweden will have the right to take part in the tests carried out by Great Britain.

July 22, 2019

Today, I wrote a post on Facebook that there are Sweden Democrats celebrating the anniversary of Anders Behring Breivik's far-right murder in Norwegian Utøya, where 69 children and young people were killed for their commitment to social democracy and multiculturalism. One of my Facebook contacts shamelessly screenshotted the post and forwarded it to one of the Sweden Democrats' local politicians, who in turn spread this in his circles. After that, I'm attacked by a furious online mob. I've been exposed to racist Facebook groups, and hundreds of people contact me.

I don't really have any evidence that the people I think celebrated the act online are actually Sweden Democrats, only that they expressed sympathy with the party. And appreciating a computer game where the player acts as Breivik and competes in murdering

It will hurt every time we try to poke holes in a created, mythical hero. Whether he represents our religious group, our political party, or the entire opposition to evil in the world, the healthy following of important leaders is deceptively close to the unhealthy worship of a man and sectarianism.

Everyone struggles. Everyone's important. Everyone's weak and has flaws. And most people quite often have a very poor understanding of most things. Everyone has their strengths. Julian Assange is exciting—and a fucking idiot—and he's done good things and bad. The same thing applies to every single person in the entire world, including myself. We have strengths and weaknesses; we've done good things and bad things.

It's possible that Julian is both a real hero and a real sex offender. The more I saw of him and his actions, the more difficult it became for me personally to see the hero. And with that, it's been difficult to portray this dual story of Julian as both. Perhaps there are simply no heroes at all, but I hope others will continue to describe all the good sides of Julian. Everyone deserves to be recognized for what they are doing that is good.

June 2, 2019

In a robe the blue color of Virgin Mary, after two years of training and one year as an apprentice, I am officially ordained as a deacon in the Uniting Church. I'm blessed by 2,500 enthusiastic conference attendees and welcomed into office. I feel so happy!

his superiors, and the movement, therefore, began to disown him. Malcolm X's first reaction was to submit to the will of the organization and accept ending up as a martyr for the good of the movement, but in the long run, it became unsustainable for him to annihilate himself in that way. In the end, he came out and spoke about the infidelities and, with them, the flaws in the organization and its teachings that led to this double standard.[60]

Mattias Pettersson drew the same parallel in December 2010 in an article in *Aftonbladet* about how gagging threatens the WikiLeaks movement:

> *Today, Malcolm X is remembered as a symbol of the fight against racism in the United States, not for the derailed religious sect he most of the time operated through. Had he not blown the whistle, he would have been forgotten today, just like any of the revolutions' eaten children. In the same way, WikiLeaks' whistle-blowing women can strengthen the fight to expose US war crimes, as it can help this movement to become bigger than just one leader and one organization.*[61]

Having double standards—that people are given different rights depending on the power they have and that leaders are excluded from criticism and responsibility for their actions—leads to double moralities. These moralities help a leader say one thing and do another in practice. The double standards and double moralities that this led to was a bigger problem in the civil rights movement than immorality. It's the same in the WikiLeaks movement.

we like him because power corrupts even the best people. We need to try everything and be prepared to use everything, regardless of who does or says what and what status that person has.

I understand all those who thought that I should've kept my mouth shut about "some little abuse" while some of the greatest crimes against humanity of our time were being exposed. Julian's crimes are so small in comparison to the oppression of the great powers and the widespread corruption and massacres of civilians. But the fact that I testified doesn't only feel important for my self-respect and integrity, not even just for women's rights, but also because double standards and abuse of power ultimately risk making all activities in an organization impossible.

Whistleblowers who reveal the imperfections of powerful leaders are more or less always accused by leaders of harming the organizations and their purposes. But in fact, it's the powerful leaders themselves who are the big threat.

In Malcolm X's autobiography, he says that he tried to keep quiet about the leaders' double standards in order to protect the movement and its aims. In this case, it was about Elijah Mohammed.

Mohammed was the leader of the movement that publicly preached that those who "committed adultery" would burn in hell and, at the same time, outside of his marriage, got several of his secretaries pregnant. Malcolm X believed that these abuses were minor in relation to the oppression of blacks in the United States. But just knowing meant a problem for

My case is about sexual abuse and has nothing to do with freedom of speech.

May 29, 2019

Today, the Christian newspaper *Dagen* is writing a major report regarding new information about Martin Luther King Jr., the leading figure of the American civil rights movement. Among other things, he allegedly watched, gave good advice, and laughed when a fellow pastor raped a woman.[59]

As a former member of the steering group and jury for the Swedish Martin Luther King Prize, I'm expected to be shocked and distance myself from either the accusations or the man. But I see no reason for that. In my eyes, Martin Luther King can be both a sexist asshole and an important civil rights fighter. And for me, who's lived in the shadow of a similar myth about a hero for almost ten years, it doesn't even feel like an unusual combination. It has—even though it's both boring and sad and has been a costly experience for me—helped me realize there are some fundamental errors in our society's view of heroes. The mythic images of heroes as all good and perpetrators as all evil are so unvarnished, they become completely unreasonable. The heroes and monsters presented become fictional characters. In reality, there are only people.

We must be able to pay tribute to all that do good. We must be able to speak out against everyone who does bad. We must constantly reflect and never sit back, lazily believing everything someone says, even if

"Good for you, Pamela! Love is a wonderful thing. This column sincerely hopes you have many happy years of washing his dishes ahead of you."[58]

May 13, 2019

The prosecutor decides that the preliminary investigation should be resumed now that new opportunities are opening up to move forward in the case. My case expired a long time ago; however, I'm now not a plaintiff but the witness I intended to be from the very beginning. A witness in Maria's case, where the crime classification is rape and therefore has a statute of limitations twice as long. A witness that Maria speaks the truth. A witness to things like him destroying condoms with his long right thumbnail.

May 20, 2019

The prosecutor decides to issue a new warrant for Assange's arrest. There's just over a year left until the statute of limitations for Maria's case.

May 23, 2019

The U.S. charges Julian with additional violations of the 1917 Espionage Act. The U.S. still hasn't brought the war criminals exposed in the Manning leaks to justice, and now they want to punish yet another messenger instead. At the same time, they help Julian confuse everybody about my case.

It does not attract much attention.

May 7, 2019

Actress Pamela Anderson visits Julian in prison and poses in a cape with printed text conveying some kind of message. She claims that she can determine the issue of guilt in unsolved legal cases merely by talking to the suspect and publicly declares that she visited "an innocent person." She also says she loves him.

People who were not previously involved in the case are furious—at me. They reach out via email and direct message on social media in shock and despair, saying it's not nice to report "an innocent person." I reply to someone that I technically didn't report him, but also point out I know more than Pamela Anderson about what he did to me.

I didn't want Julian to be hanged, and I also didn't want to hurt WikiLeaks, but that doesn't mean that I think he should be allowed to abuse me. It doesn't matter how many times I explain; at some points, nothing seems to have happened all these years.

May 8, 2019

When Julian was at my house, he had an idea that he and Lady Gaga should get married to get the papers to write about it. I don't know what preceded Pamela Anderson's plot or what their relationship looks like, but if the plan was attention, it worked. Many people write about it. Among others, Hadley Freeman, in a column in the *Guardian*:

dishes, dirty underwear, and unflushed toilets for the embassy staff but that he has also smeared poo on the walls in protest. Later in the day, he's found guilty of breaching bail. Julian was described by the judge as "a narcissist who cannot see beyond his own selfish interests".[57]

Maria's legal aid, now Elisabeth Massi Fritz, requests that the Swedish preliminary investigation into rape be reopened. Chief prosecutor Eva-Marie Persson leads the work to determine whether it should be.

April 12, 2019

I'm told that the U.S. is now requesting Julian be extradited to stand trial for, among other things, data breaches linked to the Chelsea Manning leaks. I'm surprised and disappointed. It isn't a crime to expose war crimes; it shouldn't be. It's an obligation.

I understand that the two cases will again be mixed up. I will personally once again be held responsible for everything that happens to him from now. I'm a scapegoat in Julian Assange's life. I have previously publicly commented on the case through hints. But today, I'm commenting it bluntly for the first time. On Twitter, I write:

> *"I would be very surprised and sad if Julian is handed over to the U.S. For me, this was never about anything else than his misconduct against me/women and his refusal to take responsibility for this. Too bad my case could never be investigated properly, but it's already been closed."*

to get him. He refuses to walk by himself, so the police have to carry him. He has a beard that makes it look like he was dragged out of a cave in the Tora Bora mountains, not from an embassy in central London. First, he screams and sputters. Once pushed into the police car, he looks self-satisfied and gives a thumbs up. What should perhaps feel like a victory to me feels mostly like great sadness. His nail is neatly cut, and in his thumbs up, I also see the very helplessness I saw the evening before the abuse. Again, I think he needs someone to take care of him. The policeman who drives him away looks, in my eyes, just like a parent putting up boundaries for an unruly child.

A friend of mine has been subjected to psychological abuse by her ex-boyfriend, and in a sort of summary to me, she describes the similarities she has seen between her own, mine, and several other abusers:

> *They have a kind of deep-rooted, childish selfishness that manifests itself in arrogance. A seemingly total inability to see themselves through someone else's eyes. An immense feeling of offense and self-righteousness when they are questioned. They think that the rest of us, all over the world, are in debt to them. It can be easy to accept their self-image as truth and get this feeling of caring about them. But that is a lousy basis for an equal relationship.*

I think she nails it.

There are reports that Julian has not only left

everyone to drop the question and move on. "The person is dead and cannot be heard," is his comment. He doesn't seem to regret it. Some enthusiastically agree with him.

The pattern is so clear. In every advance for women's rights, every time the structures are made visible, various ways of denying and belittling these very structures are also made visible. We want so badly to single out the perpetrator and make him a monster, labeling him as something different that is not a part of us, or the exact opposite strategy—to deny guilt and downplay the significance of the abuse, a demand for forgetful forgiveness.

But what is really needed is neither lynching nor forgetting but rectifying forgiveness.

We must be able to keep two things in our heads at the same time if we want to be able to move forward. We must be able to see that the perpetrator is not an evil monster without, for that sake, belittling or denying his crime. This still seems to be difficult, but at the same time, something has definitely happened in society since the trial against Josefin's perpetrator. There's more space for the difficult questions that Marie calls "questions that are so much bigger than a minute in the noise." It's precisely these same questions I've thought about so many times when being chased by the drive. There seems to be a wider space to ask these questions now, and that's hopeful.

April 11, 2019

Today, Ecuador withdraws Julian's political asylum and unlocks the door to the British police. They go in

March 22, 2019

Today, one of my childhood idols, Josefin Nilsson, the lead singer of Ainbusk Singers, would have turned 50 years old if she had lived. Instead, a documentary about her is broadcast on Swedish television, and it hits like a bomb. Her former partner, a famous actor, abused her mentally and physically and gave her scars for life. Under the hashtag #burnforJosefin (#brinnförJosefin), the misogyny that causes men to hate, threaten, insult, and beat women and those around them to deny and belittle the problem is highlighted and discussed. It feels like another step after #talkaboutit and #metoo in a staircase on the way to understanding and equality.

March 29, 2019

Josefin's sister, Marie Nilsson Lind, who played the piano in Ainbusk Singers, testifies on a TV couch about how much she dislikes the mob that arose after the documentary.

She comments on the fact that people want to take revenge on the actor:

"That's not how it's supposed to be, is it?" she says, describing it as a hunt for a wild animal. That there is an atmosphere of lynching, and their brother receives messages on the theme: "If it had been my sister, I would have killed that damn actor" or "why didn't you, as a man, do something?"

The actor himself thinks that he's suffered enough and has atoned for his crime (while at the same time questioning whether it was even a crime) and wants

March 10, 2019

The film *Leaving Neverland*, which wants to prove Michael Jackson systematically abused young boys, is broadcast on Swedish Television. Of course, the abuse these children testified that Jackson subjected them to cannot be compared to the abuse Julian is suspected of. But like the rapes in Bjästa or the one at Bråvallafestivalen, the defense of the suspected perpetrator has mobilized again in ways that are frighteningly similar. A man who made such important music cannot be guilty, they say. And if he is guilty, it's not that bad. And then the hunt for victims starts; people cooperate in lowering their credibility and in exposing them in a people's tribunal, judging them as perpetrators against an "innocent" star.

Every detail of the stories about things that happened in the victims' childhoods is turned inside out, and when one of the men refers to a house that wasn't built at the time of the abuse he talks about, the whole story is invalidated. I think that will probably happen with this book as well. Dates and details will be scrutinized in a way that no memory in the world can hold, and errors will be found somewhere. Errors in details about things that happened so long ago really say nothing about the credibility of testimony. It's important that people are allowed to own their stories. Of course, we can never know exactly what happened to someone else somewhere else. But we still need to give space to those who want to tell.

February 18, 2019

For a year now, I've dedicated almost every free moment to editing and finishing my book. My idea has been to show how I read the Bible's calls to build God's kingdom and that community involvement is needed to succeed. It was supposed to be the study material I thought was missing in the diaconal training, but the interest was wider than that, and now it has been published with the title *Political and Prophetic Diakonia*. Today, I'm organizing a release party with a seminar in a church in Södermalm. The food is prepared by three Roma girls from Romania whom I got to know through my commitment to their rights in the Salvation Army, and the venue is packed with exciting theologians, activists, family, and friends. A person with a very long church commitment describes the atmosphere by saying, "everyone is here!" I get to sign books and receive an amazing number of nice words, gifts, and hugs.

March 8, 2019

Today, on International Women's Day, Chelsea Manning is arrested because she refuses to testify against Julian. They are locking her up indefinitely, and I feel unspeakably sad. The political persecution I thought she had escaped once again has a decisive significance for her life. Of course, I have nothing to do with everything she is subjected to, but I still feel close.

2019

connections to Sweden, Russia, and Israel and has worked closely with Julian for several years. This raises headlines, not least because of the accusations against Shamir regarding anti-Semitic statements and Holocaust denial.[56]

October 16, 2018

Ecuador requires Julian to clean his bathroom. A nine-page code of conduct document has been leaked, and they tempt him to follow these rules with a promise of returning his Internet access.

I couldn't stand him as a guest for more than a few days and have often wondered what it's like for the embassy staff to have this guy as a resident for years. Here came one answer to that question.

Where sphere after sphere of society has swung in their view of Julian, now even anonymous, male-dominated forums on the Internet are beginning to talk about the case differently. In 2010, I felt that almost everyone had sympathy for him and mocked or hated Maria and me, but now the sympathy for us and the mockery of him is so much more palpable.

I wish it wasn't like this. I wish people could see the humanity in both the victims and perpetrators at the same time. Through it all, however, there has been a predictable constant: Male-dominated forums on the Internet are prone to mocking people even if it concerns ancient idols. But him being mocked doesn't help at all.

May 25, 2018

My project to produce study material on faith and politics as part of my diaconal training has grown into a whole book about faith, social issues, and politics. In order to reach wider Swedish Christianity, I've been in contact with a few publishers. Ideally, I want to publish the book with *Argument*, a progressive publisher with congregations as the main target group, and I know that they have now read my script and discussed it with their editorial board. It's taken a long time to get a response, but when I now finally see an email from the publisher's manager in my inbox, I get nervous. Of course, I'm fully prepared for a friendly but clear no, but I still sincerely hope that they will say yes. They write: "Now we have finished reasoning here, I can finally tell you...."

I take a breath.

"We are happy to publish this book! It has great relevance and a cutting edge and is very well written, so we would be proud to include it in our publication!"

Hurray!

September 17, 2018

The media has obtained documents showing that Julian applied for a visa to Russia in 2010, that is, at about the same time he applied for a residence permit in Sweden. According to one of my favorite newspapers, the progressive Israeli newspaper *Haaretz*, he has given a written mandate to Israel Shamir to apply for a residence permit for him. Shamir has

2018

that I will survive. Realize that people might consider seeing me again, that it actually hasn't cost everything to tell the truth. Those who stood up for me from the beginning, those who fought for women's right to their bodies, have succeeded in turning public opinion around! You publicly claim that you are someone who supports me. But I didn't see that when I needed it the most. You were one of all those who disappeared. One who thinks they are blameless just because they don't prey on women themselves. It takes more than a hashtag to change that.

November 14, 2017

Today, the media is once again reporting on WikiLeaks and the selective leaks that are believed to have damaged the Democratic presidential campaign. It's emerged that during this period, the WikiLeaks Twitter account, managed by Julian himself, had direct private contact with Donald Trump Jr., who was working for his father's campaign. Several heavyweight Americans have now officially taken their hand off Julian. Although many Trump fans support Julian in his views on women's rights, WikiLeaks' supporters generally don't seem very fond of Trump.

Olof, what you did was among the worst things anyone has ever done to me. I wanted to die. I was completely broken, got death threats all the time, and I was in love with you. You came back from radio silence and wanted to go for dinner. I was so happy for that. I guess you don't even remember what you said.

But I remember. I remember exactly what happened, I saw you on your back on a bench over there at Skanstull waiting for me, you seemed happy to see me and my stomach tingled. I remember which place we went to, which food I ordered and how, after five minutes there, you told me about your real business—that I would not mention your name in the legal process. You didn't want to risk being exposed; it was risky—for you. I didn't say anything then but screamed inside. Outwardly, I might have said "yeah," and then we chatted about other things. Maybe that's why you don't remember?

It took forever for the food to arrive. I ate as fast as I could, paid my share and went home and cried for days. I thought no one could hire me let alone love me. I felt like I had become dirty, a pariah, someone it was dangerous to support. You confirmed that feeling.

The trial (which never even happened) felt even more impossible to win. When my whole character, my sex life, all my faults were to come to light, and you, who could testify that my version was truer than his, did not even want to testify in my favor.

When I hear from you again, it's only now, when I realize

not. I tag the post with #metoo.

The support is overwhelming. I get hundreds of likes and encouraging comments from my friends. It's no longer dangerous to support me. The risks of suffering from hatred or disadvantages for taking a stand for me seem to have disappeared. It's like being cleared of my infection, at least in the circles that matter most to me.

One of those commenting is Olof. The man who not only wanted for us to stop seeing each other because of the online hate but who also explicitly refused to participate as my witness in the legal process. He writes: *"You go! You are so brave! #supportanna."*

I get absolutely furious.

"Yes," I write in response, *"I really needed support six years ago when you instead refused to testify in my favor."* He deletes his comment and instead sends a private message. He is "surprised" and says I misunderstood him, and he's upset that I don't accept his public support. It's like sadness and fear have dampened all other emotions until now. But in my life, joy has now almost completely replaced sadness. I often laugh many times every day and don't really cry at all. I love my home, my family, and my job, and the unequivocal support I now receive seems to dissolve the last of the lid of fear that has kept the anger down. I'm boiling with anger. I articulate what he doesn't seem to understand. My reply to him cannot be sent; he's already blocked me. But this is what I write:

August 14, 2017

Today, I start the second and last year of my education to become a deacon. One of the big tasks this year is an independent project, a thesis. I have outlined various proposals that connect church and social-political issues, about the deacons and the church's opportunities and responsibilities to not only help on an individual level but also structurally, to do something about inequality, racism, or climate change, how the deaconess's social mission is also political. But from the questions and objections I have received in education and the church, I have realized that it's difficult for many to even understand this connection exists. Therefore, I've decided to instead try to explain this very thing. I will produce material on how faith and politics can go together, perhaps for study circles in parishes or for courses in future deacon training.

October 16, 2017

A friend of mine writes a public post about the abuse she experienced and adds #metoo. It's an international call for all women who've experienced sexual abuse and harassment to do the same with the aim of showing the extent of the problem.

After seven years of silence, it feels right to describe to my friends what really happened that night in the late summer of 2010. I'm looking for a text I wrote about the abuse shortly after, but it was never published. I describe the details of what has so many times been called voluntary and consensual but which, in fact, was central point. Again, it's a question of who a rapist really is and who is really raped.

Jeffner: *"How far can you go before you have to blame yourself if you are raped?"*

Sara: *"Well, you can't go that far. Guys, they're a bit like that; they think you want them just by looking at them. You can dance with them, but if you start kissing them and so on and then just walk away, then you have to blame yourself if he goes after you."*[53]

It's a terrible view of men to think that men are animals or slaves to their instincts or that all men are prepared to cross a woman's boundaries if she says no too late. It's like saying that all men are basically rapists. I don't believe that.

Maybe I've been fabulously lucky, or these views are simply not rooted in mainstream male sexuality. What I encountered was awkward and pretentious, skilled and incompetent, dull and beautiful, regular and extraordinary. But this view of the frightening, threatening, and involuntary has not manifested itself among the men I have had sexual relations with. Not until I met Julian Assange.

June 9, 2017

Laura Poitra's movie *Risk* premieres in Sweden. The idea was that it would be about WikiLeaks and Julian Assange's new revolutionary form of journalism. She tells in interviews that she started working on the film six years ago as a sequel to her Oscar-winning film *Citizenfour* about Edward Snowden. *Risk* was supposed to be about the hero Assange and his important work with WikiLeaks, but as Julian's sexism is revealed, the film changes its character. Instead of just describing the heroic Julian, she illustrates other sides that become crucial to the way WikiLeaks works. In an interview with Poitras in the Guardian, she describes those sides of him as "the pompous," "the narcissistic," and "the paranoid" Julian.[54] In the movie[55], this conversation between Julian and his girlfriend Sarah is included:

Julian: *"I didn't really become famous until after the sex affair. I was well-known in media and intelligence circles but no real celebrity. I wasn't someone everyone knew until after the sex affair. So, I jokingly said to a colleague: 'A sex scandal in six months!'"*

Sarah: *"You told me that. I almost died,"*

Julian: *"It is the way to..."*

Sarah: *"'It's good for our profile, Sarah,' you said,"*

Both of them laugh.

Sarah: *"'Please don't do it! I would kill you,' I replied."*
Julian: *"What? It's a platform."*

Sarah: *"You already have a platform!"* she exclaims and giggles.

In another scene, he talks to lawyer Helena Kennedy (the woman who sent me the horrible "settlement offer" in July 2011) about how he should handle the allegations. When Kennedy says that it must not appear as though he doesn't care about women's rights, he responds that the accusations are only a part of a "radical feminist conspiracy." He refers to one of the internet's big gossips, i.e., the rumor that I'm a lesbian. Julian uses this rumor to dismiss the accusations against himself, claiming that I and the police who did the first of the many interrogations with Maria belong to "a lesbian circle" and that I have run "a dyke club in Gothenburg."

It doesn't take a master detective to find evidence that I was committed to the rights of LGBTQ people, including by starting and running Club Fever alongside Petra in Visby in 2007, which we called "Gotland's first queer club," although it's quite far away from Gothenburg. But how that has anything to do with my accusations against Julian is hard to understand.

Kennedy draws the same conclusion as me, saying it doesn't help him to talk like that. "No, not in public," he says in front of the rolling camera. And then he explains that it wouldn't be smart for me and Maria to accuse him:

An actual court case is going to be very hard for these women... They will be reviled forever by a large segment of the world population. I don't think it's in their interest to proceed that way.

He is, of course, absolutely correct. Many people will,

not least because of the falsehoods he himself spreads, forever loathe us.

Apparently, Julian demanded that the scenes showing his sexism be cut from the movie. When Poitras refused, Julian wanted to sue her. Nothing of that spirit ever materialized, but I'm also beginning to see the offer Kennedy sent me in a different light. Maybe the "offer" was that bad because Julian never really went along with her plan. After all, the offer consisted of Julian apologizing and admitting his violations against us in exchange for us withdrawing our accusations and informing the Swedish court that we no longer intended to cooperate. I'm guessing that this plan originated as an idea with her and maybe other human rights defenders as well. But it presupposes that Julian would actually also sacrifice something and begin to reflect on the fact that he committed wrong. So, when Julian refused to back down and instead continued to abuse us, Kennedy went ahead to try and get us to cooperate in clearing Julian anyway. Her plan was for us to withdraw the charges without *anything* in return.

When I watch Poitra's film, the relationship between Kennedy and Assange becomes more understandable. Only the short dialogues between them that are shown strengthen Pia's view that it's about a defense of men's rights. Kennedy should have understood that the power and responsibility—for what he was accused of and the developments in the courts—essentially rested with him all along. But she chose to ignore it.

important.

Katarina Wennstam has worked, analyzed, and written about sexual crime cases in Sweden for a long time. She believes there's a persistent and prejudiced myth about male sexuality. And it is exactly this image of the horny man who cannot think for himself and cannot take responsibility for his actions that Julian's defense has used. She writes:

> *Every time someone tells a woman that because she walked a guy home, wiggled her butt, or made him horny, she has herself to blame, we are simultaneously saying that all men "are like that," that they can't control themselves if they get horny, picked up, or see a tasty cleavage.*[51]

Wennstam also clearly describes how victims often "give up." She describes a case of such rape where a girl realizes that she will not be able to escape and therefore argues that the two guys should use condoms, partly because of the risk of infection, partly so that she will not get pregnant. The court, therefore, considers it likely that the boys perceived that she was consenting.[52] Not wanting but still agreeing to it to minimize the damage. To relax instead of resisting when it feels too costly or too risky.

Swedish sociologist Stina Jeffner also talks about the mythic images surrounding male sexuality. In the book *Liksom våldtäkt, typ* (*Like rape, kind of*), she interviews 15-year-old youths in-depth about their views on rape. Both boys and girls draw sharp lines between what they call real rape and abuse that occurs when a girl incites a boy. Jeffner puts her finger on a

I'm relieved and convinced that now—finally—we can all put this behind us and begin the next chapter of our lives.

May 20, 2017

Men get erections when they share a bed with a woman, Julian's lawyer has apparently told the court in London. I guess it's a defense against the molestation charges. Does he mean that men cannot stop their instincts and impulses? That an excited man is dangerous and uncontrollable, both for himself and for those around him? That when the blood goes out into the penis, it disappears from the brain, and the man can no longer act rationally? I don't believe that. That sounds to me the same as saying men are animals. But men are hardly more animals than women. I, and modern research, are certain that men can behave—even when they get excited.

Mythic images of sexuality have filled my inbox for almost seven years now. Opinions about abuse, gray areas, male sexuality, and what I, as a woman, should accept scare me sometimes, like the idea that men should be treated like explosives that detonate if mishandled. Or claims that men can't read women's signals and don't have the same human capacity for self-control as other people in sexual situations. That's not something feminists accuse Julian of. No, it's something his own defense uses to defend him. They explain away his behavior by arguing that he is not accountable. I'm convinced that he is. I think Julian understood that I wasn't consenting to what was going on, but he didn't care. He didn't think it was must be carried out quickly. At the time when a prosecutor does not have the opportunity to take further investigation measures, the prosecutor is obliged to drop the preliminary investigation. And it is pointless to continue the preliminary investigation without the cooperation of Ecuador.

At the press conference today, Marianne Ny says:

> *Almost five years ago, Julian Assange took refuge in the Ecuadorian Embassy in London, where he is still located. He has thus evaded all attempts by the Swedish and British authorities to execute the decision to hand him over to Sweden in accordance with the EU rules on a European arrest warrant. My assessment is that the handover cannot be carried out within a foreseeable time. All possibilities for currently pushing the investigation forward have been exhausted. In order to proceed further, it would be required that Julian Assange be formally informed about the suspicion of the crime. It cannot be expected that we would receive assistance from Ecuador in this. The investigation is therefore closed. If, at a later date, he should make himself available, I may decide to immediately resume the preliminary investigation. My decision means that it does not make sense to pursue the investigation further at the moment.[50]*

And now something strange happens. The interest in both Julian Assange and me seems to decline. There was no increase in readers for the blog post about the seven-step model of legal revenge, and no one calls to yell or threaten me either by phone, email, or Twitter.

May 17, 2017

Chelsea Manning is released as promised from Fort Leavenworth in Kansas.

"Whatever is ahead of me is far more important than the past," she says in her first comment as a free woman.

I feel hopeful and happy.

May 18, 2017

I'm watching a TED talk about orgasms with science journalist Mary Roach. She explains an old theory about the orgasm called the "up-suck method." According to it, a woman's orgasm causes the uterus to "suck up" the sperm, thereby increasing the chances of conception. The theory was tested in the 50s but could not be proven... This reminds me of a seven-year-old mystery. Why did Julian want me to cum during the abuse? It seemed so unlikely that it was for my sake. When the entire sequence up to this point was all about him, I didn't understand why he cared. It didn't fit the pattern. Afterward, I was almost unsure if it had even happened. It's taken a lot of time and effort to get hold of the memories of all the details, to understand them, and put them into context. But this detail remains unexplained. Now, seeing Roach, I get at least one plausible explanation.

May 19, 2017

Chief prosecutor Marianne Ny decides to drop the preliminary investigation of suspected rape and revoke the European arrest warrant. Ny acts in accordance with the law, which states that a criminal investigation

January 17, 2017

Manning believes she's served the punishment for the crimes she committed and applies for parole. Today the soon to be ex-President of the United States, Barack Obama, approves this. He shortens her sentence and announces that she will be released on May 17. There are many of us who celebrate and rejoice that there was still time left for Obama to act.

April 7, 2017

A man who's had his asylum application rejected steals a truck and runs people over on Stockholm's biggest shopping street, where for periods of my life, I've moved through almost every day. My friend Omar's sister is one of those who just manages to escape into a store. The crime comes uncomfortably close. Swedes of all backgrounds are shaken, and the solidarity is enormous. Churches and mosques stay open for crisis management, people give each other rides when all public transport is shut down, and the street is filled with paper hearts and messages of love.

I am being accused of complicity in the act because of my defense of the rights of both Muslims and refugees. Someone writes:

> *CIA agent, rabid feminist/ Muslim lover, Christian fundamentalist, flathead & deathly in love with Julian Assange, can you even be all that at the same time? Apparently! Anna "IS"[49] Ardin is really disturbed.*

2017

refuses to participate.

A suspect is never obliged to answer questions, and Julian takes advantage of that opportunity, which makes it impossible to clarify what actually happened. When the questions were sent in advance, when DNA testing could not be carried out, and when the possibility of going ahead and prosecuting was non-existent, the hearing in London became pointless.

The prosecutor was right all along. Going to London to interrogate him didn't work. It was Julian's reluctance to cooperate that prevented him from being questioned about the suspected sex crimes, nothing WikiLeaks-related. It seems to be simply about his unwillingness to take responsibility for his own actions, not his concern for execution.

I'm thinking a little wearily about how Ecuador views Julian's reasons for asylum. Was he granted asylum to escape because of the U.S.'s suspicions about WikiLeaks' publications, or are his grounds for protection based on the suspicions of sex crimes?

The online tribunal states that the prosecutor "lied the whole time" about the legal obstacles to the interrogation because they can now actually be removed. But despite all the nagging from Julian that he longed to give his version, he is, once again, not going to answer a single question. Instead, he presents something written in advance. Just as I thought, he has prepared answers that will not be used against him, and he refuses to participate in the interrogation at all.

He also does not take the DNA test, which he could have been forced to do during a regular interrogation, but which he does not have to in this irregular interrogation, which means that it still isn't possible to tie him to the technical evidence. He also refuses to be served a summons on suspicion of crime. As is the practice in these types of matters, Ecuador continues to comply with Julian's wishes and the conditions he seems to set on his own, so he gets what he wants.

I don't think Julian really believed that the prosecutors would clear all the hurdles and get a hearing before my case was barred; I think he rather saw it as a surefire way to have something to blame. But the prosecutor solved it; they agreed to do everything according to his demands, despite great practical obstacles. The government even signed a new international agreement. The case was tried in all instances, and finally, the prosecutor travels to London again. Now she's there for another attempt to interrogate him on the spot. There's no risk of him being taken by the Swedish police and sent to the United States, as he expressed worry about. Still, he

October 28, 2016

Michael Moore publicly admits that he is no longer quite as impressed by the WikiLeaks revelations:

"I feel like he's drifted," says Moore on the American talk show Real Time with Bill Maher.

It seems undeniable that Julian has slipped away, but I think a bigger problem is the fantasy of Julian as infallible and how people like Moore contribute to that image. The flaws seem to have become more and worse, but they were hardly absent when Julian was hailed as a hero.

November 8, 2016

Henrik and I watch the news from the U.S. about the presidential election, and it seems safe. Swedish media predict that Clinton will win, and we go to bed.

November 9, 2016

Henrik wakes me up and shows me a picture of a map of the election results in the U.S. states. The map is completely red. Donald Trump, the bully from New York, has won the presidential election.

November 14, 2016

All permits are in place, the prosecutor has handed over his questions to Ecuador's public prosecutor's office—contrary to how interrogations should be held according to Swedish law—and Julian is to be questioned by an Ecuadorian prosecutor at their embassy in London. What his fan club called the "long-awaited interrogation."

August 22, 2016

A new beginning! Today I start the two-year training required to be accepted as a deacon in the Uniting Church. My daughter is five months old, and Henrik and I will take turns caring for her. Today, she's with me in school.

August 24, 2016

A Saudi man who is referred to as homosexual in a leak from a Saudi embassy believes that he risks dire consequences if the wrong people get hold of this information.[47] WikiLeaks is once again heavily criticized for having leaked things such as private individuals' medical records, names of young rape victims, and others who are at risk of getting very badly hurt.

On Twitter, Julian calls it recycled news and stuff that isn't worth the headlines. He also points out that the journalist reporting on this "is a rat, a Jewish rat" in an internal chat that was also leaked.[48]

September 16, 2016

The Svea Court of Appeal decides that Julian Assange must continue to be detained in his absence. I have no idea how many lawyers, legal technicians, police officers, prosecutors, and judges are involved. There must be numerous. He's a suspect. And the reasons to believe so are strong. It feels like a record being stuck, repeating itself over and over again.

condoms, namely the way they broke. Both condoms have been torn off at the tip in exactly the same way.

In the evidence, it looks like Julian Assange destroyed the condoms, and my theory is that it was to be able to inseminate us against our will, but without us noticing until it was too late. In my case, he did it so quickly and skillfully that it seems unlikely that it was the first time he did it.

When I watch Julian on TV, I try to catch a glimpse of whether his right thumbnail is still long to see if he's still nursing his condom-cracker nail.

The technical evidence surrounding the condoms has been classified to protect our privacy and to allow the prosecutor to confront him with it during questioning without giving him the opportunity to prepare new lies. But now, the questioning will have to be done by the Ecuadorian prosecutor, which means that all information must be sent to the embassy in advance.

The quality of the questioning will be very difficult to guarantee, and the possibilities for relevant follow-up questions will therefore be basically non-existent. The risk that everything has been shared with Julian's defense before questioning is also imminent, and his answer will be adapted to the technical evidence. But it's still better than no interrogation. One last attempt to clarify the truth. I understand why the prosecutor is still trying.

August 9, 2016

Julian Assange appeals the District Court's arrest decision to the Svea Court of Appeal.

found in the garbage after the police requested this as technical evidence. In the State's Forensic Technology Laboratory's first analysis, not enough DNA was found to be able to determine any identities.[44] According to the police's forensic technician, this may have been due to things such as other dirt interfering with the analysis, DNA traces being wiped off, or due to the fact that some people leave only very small DNA traces.[45] They then sent the condom for an in-depth analysis.

That analysis can be found in another confidential document that Julian's defense has not seen, or pretend not to have seen, where it says that there is, in fact, DNA on the condom.[46] A DNA that matches me and a DNA from "an unknown man." But I know who this man is. And because I'm sure about who used the condom that Maria submitted from the night before she reported a rape, I'm also sure that even in that case, there are traces of two people.

Maria and the same "unknown" man as in my case.

The false information that there is a complete lack of DNA on the condom I submitted has been spread very intensively. But it isn't true. In the in-depth analysis, DNA has been identified, but the problem is that Julian does not want it to be tested to see whether this comes from him. If he had been so sure that it wasn't his DNA, he would've agreed to let the Swedish justice system swab him. It would've been an easy way to clear suspicion for an innocent person. But Julian, of course, has reasons to refuse.

There's also another similarity between these two

July 28, 2016

Edward Snowden tweets about WikiLeaks: "Democratizing information has never been more vital, and @WikiLeaks has helped. But their hostility to even modest curation is a mistake."

This is the same criticism that the chairman of Reporters Without Borders in Stockholm discussed with Julian, that WikiLeaks does not sufficiently protect individuals by the masking information that can identify them in the material that WikiLeaks releases. I don't know what Snowden means by referring to WikiLeaks as them, several persons, or who else other than Julian could have been involved in making decisions about how WikiLeaks should act. But I understand that criticism from Snowden is a serious blow to Julian.

August 8, 2016

A legal agreement is now in place between Sweden and Ecuador. Ecuador, therefore, announces that it accepts the prosecutors' request to interrogate Assange.

It's positive news because even though my case is time-barred, I'm still a witness. He will be questioned and forced to explain what he did to me as well. I think that maybe they will even be able to force him to a DNA test that the Swedish judiciary can use and thus finally prove that my testimony—not his—is correct.

Julian's online defenders have claimed repeatedly again that there was "no DNA on the condom" I

"Unbelievable that someone dared to approach this horrible person to the point that it ends up giving birth."
"The fact that this disturbed feminist still has a career after all the crap she's done says a lot about the sad state Swedish society is in. Really hope this lying feminist gets her punishment."

May 25, 2016

The Stockholm District Court decides that Julian Assange should remain wanted, despite the defense lawyers' battle to lift the arrest warrant. He's still a suspect on probable grounds. This is a higher degree of suspicion, which, according to the police, means that "the suspicion against a person appears in an objective assessment to be justified and is based on evidence in the individual case".[43] The evidence is still considered strong. But a trial is required to determine whether he is guilty.

May 28, 2016

I am informed that I've been accepted to the diaconal program at Bromma community college!

July 19, 2016

Putin allegedly supports Donald Trump's presidential election campaign in the United States, and WikiLeaks has leaked large amounts of material from Hillary Clinton and the Democrats' campaign. WikiLeaks receives massive criticism for this. On Twitter, Julian responds by implying that most of the critics are Jews.

January 21, 2016

Ecuador's attorney general rejects the Swedish prosecutor's request for questioning. As expected, a legal agreement between Sweden and Ecuador is required, and there is no such thing.

February 4, 2016

UNWGAD, the UN Committee against Arbitrary Detention, is investigating whether Julian is subject to arbitrary detention. It's silly. Since he's not deprived of his liberty, it, of course, cannot be arbitrary. Today, Julian proudly declares that he intends to surrender if they conclude that he's not being arbitrarily deprived of his liberty.

I consider it extremely unlikely that Julian would surrender voluntarily. He has evaded arrest warrants, ignored all court orders to appear for questioning, failed friends' bail bonds, and he has done everything in his power to ensure that the case never goes to trial. And when all the conditions (which are not against the law) that he set are met, he still refuses to be questioned—instead, he makes even more demands.

The idea that he would suddenly listen to five non-profits with a UN stamp makes me shake my head. There's only one explanation I can believe for such a statement, and that is that he's received advance notice that they've already sided with him.

February 5, 2016

The Committee Against Arbitrary Detention has sided with Julian. They think he should be compensated for being under "house arrest." I don't know if they mean the time he hung out at Vaughn Smith's estate or when he locked himself in the embassy, but I laugh when I hear that.

When I go to the toilet, I lock the door and call out to Henrik:

"Unfortunately, I can't do the dishes because I'm arbitrarily detained!"

I'm sitting in my voluntary lavatory arrest for a while. But then realize that I probably do have to do the dishes. It's my turn. I'm leaving when the laughter gets stuck in my throat.

The UN is one of our most important institutions for guaranteeing human rights globally. My confidence in the UN has always been high, and having worked under the UN Development Program in Geneva is one of the things on my CV I am most proud of. But their good name has now been used to defend a guy's right to impunity when he forcibly inseminates women. It's not fun; it feels terrible.

The fact that two of the five committee members did not agree and that a couple of the most credible legal systems in the world stand alongside their decisions, and that the British Foreign Minister calls the committee's statement "frankly ridiculous" does not play a very important role in that perspective. It's so sad.

February 22, 2016

Julian's lawyers are requesting a review of the Stockholm District Court's arrest decision.

February 26, 2016

My life has taken a new turn, and I feel better in every way than when it was at its worst a few years ago. At the same time, the search for the common thread that I realized I needed during my pilgrimage has continued. My beautiful family—that will get bigger just a month from now—my job, my friends, my commitment, all these are important pieces of the puzzle, but something is missing. More and more, I begin to see how my commitment to equality, human rights, and peace is more than just a piece of the puzzle. It's a framework. It's a calling. I'm beginning to understand that it's my faith that is the common thread.

How could conviction that all people are equally valuable, the very basis for what I think and do, ever be explained with logical or scientific arguments? Human value is based on the fact that we're created equal in dignity and rights. God's will is the foundation of that conviction for me. Because God exists, every human has a value that cannot be disproved. No matter what happens, deep in the universe, there's a heart and not emptiness. Believing this affects everything for me. God's calling is what holds my heart together. The church's Diakonia is, for me, a clear way of putting God's message of love into practical action. I also realize that much of the work I have done for social justice, community in civil society, and to demand that those who are not listened to be heard is actually diaconal, and I want to plunge myself into that. I, therefore, decide to apply for deacon training.

March 8, 2016

Prosecutors are sending a renewed request via the Department of Justice to Ecuador to question Assange at the Ecuadorian Embassy in London.

March 31, 2016

It's ten days until my due date, and I start having contractions when I visit my two-year-old's preschool. Just over an hour later, twenty minutes after entering the hospital, I give birth to my second child. Everything is well.

April 2, 2016

Today, I got curious about whether the trolls are still discussing me. They are. I went to a few online forums and was particularly drawn to the comments from the last time I had a baby:

> *"Recently gave birth to a son."*
> *"I guess she didn't use rubber that time either?"*
> *"Who is the father?"*
> *"Her partner, who is not a public figure."*
> *"In the same apartment, a Henrik is registered, which should then reasonably be the child's father."*
> *"I thought Ardin was an official dyke?"*

be about something completely different than the fear of being extradited to the United States.

August 13, 2015

It has now been five years since the abuse. Five years is the statute of limitations for the criminal classifications the prosecutor presented in my case. Therefore, today the preliminary investigation against Julian about the parts that concern me is cancelled.

Henrik and I celebrate with two glasses of non-alcoholic bubbly. Finally, the wait for the trial is over. Finally, my life is mine. For a long time, I felt that the whole mess, all the chaos, all the journalists who wanted comments from me—even the allegations of abuse—had nothing to do with me. Hundreds of thousands of people have helped to inflate both Julian and the allegations to absurd levels. Finally, I am officially and legally exonerated from the case. Now it's over, I think.

August 17, 2015

The police call to tell me that I have seized evidence to collect. A five-year-old unwashed sheet with semen. A disgusting little treasure somehow. I say I don't want it.

I joke on Facebook that I will sell it and make money. And then I joke that Julian's defense will take my joke seriously and organize a demonstration. Someone offers to make V for Vendetta masks from the fabric. I change my mind. Maybe I can use the sheet for something anyway. I call the police and have the prosecutor unless he gets his conditions met, so no questioning can be carried out.

Right now, Julian's main condition seems to be that he be *guaranteed* asylum in Sweden. A demand he knows is impossible to meet since our different authorities act independently according to the corresponding laws, and one authority or even the government is constitutionally prevented from giving such guarantees. Therefore, this should rather be described as an excuse. According to Swedish law, asylum applications must take place on Swedish territory. The law, being such, is an obstacle to the right to asylum. Since the right to have one's reasons for asylum assessed is a human right, in my personal opinion, reasons for asylum should, of course, be taken into account regardless of where a person is.

But the law is not written that way, and a prosecutor cannot work based on morality but must act based on the established legislature. The prosecutor cannot give special treatment to Julian Assange as he demands. In Sweden, politicians establish laws, and the judiciary judges based on these. It cannot be waived, no matter how important a suspect is considered to be. It's clear that Julian hasn't done his best to take responsibility for clarifying the truth in the case of the sex crime allegations. That it's Julian, not the prosecutor, who makes the investigation impossible.

As I see it, the Swedish judiciary has shown through its actions that sexual crimes are serious and must be treated accordingly. Julian's refusal to allow questioning of himself about the sex crimes seems to very last time before I blocked him, I see him. Andreas comes with his own stroller. He looks surprised and happy and seems to want to come over and say hello. It feels like watching a movie. I observe it from the outside; how I fix my eyes on his face for a second or so, register that he's there, but keep walking.

May 11, 2015

The Supreme Court decides that Assange should continue to be wanted for arrest.

May 29, 2015

Julian and the beaters, the people who lead the howling hounds online, have demanded that he be questioned at the Ecuadorian Embassy. But in addition to the fact that an interrogation at the embassy will probably not be able to provide the answers required for the investigation, it also entails major legal obstacles. At the same time, this is the last chance to get any answers at all. The prosecutors are therefore applying for legal assistance from the Ministry of Justice's unit for criminal cases and international legal cooperation (BIRS).

June 16–17, 2015

The prosecutor's office announces that chief prosecutor Ingrid Isgren is in London with the ambition of interrogating Julian Assange at the Ecuadorian Embassy. However, there is no permit because there's no general legal agreement between Sweden and Ecuador. Julian also does not want to see

January 8, 2015

Julian tweets about "the Jewish pro-censorship lobby," and I'm immediately accused of collaborating with it. The trolls are trying to trace my Jewish connections.

March 13, 2015

It's clear that Julian will continue to obstruct. He continues to claim that it's dangerous for him to come to Sweden, despite the fact that it's clearly and publicly declared that it would mean double protection. Both Sweden's and England's judicial systems would have to approve an extradition request.

He continues to demand to be questioned at the embassy. The prosecutors seem to see this as a last resort now that my case is nearing the statute of limitations and are formally requesting Julian's permission to proceed.

April 16, 2015

Assange gives permission to question him under certain conditions. I don't know what demands he makes, and it seems unclear even to the prosecutor.

May 9, 2015

My child has started preschool. We couldn't find a place at the one we wanted at home in Hammarbyhöjden, so we have to leave him at a place in the city center every morning. As I walk from the bus through the park by my old home where the abuse happened, where Andreas and I met each other the

2015

December 8, 2014

Julian is appealing the Court of Appeal's decision to the Supreme Court. There are starting to be a lot of courts involved. Claes is confident that the evidence is strong and that the appeal will only prolong the process, not change it.

December 21, 2014

WikiLeaks has released material leaked from the company Sony. It makes some headlines, but mainly in the gossip press, and the biggest scoop is what an employee at Sony really thinks of the actor Adam Sandler. When WikiLeaks does a stunt that brings media attention, it usually causes a new wave of hate and attacks against me. I'm usually portrayed as an enemy who wants to prevent WikiLeaks' work for transparency and freedom of expression. But this news doesn't cause any stir against me; it's a relief.

Excusing perpetrators who are perceived to be one of "us" thus goes hand in hand with a willingness to execute perpetrators who are perceived to be one of "the others." And it goes hand in hand with rejecting victims who report sexual offenses and calling them whores. There's a logic here. The logic of patriarchy.

It's far from just anonymous sexist trolls perpetuating this myth of "real perpetrators" and "real victims." The myth is reinforced every time someone calls a rapist a monster and an exception. Likewise, this happens every time someone dehumanizes a perpetrator and pretends that he's designed in some completely different way than the rest of us. That what he did is strictly individual and in no way a product of our own society. Every time someone pretends that ordinary men don't rape, the myth gets stronger. Every time sexual crimes are belittled or magnified to be used as a weapon in some debate, it risks reducing the possibilities for justice.

November 20, 2014

Through his lawyers, Julian has appealed the District Court's arrest warrant. The Svea Court of Appeal, like the District Court, considers that there's enough evidence for continuing the process of investigating the crimes the prosecutor and we accuse him of. They decide that the arrest warrant is still valid. I notice it when the usual hate messages enter my inbox, but I'm not surprised, and it doesn't affect me significantly.

Those men are never seen as guilty when suspected or convicted; they're always considered unjustly accused.

It seems that in the strict hierarchies of patriarchy, there is a group of men who "can't" rape. They can perform the acts, sure, but nothing they do will count as rape. Nice guys don't rape. Handsome and popular men don't rape. "Ordinary men" do not rape. In their world, Julian belongs to the category of men who just can't rape anyone. What happened to me cannot, therefore, by their logic, be abuse. It must have been consensual, and if not consensual at least legal, and if not legal still fair since I deserved it.

Women seem to be counted as objects, things that can belong to men. If it is "your" woman—that is, a woman who belongs to your own tribe and worthy of protection—it's your business what you do with her. You have a right to her body. But if you're not one of these men, if you're "one of the others," you will instead become a monster if you claim the right to her body. As an outsider, preying on a woman who is among the patriarchy's protected objects is considered a very serious crime.

Nothing a "nice guy" does seems to count as abuse in the eyes of Truthbomber and his ilk. And reporting "a nice guy's" abuse to the police arouses their hate. It even seems to be considered a crime to report, and they believe that other victims and I deserve to be raped as punishment for this violation. Women who demand to own themselves, to take control of their own lives and their own sexuality, and who refuse to be treated as a man's property are consequently considered whores.

same men who defend Julian's abuse of me. It seems illogical. But there should be a kind of logic here. I take a closer look at how these men describe what they perceive as a "real victim" and a "real perpetrator."

A "real victim" is rarely mentioned by name in their world. She is not described as a person but rather treated as a symbol to defend, a symbol that doesn't seem to think or feel anything.

It's clear that I do not at all fit their sexist template of the victims they want to protect. The fact that I show myself to be both sexually, politically, and relationally active is described in various ways as a reason for why I'm not good enough as a victim, as if I somehow wrung myself out of their protection.

A "real perpetrator" for these men never seems to be someone belonging to their own group. Someone considered a real perpetrator is rarely white, and if he is white, then he's of another religion, has a mental diagnosis, or something else is used as an explanation. The perpetrator is described as a person whom it is in no way possible to understand or identify with. Perpetrators are dehumanized and portrayed as monsters. The question: "How the hell is your brain wired if you do that?" is constantly hanging in the air. An unaccompanied refugee boy from Afghanistan who groped someone at a festival should, according to them, be deported and preferably beaten before then. He's a monster that moves like a shadow in the dark. It's a stark contrast to their post, which discusses cases where the perpetrator is someone who could be themselves, their friends, brothers, or sons. Nice guys.

August 31, 2014

I continue diving for truths online, and what I find is interesting. Person after person who posted about me online turns out to have previously been involved in other discussions about sex crimes. The same men who want me raped as punishment for the accusations against Julian say they want to kill rapists. The same men who call me bad and dangerous because I testify about abuse put a lot of effort into discussions about protecting women from abuse. Without much protest from others in the same online forum, they are allowed to advocate such things as castration, deportation without trial, beating to death, and the execution of sex offenders.

Several of these men have also been extremely involved in online discussions about Bjästa and in the Austrian Fritzl case, where a man kept his daughter locked in a secret basement apartment for 14 years, in which he repeatedly raped her. Like in the case of Hagaman, the Swedish serial rapist who ambushed unknown women in dark parks, and the pedophile Anders Eklund who kidnapped, raped, and murdered a small girl. The commitment is not least visible in real—or invented—cases where men with a foreign background have committed gang rapes.

They put a lot of effort into creating and maintaining an image of sexual abuse as the worst thing anyone can be subjected to and give an image of the rapist as an inhuman being completely outside of society's norms. The term "headshot" is common. Dissociating from rapists seems to be central to many of them, and yet time and time again, it is those very might have sent out were not interesting. But now, when the man is perceived as belonging to the commentators' own group, her features suddenly play a very decisive role.

Even the view of the abuse itself is changing among those who discuss the case online. It is no longer considered a "real rape" since the penetration was performed with fingers and not with genitals, and since it cannot be considered certain that she didn't want him to strangle her from behind, it apparently seems far too rough to speak of rape. It becomes important not to "water down the concept."

I recognize this so incredibly well, and want to try to understand; why is it so important to so many to acquit some rapists and convict others?

What drives the men with usernames like BleachDrinker, XXXNNN, Engelbrektsstrategy, CounterRebellion, Mojave, MoLeK, UglyAgent007, 8truthbomber, MunichCalling, wolfhard, DRD47R, Raedwulf, Battuta, BananAnus, KnudKragballe, almain and many others who have mocked and threatened me year after year? I decide to dive deep down into these men's online discussions about my case and other sex crime cases to try to understand their thinking.

then, people online have written long, aggressive posts about the horrible attitudes towards women that men from "other cultures" supposedly have. Many are completely convinced that the perpetrator is a refugee, an unaccompanied youth from Afghanistan. But it turns out that it is, in fact, a white Swedish 19-year-old guy from a medium-sized Swedish city who lacks mental health diagnoses. Hanna Gustafsson, who writes on the website *Politism*,[42] analyzes that the energy in agitated discussions goes down just as quickly as it went up. She notes that the tone becomes much more conciliatory towards the perpetrator, knowing he's white. But there's also something else happening when the online communities understand that the perpetrator is white: the responsibility shifts from the perpetrator to the victim. Choking someone and running your fingers up between someone's legs—which was recently considered an unacceptable behavior by men from "another culture"—is suddenly just a result of being exposed to "vague signals that girls send out at festivals." According to many of the comments I read in various discussion forums, apparently even the very best of men can behave that way, especially if the man in question happened to drink a little too much. When it turns out that the perpetrator cannot be singled out as different, the people's tribunal online seems to start working to exonerate him. Instead, the victim becomes the focus, and the responsibility is placed on her.

When the man was assumed to be a foreigner, one of "the others," the girl's behavior and dress, her past behavior and background, and what "signals" she

2016

to go in and pick up a paper bag marked with a diary number, a bag that I stow deep in the storage room.

Apparently, someone else has also requested the sheet. There's even someone who's claimed the broken condom that's also seized evidence, but I ask the police to throw it away.

December 22, 2015

The prosecutor still wants to question Julian about Maria's accusations, but when he doesn't agree, the help of Ecuador's prosecutor is needed. The Swedish prosecutor sends a new request to Ecuador via the Ministry of Justice to interrogate him at the embassy.

Sarah: "And that you set out to impregnate girls. It says you said to one of them you would call their baby 'Afghanistan.' Well, that does sound like you. I've heard you say that sort of thing about naming babies after your campaigns. But you wouldn't leave all these girls to have babies on their own, would you?"

Julian: "Sarah."

Sarah: "I'm just asking. Have you been at the births of all your children?"

Julian: "All except one."

O'Hagan is surprised because Julian told him that he only has one son, and he begins to realize that Julian is lying to him.

July 16, 2014

Julian has requested a new trial of the Stockholm District Court's arrest decision, and today they decide that he should remain in custody because he's still suspected of a series of sexual crimes on probable grounds. In other words, the court still thinks there's reason to believe he's guilty.

July 30, 2014

A few days ago, there was a rape at the Bråvalla Music Festival. A young man pulled down a 17-year-old girl's pants in the crowd and strangled and raped her. Since

March 6, 2014

Andrew O'Hagan, the ghostwriter for Julian's *unauthorized autobiography*, writes about his experiences working with him in an essay for the *London Review of Books* entitled "Ghosting." Among other things, he describes how difficult he found it trying to save Julian from himself. That Julian doesn't seem to understand that he can come across as very unattractive and how they try in vain to make the book go deeper than Julian's defense strategies which O'Hagan says are "infected with his habits of self-regard and truth manipulation."[41]

He confirms much of the behavior I saw as well. Julian still wants to check bushes and parked cars to ensure that the scouts will not be allowed to watch him undisturbed. But now it's his personal assistant/girlfriend Sarah who does the checking rather than himself. And the scouts of his fantasies have also been upgraded to "hired killers."

I'm also told that Julian suggested the title *Ban this book: From Swedish whores to Pentagon bores*. He himself uses the same language about us as many of his online defenders as a "joke."

O'Hagan quotes a conversation between Julian and Sarah, who is reading Leigh and Harding's book *WikiLeaks: Inside Julian Assange's war on secrecy*:

Sarah: "It says here you carried abortion pills around with you that were really just sugar pills."

Julian: "What?"

2014

December 28, 2013

Nine days early and four minutes after I was registered at the Södra maternity ward in Stockholm, my child is born. He's so beautiful, and I'm so happy! And relieved that we made it in time, and I didn't have to give birth in the taxi. I am also completely disconnected from all trolls and live my life.

leader or teacher or the smartest person in the room. Who wants a family, a workplace, or a party made up of victims?

In an attempt to get my dignity back, I request the floor and say that the skit was fun, that she did not lose herself at all, and that humor can be a support. But it's kind of too late. In this room, I've already been reduced from sister to guilty conscience, from feminist equal to laugh with to a victim to slowly back away from.

December 6, 2013

At work, we arrange the Civil Society Gala—a big gala as the last thing before the think tank's closure. We hand out prizes, give away all our books, and thank everyone who got involved. My mother is there, and she's proud of me. It's one of the most successful events I've arranged.

December 9, 2013

Henrik and I are moving in together for real, in a three-room apartment south of Stockholm. I have paid vacations, a home, a job waiting, and soon a whole family. I still get nasty comments as soon as I'm seen in public online and as soon as Julian makes a move. But on Twitter, it's a small number of his supporters who've been responsible for almost all the hate, and blocking them has been like cleaning, and gaining peace and quiet.

Spring is coming.

by the head of one of the organizations, and even though I'll give birth to my first child in January, we talk about starting to work for them in April.

November 23, 2013

The Socialist Forum is going on at the Workers' Educational Association (ABF) in Stockholm, and I am eight months pregnant. I attend a seminar on humor in the Zäta hall, the largest hall in the ABF building, with several hundred participants. The question for the day is, "Can we joke about everything?" It's fun. One of the comedians on stage talks about an incident at Maria Sveland's release party where she did a skit about Julian Assange. She says she felt uncomfortable knowing I was in the room, and despite the fact my full name isn't public, neither at the party nor in the media, she mentions my name now, with incorrect, English-sounding pronunciation.

I remember the skit, and I thought it was very funny. It felt like a vindication to be allowed to laugh at hatred and abuse. A release after guarding my tongue for so long. But today, at the seminar, I'm once again reduced to a victim. A fragile survivor who can't stand jokes, someone you talk about but not with. There's nothing attractive about staying in a victim role or having it become a part of your identity—it's horrible to be singled out as a victim. It's like someone looking at you and feeling pity, someone looking at you from above, giving you a pat on the head, a candy, and then waving goodbye.

A "victim" is not supposed scream with laughter and dance with dildo shoes. A victim cannot be a

Courage is contagious. It's the kind of contagion I wish WikiLeaks had continued to be associated with.

September 13, 2013

I receive an email from a woman in southern Europe who tells me that she once contacted Julian with encouragement about what she perceived to be very important work. He responded positively, and they started emailing back and forth. He asked her to send pictures, started making sexual suggestions, and wanted to meet her in person. His reaction, immediately asking for pictures and pursuing sex, is similar to what I witnessed when he lived with me. She sounds believable. At first she was interested but eventually decided to cut off contact. He continued to contact her and then became more and more threatening. In her message to me, she writes that he didn't email or write to her in any chat programs but directly in documents on her computer. She's also convinced that even now—in real time—that he sees our conversation. I'm not sure she's telling the truth, but the awareness of the risk of Julian accessing my accounts is always there.

September 15, 2013

It's decided that the think tank I work at will be shut down by the end of the year. When the news gets out to all our member organizations, several of them contact me and ask what I'll do now and if I'd be interested in working for them. I definitely seem to have defrosted in the job market. I'm invited to dinner

June 10, 2013

Henrik's apartment has been completely renovated and is to be sold. We're getting a broker who can sell both his apartment and mine because we need to move to something bigger. We're expecting a child!

July 30, 2013

Manning is acquitted of the charge of "aiding the enemy" but is convicted of 20 other crimes. It's so wrong and so upsetting.

August 21, 2013

Manning's sentence is set at 35 years in prison, dishonorable discharge from the Army, and to be sent to a military prison at Fort Leavenworth.

I'm so sorry. I really thought there was a chance of an acquittal.

August 22, 2013

We learn that Manning is a woman. In a statement via her lawyer, she says that she's felt like a woman since childhood. She asks to be referred to by the pronoun she and the name Chelsea. She also expresses a desire to undergo hormone therapy. I start to cry. This is a truly brave person. A role model. A woman who not only stands up against the whole U.S. military power but now also against the rigid gender norms of the entire world. Chelsea's courage is something to organize and spread further.

former peers, political opponents, Sweden Democrat supporters, anti-feminists, Jew-haters, the perpetrator's friends, and his mother decided—and mobilized—to convince others that I was lying.

One fantastic story after another was lined up about me in tribunals with anonymous judges and wildly guessing witnesses. It was easy and painless for anyone to join in who wanted to. The exact same thing, the same bullying, now strikes Omar. Bullying can completely destroy people. But it's often not something an individual suffers because of his or her person; no, it's often structural. The lies spread about individuals don't arise in a vacuum but are often based on prejudices and myths about entire groups. It is a weapon to solidify illegitimate hierarchies of power, solidify men over women, women over transgenders, whites over blacks, Westerners over Arabs, and rich over poor. It is a weapon against individuals who threaten to change something of the order of power. A kind of violence with the potential to destroy entire societies.

But in my case of bullying, I also received support. First, a few, then more and more. And after a while, it became obvious that everything said about me was not true. It became OK to talk to me without risking your own skin. But without the first ones who stood up, I don't know where it would have ended. I want to be one of them; one of the people who stand up to bullying. I want to stand up in stormy weather, even though it's hard.

There was never a feminist conspiracy to put Julian Assange in jail, but there is a feminist organization to provide redress for women who have suffered the hatred of anti-feminists.

April 13, 2013

In Sweden, there is an intense campaign against one of my closest political friends, Omar. He's an extremely competent, friendly, and progressive young Muslim man who was elected to the national board of the Social Democrats—a fact that awakens enormous Islamophobia. I help organize the defense for him and am accused myself, above all, of behaving strangely. Many people think that I'm "inconsistent" because I defend the rights of women, homosexuals, Jews, and Muslims at the same time. It's expressed in the same way as when young Muslim Assange supporters thought Omar was strange when he defended both women's rights and the importance of exposing U.S. war crimes in the Middle East in defense of me in 2010 and 2011. In comments on blogs, on Twitter, and in emails, I have been called stupid, naive, "as close to an idiot as you can possibly get," Muslim lover, not a Social Democrat, not human, anti-feminist, horrible, disgusting, and mentally sick.

Many, of course, bring up Julian as usual. Once again, some block me online and distance themselves from me, and I notice how I once again end up out in the cold. It's like that with bullying; it comes with a price if you refuse to participate. It will cost you to speak out against those who have the power to bully. After I testified about abuse, it happened so fast;

do not need to be held accountable for their behavior towards women. Many felt that we had ourselves to blame for not backing down.
But when the online hate rolled in, there were some who took a stand. There was a group that, within just a few days, started mobilizing support.

The feminists.

The feminists in the Witches of Berlin who collected 38 euros and demonstrated for women's right to their bodies, even though Europe's press seemed to agree on the need to excuse abuse to protect free speech. The feminists in the comments sections and on Twitter. The feminists in the Talk About It campaign. Feminists in Stockholm's workers' commune. The feminists on nyheter24 and in the magazine Neo. The feminists. I really just want to say one thing. Thank you.

Thank you for saving me when life was hell. Thank you for being there. Thank you for standing up. You are so incredibly important to me. Thank you.

Afterward, tears flow down my cheeks in a mix of sorrow and joy. The after-party is one of the most fun I've been part of. I borrow actress Lo Kauppi's shoes with heels made of dildos and dance in and out of the VIP room.

women," where the evening's protagonist Maria Sveland was number 1.

It's a cavalcade of feminist role models who speak before me—writers, researchers, activists, and artists. I'm grateful that I get to be part of this context among the very people who I feel saved my life. Then, it's my turn. Mian introduces me as "number 13," and after the initial applause, the audience does not stop applauding. Instead, they stand up in the pews and continue. I'm so moved that I completely lose track. To receive such an avalanche of love after two years of hate is incredibly overwhelming.

I want to convey my speech this evening to all the world's feminists and women's rights defenders:

> *Since 2005, when I started my blog, I have been threatened from time to time; there have been letters that I am better suited in bed than in politics. Unknown men have called at night, told me they want to pull out my teeth and rape me like a toothless crack whore. A dose of hate has become a part of my everyday life.*
>
> *Just over two years ago, it was much more than a dose. Threats of sexual violence became global. I needed police protection, had to quit my job, move out of my apartment, stop blogging, and I was also told not to sign articles with my own name. I felt like a hunted animal.*
>
> *Many backed down, perhaps because of the risks of being affected by the hatred themselves. For a brief moment, it felt like I, the other woman who reported the same man, and our loved ones were alone in a storm. Many felt that heroes*

when he was away, and it's clear that she was charmed by him or his halo—perhaps Julian's "dazzling effect on his admirers" that Bennett[40] described back in 2010? Khan's involvement in the film is news to me. But it also seems that having scratched a little at the grandiose surface, she has seen the same things that I saw.

I haven't seen any direct apology for the suspicion she stood for, but what she has effectively done with this film is, to me, both reparation and sisterhood.

February 28, 2013

Manning pleads guilty to leaking military information but pleads not guilty to aiding the enemy and eleven of the other most serious charges.

March 6, 2013

Tonight, there is a release party for Maria Sveland's book *The Hate: a book about anti-feminism* at Södra teatern. "Love: a party for the feminists" is the theme, and I am invited to speak. Although I'm only introduced as "Anna," this is the first time I've officially appeared as a plaintiff in the high-profile case. Nicke and Hasse, the journalists making a documentary about the case for Swedish TV, are involved and filming. I got a free ticket, which I gave to Maria, and even though it's full and there's a queue, the organizers still get a ticket for her friend as well.

Conference presenter Mian Lodalen is wearing a t-shirt with the number 17. The number she got on a list compiled by trolls of "Sweden's 100 most dangerous

January 10, 2013

Henrik is going to renovate his apartment and has planned to move in temporarily with his sister in Sundbyberg, a city in the greater Stockholm area.

"But why there?" I ask. "It's far away!"

We've only known each other for a month, but we totally agree that we have a long relationship ahead of us. There's no reason for him to live with his sister when he can live with me. And then he moves in. His name is on my door.

January 21, 2013

The HBO film has been named *We steal secrets*[39], and today it premieres at the Sundance festival. According to the reviews, it shows Julian and the development of WikiLeaks under his leadership just as the production team told me they'd portray it.

Jemima Khan is the executive producer of the film. She was also one of those who bailed for Julian. When Julian went to the Ecuadorian Embassy instead of appearing for extradition to Sweden, she had to pay large sums to the British justice system. Khan is a British cultural figure who tweeted about my alleged vindictiveness because I was once linked to that seven-step model of lawful revenge, and this very thing remains one of the main charges against me by the drift tribunal.

Moreover, Julian seems to have stayed with her

2013

buffet upstairs. Henrik finds himself easily in this context, and I get a kiss on the mouth on the dance floor.

When we finally get home to Söder late at night, where it turns out we both live just a couple of blocks apart, we wander back and forth between each other's apartments, unwilling to let the other go. Then, we also get to the moment where I tell him. It's a bit like coming out.

"It's me; I understand if you think it's unpleasant. If you think it's a risk. If you don't want to see me anymore." He doesn't seem to see either the risk or the discomfort, but he's a bit put off. He's silent for a moment before saying:

"In that case, it's too late. I think I'm already in love with you."

December 16, 2012

Henrik and I have met every day since our date and all weekend. It feels absolutely magical and so logical. I didn't know it could be this easy to be with another person. It's easy to talk to him; it feels like he understands so much. He makes me feel calm and safe in a way I haven't felt in a long time. He's caring and perhaps one of the most underrated things in men—he is kind.

I ask him if he's a feminist, and he looks at me and asks: "What do you mean? Do you think I seem like someone who wants to chain women to the stove or…? Of course, I'm a feminist." In the days between Christmas and New Year's Eve, I will meet his parents.

know who I am and is a journalist who intends to frame me.

December 12, 2012

Today, Henrik and I are going on a date, and we have decided to meet at a museum. It's been more than two years since the abuse began, but I'm still involuntarily attracting media attention. I wasn't infected with HIV, but I was infected with something else. Something chronic. A virus that makes being with me unpleasant and dangerous even though it really has nothing to do with me or my personality. I have an escape route. We'll meet for a limited time, and then I'll go to a party with a friend.

I meet Henrik at Slussen. I'm late, of course. He smiles generously and gives me a hug.

"How lovely to see you in real life!"

I quickly understand that he doesn't know about my infection. He has no other preconceived notions about me than what I myself have said. When it's time to go on to the party, I don't want to leave him. I invite him to come along, and he accepts.

We go to Skogås and wait for my friend to show us the way to the party, but she misses the train and won't arrive for an hour. Henrik and I decide to have a beer at a neighborhood pub, but the pub recommended to us turns out to have been blown up in some criminal settlement. Instead, and by chance, we end up at a big Syrian wedding and are warmly welcomed. When my friend finally picks us up and takes us to the party, they have a punk gig in the basement of a big townhouse and a vegan Christmas and I get a new hairstyle with the help of a wig. When I see myself in the mirror, I laugh.

"Oh my god, I look exactly like Lisbeth Salander when she's in disguise in the movie *Men who hate women.*"

Alexis laughs and turns to the make-up artist.

"You did that, didn't you?"

The artist that did my make-up had also done actress Noomi Rapace's make-up. The resemblance to the character Lisbeth Salander was intentional.

December 9, 2012

A guy named Henrik contacts me on a dating site. He says I resemble the Russian Jewish anarchist democracy activist Emma Goldman and it feels like he already knows me. I respond by saying that "Yes, Goldman is great. Freedom, harmony, and real social justice that she strove for are the only political goals we need, but maybe... she was a little too violent?"

Instead, I suggest a comparison with Rosa Luxemburg, the Polish-German Social Democrat who was murdered in 1919, and I quote her: "Without general elections, unrestrained freedom of press and assembly and free struggle between different opinions, life dies in every political institution." Undeterred by my nerdiness, he laughs, saying OK, you can be Luxemburg; I can be Karl Liebknecht, referring to Luxemburg's closest ally. He's so cute, but the thought that he could find out my identity at any moment and then want to withdraw scares me. I find his Facebook account and see that he has liked WikiLeaks.

I immediately start to wonder if he might already

as exactly the game changer, superhero, and elusive Scarlet Pimpernel-figure he was described as in the summer of 2010. They also want to show how things turn when power gets to his head, when he demands gagging within the organization and starts firing and threatening anyone who speaks out against him, and when he is accused of sexually assaulting women. It's hard to believe, but they seem sincere in their desire to show both sides of Julian—WikiLeaks and the harassment. When the tidal wave of disinformation and the interest in using everything against me has been so great, it's almost hard to understand that they really do want nuance. I recognize myself in the story they want to tell and am convinced. My hand is shaking, and I feel a cold lump in my stomach, but I sign the contract. In the email, I get the questions for the interview, and we set a date for about a week's time.

October 29, 2012

My interview with HBO will be recorded today. I'm so nervous that I'm going to say something that will be misunderstood, something that could complicate the trial once it comes, and I've prepared meticulously. I've tried on clothes, read the questions, written down answers, talked about them, tested my answers on different people, and practiced in front of the mirror. Now, I go to the Grand Hôtel in central Stockholm to meet the team. I have an expensive gray pencil dress, and at the suggestion of the producer, I will be made anonymous by being filmed obliquely from behind and lightly disguised. A good artist does my make up,

Then, he quickly moves on to conflate it with Julian's efforts to stay out of the way and avoid taking responsibility for the sex crimes he's suspected of having committed. I can somehow understand that it's not so easy to be nuanced when you have an image of someone being a heroic champion of freedom. The idea that people can be divided into good guys and bad guys is so strong, and for so many people all over the world, Julian is still a good guy. In the Swedish debate, it looks like Julian isn't particularly popular anymore. I'm not sure if it's because some—like Jan Guillou—moved him to a different category other than the heroes or if more people see both sides of him. Regardless, there's a clear difference in my life. The air is easier to breathe.

October 20, 2012

The HBO production team has approved my request to participate in an interview for the WikiLeaks documentary. I have said that, of course, I don't want to be paid to participate, but that I want the right to see and approve how I'm portrayed. They also pay for me to have a qualified contract lawyer review the contract I sign with them so that the recording cannot be used against me. In the company of my lawyer, Pia, and the contract law lawyer—a 75-year-old man with a hat and long coat—we go to a studio in Frihamnen to see the material they have so far and get an explanation as to the layout of the film. Their idea is to start by showing the importance of WikiLeaks' work; how heinous war crimes are revealed, how Manning was betrayed and imprisoned, and how Julian emerged

Even the very best of societies must be built on precisely the flawed human beings that we all are.

I sense that I might have a place in this world, the thing I doubted so much. But I need to understand where or what that place really is because it's obviously not as Andreas' other orange half. I need to find a theme song for my life, a common thread to understand and explain what and who I am and how the things I do are interrelated. This is one big step forward. To start searching and describing this thread with words that make sense, the flesh string that my torn heart needs to function normally again, even if it may never be mended.

August 16, 2012

Ecuador grants Julian asylum. The president is making a political point and seems to have the support of his population. The debate about women's rights to avoid sexual violence seems subdued in Ecuador.

Within the left in Sweden, it has been expressed that Julian deserves support. As "despite his views on women, he is no choir boy," as a couple of his defenders from my own organization put it. In Ecuador, however, large sections of the left, side by side with the extreme right, like Glenn Beck on Fox News, seem to think that Julian deserves support not despite his misogyny but because of it.

August 21, 2012

Michael Moore tells us that he, like me, is grateful for WikiLeaks' revelations of human rights violations.

August 3, 2012

The hike is over. We have walked together, and I have walked alone. He took the bus between several of the cities—I couldn't stand his company, his love. I got angry when his foot hurt. I wanted to be quiet and think, I wanted to talk to anyone but him. When I drank wine, I drank way too much; I opened up in intimate conversations with others in another part of a venue, disappeared from him without a trace to an after-party, and didn't turn up at our hostel until eight the next morning. I don't think I've ever behaved this badly or been so mean to another human being. I've listened to all the songs that make me remember Andreas. Among others, *Ojalá*, by Silvio Rodriguez, a song about the hope that something drastic will happen in order to avoid seeing a lost loved one in every dream. I walked mile after mile, several times two normal days' journey, in one day. My friend has cried, and I've begged for forgiveness, saying we have to continue walking and dating, without really understanding why myself, without understanding how he, or anyone else, could really make use of me.

Today, we finally part, both with completely broken hearts. Me with mine that has been broken so long ago it's congealed, and his freshly crushed and bleeding.

I thought perhaps that the pilgrimage would help me to let go of Andreas, to find joy and peace, but my realizations are of a completely different kind. I realize that I'm not a good person, that no one is. That goodness is not tied to people in the way I previously thought but must be created in our communities.

June 20, 2012

Over the last year, I've had some contact with a person who knows Julian and the people around him well. Today, I receive an email from her:

What a spectacularly misguided move JA has just made. For your sake, I'm so sorry he can't act more honorably than this. I wish he'd have the backbone to do the right thing. It's as if he cannot have his lie revealed, so he has to bolt—to tell another, bigger lie and "escape" somewhere rather than have people know he was bullshitting all along. Since he didn't report to the police by 10 p.m. tonight, he's broken his bail conditions. The people who put up the money for his bail are worried. They knew nothing about this. I hope you're OK. Take a deep breath. This is a development that will serve to undermine JA's credibility. But the delay must be tough on you.

July 17, 2012

I've wanted to make a pilgrimage to Santiago de Compostela for a long time. Being lonely and hunted, it's felt even more relevant to finally be able to follow in the footsteps of perhaps the very first tourists as a tribute to human encounters and the search for meaning in everything that so often feels meaningless. I have asked my friend, maybe my boyfriend, from the human rights organization if he wants to come along. Today, after all the video calls, we will meet again in northern Spain.

WL, Manning hearings, government secrecy, and the accompanying media storm. You're a voice of reason ... and it makes me glad.

The email makes me glad.

June 14, 2012

The Supreme Court rejects Julian's request that the negotiations be resumed, and the extradition is confirmed. Pia calls.

"Now he is coming to Sweden," she says. "It's probably time we start preparing for trial."

I say as I said to my mother, "We have not seen that yet," I laugh. "He might as well go to the moon next time."

Pia laughs and agrees.

June 19, 2012

Pia calls again:

> "It didn't turn out to be the moon," she says.
> "Nah, but almost!" I answer.

Julian has requested political asylum at the Ecuadorian Embassy in London. One of the guests he interviewed on the Russian talk show he hosted some time ago was the president of Ecuador. Maybe it's that contact helping him now.

May 31, 2012

Claes calls me.
"I got a question that I think might be interesting. HBO is making a documentary about WikiLeaks and wants to talk to you."

I say it's OK for them to contact me, and they do so this evening. Someone is on their way to Stockholm and wants to meet me. Maybe this is an opportunity for me to somehow show the world that I am, in fact, a human being.

June 3, 2012

Alexis, one of the people working on the HBO film, invites me to dinner. We eat a bowl of pasta at a place near my home, and I tell her about the case as I see it. About the abuse, the harassment, and why I got involved with WikiLeaks. She understands what I think is the most important thing in this story—not to let human rights and women's rights be pitted against each other. I decide that I'll accept the offer to appear in their movie, but until the case is settled in court, I do not want to talk about what is legally relevant— neither the sexual abuse against me nor my testimony in Maria's case. We agree that I will talk about all the rumors. All the false claims and secret motives I'm supposed to have for reporting him, and all the hatred. Later that evening, I receive an email from Alexis:

> *Was really nice to meet you, A. Somehow you seem like one of the sanest people I've met on this journey through*

rights in the debate about the Assange case. It's so nice to hear about all the support unknown feminists have mobilized these past years.

May 4, 2012

I have been abroad for two weeks to visit a friend—a passionate activist with a huge heart—who works at an international human rights organization. Among other things, he works with people who have been driven from their land. We have traveled among ripe fruit in organic plantations of mangoes and peppers. He's told me that he's in love with me, and it shows. Receiving his unreserved love is like a numbing drug. He reads what I wrote about the case so far, and he boils with anger. He is 100 percent on my side, and he says he's crazy about me. Already at the first kiss a few days ago, I thought about how I could stand this. I panicked and felt like I should go home early, only to think the next second that I can't live without him. Now that I'm sitting alone in the airplane and he's still on the ground, I'm longing for him, or at least his love, again.

May 30, 2012

The U.K.'s Supreme Court announces they've decided to reject Julian's appeal and that he will therefore be handed over to Sweden. The mandatory messages trickle in. "Can you stop now? Hasn't he suffered enough? You're the one who should be locked up." Like I'm in charge of the courts.

soldier.

But he also believes that in reading it, it is difficult to "separate well-founded fear from what must be described as pure persecution mania, especially when it is combined with megalomaniac claims to have single-handedly changed the world." Kolmisoppi refers to Julian's paranoia in that he sees traitors everywhere, both within his own organization and in the corridors of the established media, how he engages in slander and portrays himself as a Jesus figure surrounded by Judases:

> *It is unfortunate, not because he comes across as moody and unsympathetic, but because he thereby stands in the way of a larger discussion about the revolutionary importance that WikiLeaks and similar organizations have had and may have for revealing journalism and the democratic discourse. (...) each smear attempt pushes the issue of the leaks further down the agenda. (...) Nowadays, regimes and opponents do not have to make the slightest effort to smear the organization. It manages that all too well on its own.*[38]

March 30, 2012

Twelve years ago, many other young people from 41 different countries and I worked on an environmental organization's pavilion at the world exhibition in Germany. This week, we're having a reunion in London of all places. I'm worried about being recognized or that the press will somehow find out I'm here, but of course, the fear is exaggerated. I'm just one of all the regular tourists. However, I meet an artist and an activist who are committed to women's

February 7, 2012

The autumn and winter have been tiring, but I still feel like I'm slowly but surely getting stronger as the debate becomes more nuanced, and more people seem to share my view of both Julian and the events of 2010.

February 29, 2012

Today, Julian's autobiography, *Julian Assange: The Unauthorized Autobiography*, is beginning to get reviewed in Swedish newspapers. It's been issued against his will and is marketed with Julian's quote, "all memoir is prostitution." He has received an unbelievably high advance of six hundred thousand British pounds from this British publisher, which he's reportedly used to pay his lawyers. Now, however, he no longer wants to publish the book. The publisher has done it anyway, according to the agreement. Julian accuses them of wanting to make money.

The author, Mats Kolmisoppi, who is well acquainted with the movement for a free Internet in which Julian had much of his support, reviews the book in *Helsingborgs Dagblad*. His analysis shows, at least to me, that the nuances of the public conversation around WikiLeaks are definitely about to emerge more clearly. Kolmisoppi lauds the descriptions of WikiLeaks' important world-changing work and highlights WikiLeaks' work with war crime leaks, criticism of the contemporary lack of journalistic integrity, and the fear that arises when debaters demand that the leaker be executed as an enemy

2012

November 26, 2011

A guy who calls himself a "social entrepreneur" messages me on OK Cupid, the same dating site I found Julian's profile on. He has contacted me several times before, but I haven't been very interested. Now, he gets in touch again to tell me that he understands who I am and that he regrets it. He feels disgusted and cheated. It turns out that I'm familiar with his girlfriend. But his regret is not about himself, looking for other women online behind his girlfriend's back. No, it's about Julian Assange. The man is apparently involved in freedom of expression issues and has a working relationship with Julian; they intend to do some seminars together. The relationship between them seems like a crush, a bromance.

The entrepreneur's hatred of me is personal and he writes a long and nasty message. He seems to perceive the accusations against Julian as directed against himself. He says I messed up something nice and that it's unforgivable. He uses the words "disturbed" and "disturbing" to describe me. This guy goes from liking what little he knew about me to completely judging me as a person. Again and again, I am overshadowed as a person by the persona that others have invented.

case, it is clear that Julian Assange is innocent of the alleged rape charges," he says.

The news about the PR assignment saddens me. But I still get on my bike to cycle home through Fleminggatan. As I cycle, I start to feel worse and worse. I can only breathe in short spurts and am starting to experience a lack of oxygen. At the height of Sankt Eriksgatan, I feel so bad that everything spins, and I vomit. I fall off the bike. An orange I have in the bicycle basket rolls away and is crushed by a passing car. I sit on the curb and wait for the shock to wear off. As usual, I quickly pull myself together and go home.

November 21, 2011
For several weeks I have been unable to sleep at night and stay up until three or four a.m. Sometimes, I'm awake around the clock. The hatred that never ends, against Muslims, against women, against me, has crawled under my skin. Stressed out at work. Going on failed dates. My life is misery.

November 24, 2011
Johanna Koljonen and Sofia Mirjamsdotter win the Grand Journalist Prize in the innovator of the year category for #prataomdet. It feels like recognition for me too. It feels like it can actually make a difference about daring to speak. Like the report on Bjästa, #prataomdet has become an important milestone for the Swedish sexual policy debate.

November 2, 2011, my mother texts me that the High Court in London has decided Julian should be handed over to Sweden. She thinks it means the trial will be soon. "We haven't seen that yet," I answer.

November 11, 2011

A Swedish Social Democrat with a PR agency has offered to "cleanse" Julian to help him avoid being associated with abuse in the public debate. Whether it's a non-profit commitment or whether it was also paid with WikiLeaks' money is unclear. There's only one way for Julian to be cleared of suspicion. For a brief moment, I think that's what's going to happen. That Julian should be supported to participate in the legal process and, once and for all, get a chance to clear his name. However, it turns out that the purpose of the PR campaign is not to be fair, but to smear me. I have previously had several quarrels with this PR consultant when he called male feminists "sissy knights" or used his positions of trust within the Social Democratic Party for anti-union and commercial purposes.

But now I notice that he's been actively spreading scorn and hatred about me in various comment fields and threads on social media for some time. Offensive comments on mutual acquaintances' social media updates. Laughter at completely unrelated posts and short jumps like "she's probably lying about this like she's lying about Assange." And now this PR bully is being interviewed by newspapers as the official representative of Julian: "Having put myself into the

and only appreciated if they were useful."
"In what way did he offend you?"
"Eh, he came with threats. I can't go into details."
"Why not?"[37]

She doesn't answer but just shakes her head in despair. I hope one day she tells me what she knows about Julian's behavior towards women. I think she saw some of it.

October 24, 2011

Many WikiLeaks fans regret that the media treats Assange synonymously with WikiLeaks. "Many who worked with the organization were concerned that this case was linked to WikiLeaks. They must have had a party at the American Embassy when this happened," said Birgitta Jónsdóttir in *Agenda* yesterday. And yes, it has been so. And yes, that is a problem. But one of the biggest reasons for the media's treatment of Julian and WikiLeaks as synonyms is the fact that he himself has done and is doing everything to make it a fact. Those who suggested Julian take a break as a spokesperson for WikiLeaks while the sex crime allegations were investigated had to leave the organization. But Julian Assange is not WikiLeaks. And WikiLeaks wasn't Julian Assange either when I chose to support their work with my involvement. Criminal suspicions against the person should not have been allowed to spill over to the movement, just as the success of the movement should not have been attributed to a single man. I wish WikiLeaks had been allowed to continue to be bigger than the man who clung on as a face.

cannot and must not escape. It would be a clear case of abuse of power. The kind of abuse that WikiLeaks in any other situation would try to prevent.[36]

The right to leak classified documents that the public needs to see should be the highest priority for an organization like WikiLeaks. That Julian Assange should avoid standing trial for his personal shortcomings should not be the highest priority, and that he should avoid a follow-up questioning about whether it is the case that he forces and tricks women into their sperm should not have been an issue for WikiLeaks at all. The distinctions between the person and the organization are becoming increasingly blurred.

Domscheit-Berg also believes that Julian suffered from delusions of grandeur and testifies to threats. Among other things, he writes this:

He threatened to seek me out and kill me if I messed up, that is if I endangered any of our sources. He became very paranoid in his behavior toward me and others. It was all about alleged conspiracies and alleged betrayals. {Domscheit-Berg, 2011 #59}

Even the Icelandic former WikiLeaks employee and parliamentarian Birgitta Jónsdóttir testifies in the TV program about that part of his personality:

"What happened was that a lot of threats started coming. It felt offensive to work in an environment where people were objectified

he blocks me. Both on the dating site and on Twitter. I'm convinced that he hadn't understood that I was the one who reported Assange when we spoke earlier, but when he did understand, it became unthinkable. Unthinkable to be associated with me in any way. I feel like a fucking idiot for thinking that was over now. It's been a year and two months since the abuse.

October 23, 2011

A feature in the program *Agenda* on SVT is about WikiLeaks. The dissatisfaction that exists within WikiLeaks against Julian's "dictatorial" leadership style and his inability to distinguish between WikiLeaks and his own person is clearly stated by several who worked very closely with him. Co-founder Daniel Domscheit-Berg says, among other things, that if you advocate openness, you must be open yourself. You must live up to the demands you place on others.

Domscheit-Berg also wrote the book *WikiLeaks: the story behind the site that changed an entire world* and explains even more clearly there. He writes:

> *It is clear that Julian deserves support in principle. It is scandalous that American politicians and journalists, in front of rolling cameras, are advocating that he ought to be killed. And above all, he mustn't be extradited to the United States. That would be a serious precedent, and it must not happen. But how you can be against Julian being interrogated in Sweden and possibly brought to trial? Someone needs to explain that to me. That procedure, which has nothing to do with WikiLeaks, but only concerns Julian's private experiences with two women, he*

October 12, 2011

Nicke and Hasse, the two reporters who recently received the Grand Journalist Prize for their documentary about Bjästa, come to my home in Tjurbergsgatan. Since so many journalists have been hounding me for over a year, it's strange to speak completely openly with some of them. It feels like finally getting witnesses to the abuse that's still going on. They want to follow up on their previous report and see very clear parallels between my case and Bjästa.

Our conversation strengthens the parallels, and we decide that they should start gathering material to make a documentary when the legal process is complete.

October 14, 2011

Today I chatted with a guy called Tomas; he has been single for quite a while and is looking for a long-term relationship. He seems super nice and suggested we meet today. I've accepted. It's Friday night and my shoulders hurt after a very intense week at my new job at the think tank, so I've made an appointment for a massage near work. After the massage, the staff at the salon have an after-work meeting, where they talk, laugh, and drink wine; they invite me. It's like we're old friends who enjoy the same jokes. Life feels fun. Then, I send a tweet to Tomas that we will see each other soon. My last name is visible. Within just a few minutes, he replies that he can't. And right after that,

The criticism against the black-and-white and dogmatic is important because the absolutism in the notions of good and bad, and the categories which are sometimes so fixed that they risk being completely wrong in the end, deserve their criticism.

October 6, 2011

"Is it a criminal offense to force your bodily fluids onto someone?" asks the journalist Hanne Kjöller in a text in Sweden's biggest morning newspaper, *DN today*. She believes it's "strange if there is no real legal scope for intentionally exposing a woman against her will to the risk of becoming pregnant or being infected by a venereal disease".[35]

She thinks it sounds more like the Saudi Arabia of patriarchy than that of feminism. Finally, transferring bodily fluids against someone's will is at least on the agenda. The chances of being able to improve the law on this point increase when it's discussed publicly.

October 11, 2011

The ten therapy calls I received from the insurance company have been completed. Among other things, the therapist made me write encouraging letters to myself as a little girl. The purpose is to build relationships with the person I once was, to understand and love myself. Today, I see the therapist at my own expense and realize that I actually feel ready. I have been given valuable tools to move forward in life, but now the conversation has come to a standstill. I do not book any more appointments.

movements, and individual activists who want to communicate and collaborate worldwide, with openness and accountability of the figures of power as the highest goal. The thousands of people who have been part of the collaboration to do the job have been both responsible and patient. And many, including Manning, have had to pay too high a price.

October 2, 2011

Today, I read yet another text that casts doubt on our sex crime charges against Julian somewhat by mistake. Since the text is written by a left-wing debater I look up to, I assume the text to be good. After a while, however, I realize that she means that because Julian is an important person, the accusations against him are not credible, and thus we who accused him are not credible either. I am so terribly disappointed. Disappointed that the list of *former* role models is growing. The people I saw as my own ideological leaders so often ally themselves with the very men who scream that I deserve rape rather than trying to see multiple perspectives. I understand that it was easy to draw that conclusion a year ago, but now? When more and more people show that they can keep two thoughts in their heads at the same time, when it's becoming possible to see shades of gray, she wants to reduce the debate to black and white again? Innocent freedom fighters against falsely perjuring whores—although, of course, she does not use precisely those words. I suddenly understand, in-depth, some of the libertarian and liberal criticism directed at the same left in which I have been involved for so long.

irregularities.

Manning (unlike Julian) is not entitled to a public defender and must therefore pay for his own trial. But it isn't just a lone soldier's battle; it's our battle. It's about whether we have the right to know about what's happening in our name—about our right to live in a world where human rights are respected.

Therefore, I have been planning a party in favor of Manning's defense for a week or so. An American-style fundraiser with a large glass jar for a voluntary entrance fee. I didn't really think it would work, but it does! A lot of people show up, and they put quite a few hundred notes in the jar. When the party's over, I immediately transfer the money. The entire sum.

Transparency, truth, and openness are the basis for all forms of community building. The grassroots organizations that work based on these principles are a creative global resistance that I believe is absolutely necessary to prevent wars and corruption from tearing the world apart. It's because of this I chose to get involved with WikiLeaks. It's disgusting when countries' governments try to bring these organizations to justice for the work they do in the service of democracy—such as publishing documents that we should all have the right to access. We need to stand up for movements that were formed in defense of our right to disarm power and our right to know what our governments, politicians, and multinational corporations are doing behind closed doors.

WikiLeaks tried to expand the opportunities for whistleblowers in the world. The organization had the potential to bring together networks, solidarity sides. His positives have been rightly praised, and his negative sides magnified into absurdity.

Julian is a guy who got laid an unusual number of times, despite his social difficulties, perhaps because of celebrity and power. And he has received support from the outside world, which in many cases was genuinely aimed at supporting WikiLeaks, but which, as far as I can see now, ended up having exactly the opposite effect. The more we let people get away with their infringements, the bigger their abuses become. When more and more people began to realize that even Julian had flaws—flaws exacerbated by the carte blanche to behave badly so many gave him—and his heroic glory fell, the whole of WikiLeaks' brand was drawn into the case. This is not my fault. We cannot save something beautiful by keeping silent about what is ugly. If we deny the darkness, it doesn't disappear; it grows.

October 1, 2011

I'm having a party tonight! A party for Manning.

"I was that young man," says Daniel Ellsberg in a quote I framed and put up on the wall in honor of the evening. Ellsberg was the one who, similarly to Manning, leaked secret war documents, namely the Pentagon Papers about the Vietnam War in 1971. He was charged with espionage and threatened with 115 years in prison. At the time, the world's, and the U.S.'s, laws on freedom of communication looked very different, but Ellsberg was acquitted entirely. The court recognized the right to report war crimes and wake of the incident. And perhaps above all: why didn't I warn Maria?

Why did I even try to help him get to her? Why did I put her at risk? The thousands of others who've found fault with me—those who've faulted every syllable of what I've written in my blog—have created an image of me as a person who's essentially wrong, doing wrong, being wrong. I thought they were right, that Johannes was right. Of course, it was unpleasant to be exposed, but it wasn't that bad, was it? Absolutely no reason to make all this fuss...

But that's enough now. None of what's happened, not what happened to Maria, not the bullying I was subjected to, not the crap that hit WikiLeaks, not the excessively negative publicity that hit Julian, not the bad image of Sweden's justice system that was spread around the world, or anything of all this other stuff I wish hadn't happened, is my fault.

I was not the one who set the series of events that followed in motion. It was *him*. All the bad things that happened started with what *he* did. He did what he did to me, and it wasn't OK. I told the police about it. That was the right thing to do. I have both a legal and moral right to decide over my own body. I couldn't have done more or less. What he did to Maria, or any other woman, isn't my fault. It no longer matters that hundreds or thousands of people demand that I feel guilty. It doesn't matter that they decide I'm crazy because I no longer feel this guilt. The patriarchy is wrong. When a man abuses a woman, he is to blame, not her.

Julian is a person with both positive and negative

that convinced me to go to the police. He's far from alone in this thought process.

The lists of everything different people think I "should have done" are very long, and many times I have thought exactly what they say myself. There are a thousand conflicting things I should have done and a thousand things I did that went wrong—which somehow makes it easy to think that I've myself to blame. I've gone over every detail, from where every body part was from the time, I walked into the apartment the first time we saw each other up until I fell asleep after the assault and beyond.

Over and over again.

I shouldn't have made the decision to let him kiss me; I should've resisted when he wanted to take off my nightgown; I had so many opportunities to say no, to stop it before it went that far. Perhaps even more, I shouldn't have been impressed by him, I shouldn't have given him any encouragement, I should've protested, cooled the situation, spoken up afterward, reported him, gone to the police earlier—no, I shouldn't have gone to the police at all, I should've kept quiet. I should've screamed, so I woke up the neighbors, and I should've thrown him out right after the assault. And I absolutely should never have met him again.

I've even cursed myself for not recognizing and compensating for his difficulty understanding social codes sooner and for not excusing his behavior more—maybe he couldn't handle it? I should've taken responsibility, not only for myself but also for his shortcomings and for everything that happened in the admit they did wrong and change. Reconciliation requires truth, and victims receive restitution and reparation. Linnea needed to have her story recognized and Oskar had to take responsibility. Then the consequences of the event could have looked completely different.

August 20, 2011

It's been a year since we went to the police. It's been one of the worst years of my life, and it feels like it's time for the annual accounts. I want to close something. I stopped being ashamed of the abuse a long time ago but still resented it in different ways. It's like a byproduct of self-accusations, a churning of wishing I'd acted differently. I know women often feel guilty after sexual assault. I've long been involved in organizations, online forums, and very secret groups where we warn each other about men who prey on women. I have also tried to find structures and language around sexual abuse in books, lectures, and debates. I've actively pushed that women should be taken more seriously and participated in trying to explain how the mechanisms work to counter girls' and women's sense of guilt. "It's not your fault!" I've wanted to say, over and over again. Then I was exposed myself. And it suddenly turned out it was extremely difficult to shake that feeling of guilt and shame off completely.

Johannes believed me, and he understood my upset. But he thought it was "unnecessary" to go to the police. "Why didn't you just punch him instead?" he asked. Like he thought it was the feeling of revenge and change, and that, step by step, dismantles patriarchy and replaces it with equality. The forgiveness of taking responsibility and making amends. Never apologetic, never glossed over.

I wrote about the report from Bjästa on my blog when it was broadcast, about the importance of seeing the humanity in the perpetrator. That people, after confession and repentance, should be able to be forgiven. Hanging the perpetrator is not necessarily the best way to show support to the victim because the truth is that both he and his defenders are human, just like the rest of us. People do good things sometimes and end up completely wrong at other points. Neither the inhuman rape monsters nor the allegedly greedy attention-seeking whores are very often found in reality. If ever. The reality is not that black and white.

Talking about the kind of forgiveness that I did on my blog back then, according to the internet mob, is something very controversial. It becomes a kind of proof that I am a strange, irrational, and perhaps even a "mentally disturbed" person. Talking about the gray areas of reality with people who have decided to think in black and white is very difficult. This is made clear in the comments on the post. I still mean that yes, of course, Oskar committed abuse, and of course, the priest was completely wrong when he allowed a convicted rapist with a restraining order to be present at the graduation, but reverse lynch mobs after self-sufficient and unreasonable sentences by an uninformed public do not help anyone.

It must be desirable and welcome for offenders to

were subjected to brutal threats, as well as against the priest who welcomed Oskar at the school graduation and even against another boy at the school who was just unlucky enough to be named Oskar, unlike the rapist, whose real name is actually something else.

There seems to be a strong desire to keep abuse as far away as possible. So strong that it leads many to try to dissociate with the perpetrator or the victim—or often both—from a collective "we." It would of course have been more constructive to instead try to understand the events and the psychological mechanisms that led so many to defend Oskar and smear Linnea. But that is not what generally happens.

In this specific case, the Swedish public even seemed to want to dissociate from the whole village of Bjästa. But the problem is not—as it is claimed—some particularly strong inbreeding in Bjästa. It is not the guy who happens to be called Oskar who's responsible for Linnea being canceled; it's not the priest, Oskar's family, or even the rapist's fault. The problem is much deeper. It's about a structure that so many of us participate in and maintain. And to me, the structure seems to be the same for a woman who has been captured and raped hundreds of times in wartime Congo and then not allowed to come home once she has managed to escape, as when a girl is forced to have oral sex in a school toilet in Bjästa and cannot go to her own graduation. It is a structure, an order of power, and it is called patriarchy.[34]

I think the solution is very far from scapegoats and new lynch mobs. The solution is instead forgiveness. Real forgiveness, that's based on insight happened. Julie Richter, who works with young sex offenders at the Bärby Youth Home outside Uppsala, wrote that without the massive support that Oskar received from those around him, the second rape probably would not have happened. Richter said that when young people are treated for sex crimes, it's extremely important to make them understand what they have done. Many deny and minimize in various ways what happened. At an early stage, Oskar admitted, but a large part of his entourage denied what happened and placed the blame on the two raped girls.[32] Cecilia Kjellgren, a sociologist at Lund University, confirms this picture. According to her, young offenders have a tendency to confess more often than adult offenders, but when society—and the social context—continues to assert the perpetrator's innocence, it can be extremely difficult to maintain one's guilt or even understand it.[33]

The documentary actually affected the case and made the sympathies swing in the case of Bjästa. Finally, the crimes were taken seriously, and Linnea was defended. Swedish public opinion underwent an educational journey. This was a big and important step forward to do away with the rape culture that characterizes so much of the power relations between the sexes in Sweden. It would have been nice if the story had ended there. But it didn't. Instead, the pendulum swung completely and struck back. Hard. And with that, the attitude towards Oskar changed. From having been "a really nice guy," he was suddenly seen as a monster, hardly even a human being. The mob raced on. Both against Oskar and his family, who

"Absolutely sick as hell, I was skeptical before I read the verdict. But now that I've read it, I hope that this girl is raped for real."

One of the young girls who wrote offensive comments about Linnea in defense of Oskar is asked by the reporter why she did it. She replies that she thinks "it's too hard to think about whether it would be true." If so, she doesn't want to know.[31]

The sexual abuse I suffered was different from Linnea's. The circumstances, details, and legal process differ. But what I was subjected to by the perpetrator's online support groups is very similar to what Linnea suffered—right down to the details. She testified that "the school's most popular guy" had assaulted her. I testified that one of *Time* magazine's top candidates for Man of the Year 2010 had committed an assault. Linnea was threatened with death and accused of making false accusations to make money from them. She received messages from men who said that they carefully studied the case and that they *usually* react differently but that *this particular* case is so special that it is necessary to take the man's side. Linnea was not believed. She was subjected to allegations based on unsubstantiated and fanciful stories about what "actually" took place. All this has happened to me in a similar form and still happens. Both Linnea's and my perpetrators were forgiven without having to ask for it.

The report on the rape in Bjästa attracted a lot of attention, and afterward, many contributed important analyzes to the collective understanding of what a white rose and a hug from Oskar. The footage was used as evidence of his innocence. Would the girls in the class have hugged him if he really was a rapist? They believe that Oskar is brave. "Hope the liars get caught," someone writes in the Facebook group. Bjästa's lynch mob tribunal acquits the convicted rapist and sentences his victim.

That same evening, Oskar rapes again. This time, too, he is convicted of rape in both the District Court and the court of appeal. But not even two proven rapes make the people of Bjästa leave Oskar's side. "Poor guy," says the priest when he learns this in the interview, not "poor girl." The support group and its thousands of members are ready to judge this victim as well:

"I don't understand how you can be so desperate for money that you do this. Then there's something fucking wrong. Damn, I'm getting tired of hoes like this."

"It's stuff like this that makes me ashamed to be a girl. Reporting someone for rape just to get revenge indicates huge mental issues. She should get mental health care..."

"Justice will prevail. Poor Oskar and fucking sluts who lie. Should it be like this in Sweden?"

"Hope those pigs are exposed or raped so they are punished. Fucking cunts. Hope Oskar will be released!"

supporter who accompanies her to school. Oskar's mother and brother start a Facebook group to support Oskar. The group has over 4,000 members, more than the number who live in the village. At the school, the students go on strike to get Oskar back.

Chamber prosecutor Stina Sjöqvist describes in the report how difficult it must have been for Linnea. First, the physical abuse happens, and then she must go into detail and explain what happened to relatives, to the police, and in front of a court with unknown people listening. And then again during the campaigns.

The spread of rumors and the pressure is enormous before, during, and after the judgments in the District Court and the Court of Appeal. At school and at the recreation center, the adults choose to be "neutral" about the incident—even despite Oskar being convicted—and no one checks what Linnea is exposed to online.

As the summer holidays approach, it is, as usual, time for graduation, which takes place at the local church. Oskar no longer attends school but asks the priest, Lennart, if he can still come and leave flowers for his old classmates. The priest says that he doesn't want to take a stand and that he thinks it's a nice and strong manifestation for Oskar to come there. When *Uppdrag granskning* asks, he says that he did not know that Oskar was convicted of rape and had a restraining order but that he can imagine it. Linnea's mother decides that she and Linnea will go away so that Linnea doesn't have to be part of the event. After the graduation, Oskar's mother posts a video of the ceremony online, showing smiling classmates receiving

"He's a really nice guy. If I looked at him, I would never think he would do something like that. He cares about others."

Students say that they have had a hard time believing he could be guilty, despite the fact he was convicted of the rape. Oskar is described as social and is considered popular among girls. Why would he rape someone?

A woman participating in the program believes that Linnea's claims about Oskar do not fit well with reality. After all, he's a guy who looks good and is kind, so he "doesn't look like someone who would have to [do] that." Another, older woman, thinks it seems unlikely that a guy can force a girl into a blow job: "It's just a matter of biting," she says. The rumor also says that Linnea is a slut.

On the Internet, rumors are spread further, and they ultimately create an image of a course of unrealistic events. The village's conclusion is, therefore, that everything is a lie. Most of the people whom the editorial staff of *Uppdrag granskning* speak to have heard what they "know" about the case from "an acquaintance" or from a "friend of a friend" and not from Linnea or Oskar. Many turn their backs on Linnea. She says that apart from the rape itself, the worst betrayal comes from friends she trusted. That those whom she laughed with and listened to when they were having a hard time now turn their backs on her and join the crowd calling her a liar. That her friends aren't there for her when she needs them. Linnea becomes more and more isolated, and she receives personal protection in the form of a peer that Linnea was shaken and sad immediately afterward.

At first, Oskar denied the accusations. But in the third interrogation, he admitted that he put his legs on Linnea's arms so that she could not leave and that he pried open her jaw to force her to perform oral sex. He also said that he thought it was a relief to be able to confess and said that Linnea asked him to stop five or six times.

Oskar's description of the incident contained details that only he and Linnea could know. For example, what he and Linnea said afterward. That he said sorry because he was aware that he had forced her and raped her. The recorded interrogation matches well with Linnea's story. But two weeks after the confession, Oskar changes his mind and instead says that Linnea wanted to have sex. Oskar is sentenced in the District Court for child rape because Linnea was 14 years old at the time of the abuse, and when the verdict is appealed, the Court of Appeal makes the same assessment. Linnea's story is credible, but Oskar's changed version is not. Oskar is sentenced to 130 hours of youth service, transferred to another school, and given a restraining order. He is thus forbidden to go near Linnea.

When *Uppdrag granskning*'s reporters come to Bjästaskolan in 2010 and ask questions about the rape following a tip from Oskar's support network, the students have been discussing the incident for over a year. In the report, it is extremely clear that the popular Oskar is the one who is believed and gets support, with only a few exceptions.

"That's exactly what they said. Can I give them your number?"

"Of course."

I remember the report on the rape in Bjästa in the investigative journalistic program *Uppdrag granskning* (Mission Investigation), which was broadcast in March last year. I definitely want to talk to these reporters. Their work has already been important to me.

In March 2009, 14-year-old Linnea from Bjästa outside Örnsköldsvik went to the police to report that she had been raped by a then-15-year-old boy at her school. In the documentary, he's called Oskar. The rape took place in a school toilet in the middle of the day. As is so often the case with rapes and sexual assaults, there were no witnesses to the incident itself and no DNA evidence. Only Linnea and Oskar knew what had happened.

Immediately after the assault, rumors about the incident began to spread in Bjästa. A bunch of guys say on camera in the documentary that a rumor tells of Linnea claiming she got his semen in her eyes, that she got pregnant, and that "her pussy was cracked." And since she was wearing tight jeans in the days after, this rumor was taken as evidence that she lied about the rape. More and more people distrust Linnea.

One of the few who found Linnea credible was the prosecutor. She argued that although there were no witnesses, Linnea's story was supported by other evidence. Among other things, there was a forensic medical certificate that supported Linnea's story about how the abuse took place and a teacher who testified

August 15, 2011

I get a new job!

My future boss tweets after we sign the contract: "I just hired a rabid Muslim-loving feminist whore agent. I mean, how many are there? #epicwin"

I have a good laugh at that. Somehow, all the negative attention I've received over the past year still doesn't seem to completely shut me out of social life. To handle it all with openness and humor feels like a good strategy.

The job is at Sektor3, the think tank for civil society. In my opinion, this is one of Sweden's most important think tanks. Now I will be able to devote myself full-time to idealism and freedom of association. At the same time, I maintain my involvement in Faith and Solidarity in my spare time. Now I'm running for the national board.

August 18, 2011

Claes gets in touch.

> "I know you generally turn down interviews, and most requests I don't forward to you, but here is one that I think is worthy of passing on to you."
> "Okay, tell me."
> "Well, you know the guys who did the documentary about the Bjästa case? They got in touch and want to talk to you."
> "Yes, in many ways, this has been just like a global Bjästa!"

Everything feels fine and we go to a restaurant called the Elephant Boy. A little while into our dinner, it emerges that he has a special reason for meeting. He wants guarantees that I'll never mention his name in connection with the story and in connection with me. He also says that, unfortunately, he absolutely cannot testify I slept at his house that night.

"You have to understand that," he says. Our topics of conversation are running out. I pay what he suggests, give him a hug, and go home crying.

August 10, 2011

I can't stand living alone and going home alone every day anymore. I don't want to live like this.

August 11, 2011

I've blocked the woman Andreas lives with on Facebook to avoid reminders that she exists. But today, I remove the block and write her a short message telling her that Andreas is still in touch. I tell her, truthfully, that he recently said he loves me more than her and the fact that he said our love was much greater than theirs. A few hours later, Andreas calls. I actually answer. He's furious.

"Do you realize what you've done?"
"It's not me; it's you," I tell him.

Finally, *finally*, he will let me go. I can feel it.

with the headline that the Swedish prosecutor is "biased against men." The article is illustrated by a picture of Helena Kennedy happily kissing Julian. "It's not *human rights* that are in focus," says Pia. "It's *men's rights*. Especially the rights of a certain man."

July 21, 2011

The last few weeks, I've been dating like crazy: Jakob, Erik, Gabriel, Ali, Samuel, Sam, Janne, Jonas, and Martin. And between each potential crush, between hopes for a new love and text messages that go silent, I myself disappear from the radar and think about Andreas and my failed life. Today, I received a postcard from him in which he tells me he's depressed because he misses me. A grain of confirmation. I don't answer, but inside I keep waiting and breaking down.

July 27, 2011

A few days ago, Olof, the man I stayed with when I ran away from my apartment, called and wanted to have dinner. Even though he abandoned me to save his own skin last year, I was so happy to hear from him. Happy because I want to meet him and because maybe life can start to get back to normal. If I'm only going to spend time with those who were there for me when it was really bad, I'll be too lonely. I'm ready to forget and forgive. We decided to meet today.

It's getting hot and he's lying in the sun on a park bench at our meeting place over at Blecktorn park. Cute Olof, who got scared. Who wouldn't be when a pack of British media hyenas attack?

still believes there are ways. The politician is diplomatically neutral when he acts as an intermediary.

I'm honestly trying to understand what they mean. Do they really think I would have anything to gain by refusing to participate in the legal process or by suddenly retracting truthful information? If I change my story to something that suits Julian better, how exactly would that benefit human rights? Kennedy refers to my reputation and says that Julian would help restore it. But how could this suggestion affect my reputation other than that I will forever be known as the one who lied about a rape? When credibility is so often a sex offense victim's only asset, it means that I will essentially be disenfranchised if I find myself in a similar position again in the future. To me, this proposal just looks like an attempt to lower my credibility for good. However, I can't stop thinking that it's a kind-hearted woman who comes up with it, so I must have missed something. There should be some advantage for me if someone like her is even going to do the math that it's worth putting forward. I'm puzzled.

My legal assistant, Pia, who's also present during the conversation, has seen this before; she is not the least bit surprised. Rather, she's really pissed off.

"So-called representatives of human rights show once again that they do not think that women's rights are actually part of their work. Women should back down, not have their case tried, settle for an apology, and assure the world that the perpetrator is a good man. It's insane!"

She goes on to show me an article from February

She has convinced a Swedish politician with a focus on human rights who I know to pass on some kind of settlement offer from Julian. They think you should withdraw your accusations against him making certain avowals."

"OK, what kind of avowals?"

"As I understand it, he would publicly declare that you are not hired by the CIA as he indicated earlier."

"And?"

"No, nothing more."

It's quiet for a while. Then:

"So, I'm going to go out and tell lies, and in return, he would take back his own invention?"

"Yes, you can probably interpret it that way," says Claes.

I laugh. It's so absurd.

"But in fact, no one really believes that about the CIA anymore. Hasn't he even said it himself already, that it's not likely?"

"I take it that you to mean that you want me to decline?" Claes asks.

After our conversation, Claes explains to Kennedy that the Swedish justice system doesn't work that way, that this case falls under general prosecution—regardless of what we say about the matter. I simply cannot stop the legal process, even if I wanted to. Nor is there anything that makes me want to stop it.

Kennedy replies that she is aware of how public prosecution works but tries again. She writes to the politician that she thinks can persuade me, that she

July 8, 2011

The Political Week of Almedalen is going on in my hometown, Visby, and I have traveled here to participate, along with the elite from political parties, enterprises, and civil society organizations. An unknown woman approaches me and tells me that she has been hoping to meet me here. She is very keen and tells me that she knew Julian before, and she knows I'm telling the truth. And when she tells her story, I know just as well that she is telling the truth too. She says she spent time with Julian before he became famous for the Manning leak, before the footage of the Apache helicopter murders, and that he subjected her to abuse similar to what he subjected me to. We both know we're telling the truth. Not because of intuition but because we've never heard any other story even remotely like how Julian behaves. She wants to know how she can proceed to testify. I give her Claes' number.

July 18, 2011

Claes calls me:
"I want to start by apologizing, this is something rather bad and silly, but I still feel that I need to tell you so that you can make up your own mind."
"Yes, go on," I say.
"Well, Helena Kennedy, do you know who she is?"
"Huh?"
"An internationally renowned lawyer and human rights defender who works with Julian's legal team.

describe me as someone completely different from who I am, to claim that I stand for completely different things than I actually stand for, and to direct hatred towards me for that. That I am hated for claims that I would like to reduce freedom of expression and harm human rights when strengthening and protecting this is so extremely important to me. It hurts, physically. I am once again listening to the Gotland feminist group Ainbusk, and Josefin Nilsson singing *Love me for who I am*. Thinking that if loving me isn't possible, they can at least hate me for who I am.

At the same time, I'm beginning to sense that what really made me sick is a thought in the back of my head that has barely come to the surface. Something I know isn't true and that I don't want to be true, but that overshadows all other details and pierces my heart. Something that I come back to again and again and from which I cannot free myself: "The world is evil, and I have no place in it."

May 25, 2011

The tension in my muscles is killing me; my shoulders are stiff as planks, and I have a headache. I go to an osteopath, but I don't feel it helps. My project employment at the community college is about to end, and it doesn't look like there's money available for an extension.

stay with me, why I didn't do more to stop him, why I didn't realize right away that he actually broke the condom and abused me, and how the feeling of having his hands locked above my head still sits as an extremely clear bodily memory. I talk about how the retching returns at the memory of the stench of his burp.

May 23, 2011

Second therapy session. I begin the session by continuing to talk about the abuse. It surprises me a little, but I find that it doesn't actually upset me very much. It feels more like I'm at a party and talking to another one of the curious acquaintances who want to question me. It's more like a job than help because the shame he created is no more. The thousands of people who have investigated me, blamed me, and shouted at me to be ashamed have worked in vain. I've apparently already processed the incident and put all the responsibility for what happened where it belongs: on him. That is a great and important insight.

At the same time, I think that it's what the insurance company has agreed to replace. The psychological damage from the abuse. But the therapist confirms it's okay to talk about other things. That there is always something else at the bottom, something else that is activated, something else to treat to continue on and come out stronger on the other side.

In my case, the hate arouses stronger emotions than the abuse. Specifically, the hatred directed at me for unreal reasons. That it has been possible to visible in the background.

Julian's defense also does not think that I "look raped" in the picture from the dinner with the leaders of the Pirate Party. The police ask for my opinion on this. And I explain it as it was, that it hadn't even felt real that he would do something as sick as destroying a condom. That I could barely admit to myself that it had happened at that point.

The interrogation completely exhausts me.

May 14, 2011

I experience a nasty anxiety attack in a way I've never experienced before. I've hyperventilated and have cried so much, but this is something completely different, something completely uncontrollable. It feels like being alone in the dark.

At three o'clock in the morning, I call the psychiatric emergency department. When they estimate there's no risk of me harming myself, there's not much they can do. But the mere contact with someone allows me to pull myself together enough to fall asleep.

May 18, 2011

It turns out that there is only one Swedish insurance company that does not require a conviction to provide support in the event of sexual abuse and that my home insurance is with them. It feels like having a winning lottery ticket. I get ten hours with a psychotherapist straight up. Today, at my first appointment, I talk about Julian. About why I let him gained a view of myself in which I believe the periphery is my place and that it's OK if that's the best I can get. *What a small person he is*, says EvaMaria. *If he's a little person and I'm his satellite, then I'm hardly anyone at all*, I think. And that does it. Today, I finally manage to block Andreas on Facebook and Messenger where we constantly see each other and are in contact. That's enough. I decide he doesn't exist for me anymore. I decide to become my own person again. It's hard but also such an incredible liberation.

April 27, 2011

Police hearing, again.

New accusations and fabrications circulate online. Among other things, the various conspiracy theories that Julian's defenders, the self-proclaimed legal experts in collaboration with the media, have presented. The police take them seriously, or at least they want to eliminate the risk of missing something, even if it may seem unlikely at first glance. They document my responses to how I feel regarding the utterly creative claims about the course of events and both real and invented personal connections, where random coincidences—such as the fact that both Maria and I visited Zimbabwe on different occasions many years ago—are presented as evidence of long-planned conspiracies. I get to explain I had no idea who Julian was until last year. Most police officers we met at the station didn't even seem to know who Julian was when we got there. He simply wasn't that famous. One of the earliest press pictures of him used in the media is from our seminar; a piece of our logo is happen several times now. Because the myth of the infallible hero is so strong, it's like there's a need to change his category to be able to recognize him as a sex offender at all.

Creating role models and heroes by ignoring a person's flaws is an all too easy way to create hope and meaning. Similarly, it's easy to create villains by ignoring a perpetrator's good sides.

It's tragic that Julian lets Manning down, but at the same time, it undeniably helps my cause. This betrayal makes it possible to take him down from his pedestal. And once he's down here, among us mere mortals, it's much easier to place him in the rapist category, a category that leaves no room for being a hero. The reverse also applies here; keeping him in the category of a freedom-of-speech hero apparently makes it difficult or even impossible to accept that he's on probable grounds for suspected sexual crimes. It's unfortunate that it has to be this way, but Julian is a human being, neither demigod nor monster, neither infallible nor worthless. It is possible to be both a fighter for freedom of speech and a rapist at the same time.

April 26, 2011

I've spent the whole spring feeling bad. The constant hate attacks were mixed with desperate dating and longing for Andreas all the time when we didn't see each other. He's continued to see at least one other woman and me simultaneously. He both comforts and betrays me, and I have been close to perishing. I have accepted living in his periphery. More and more, I've

Pilger, Michael Moore, and Tariq Ali seem to be backing this campaign."[29]

In the same article, Guillou also describes "a legal scandal far removed from Julian Assange's self-absorbed idiot campaign." That is: not that Julian Assange is suspected of sex crimes, but that Manning, Julian's source of material, risks life in prison for the enormous revelations:

> *But that doesn't seem to worry Assange himself or his cheerleaders. For them, lawyers for Assange are more important than lawyers for Manning. Quite apart from the issue of guilt in the rape story, you can therefore safely say that Julian Assange is a repulsive little chap without principles. To again express the matter carefully.*[30]

Together with Peter Bratt, Jan Guillou was the last in Sweden to be convicted of espionage through journalism when he revealed the so-called IB affair, showing that the Swedish state had registered citizens' opinions. Because of that case, the Swedish constitution was then changed to increase the freedom of the press to prevent similar verdicts.

His article today is a turning point for me. A turning point so that the Swedish public debate no longer automatically confuses Julian's work with WikiLeaks and his sexual crimes. In Guillou's article, Julian is also put in a new category and is recoded from the "good person" category to the mutually exclusive "bad person" category. I have seen this have been victims of abuse.

I'm turning 32. Andreas comes to visit with flowers and says he loves me.

April 24, 2011

The columnist Jan Guillou writes a text in *Aftonbladet* today with the title "Julian Assange – a repulsive little chap without principles":

> *It is embarrassingly clear that Julian Assange, the leading figure of WikiLeaks, is no male role model if I express myself carefully. Whether he is also guilty of some form of rape and sexual harassment, I cannot know. But neither can his ardent supporters, who claim to know that he is innocent.*
>
> *The fact that we do not know is due to Julian Assange himself, who refuses to appear for questioning in Sweden. Which, if he were as innocent as he and his supporters claim, would be a quick and easy way to get the suspicions dismissed. Most people who are suspected of sexual crimes in Sweden actually go free, depending on the fairly high standard of proof.*
>
> *Instead, Assange has started a campaign against the Swedish legal system. He compares Sweden to Saudi Arabia and believes that here innocent men are sentenced to an assembly line because our country is controlled by iron-fisted feminists. In addition, he talks about a conspiracy that involves getting him extradited to the United States via Sweden and false accusations of rape.*
>
> *Even for those who, like myself, have devoted themselves to criticizing flaws in the Swedish legal system for decades, the legal reasoning from Assange and his circle appears so pretentious that they are not even worth taking seriously. Even more embarrassing is that well-known radical social critics like John*

the condom with different tools and examined and compared the cut surfaces. They determine the damage present when I handed in the condom was not done by tools such as scissors or a knife and that it isn't a question of the material becoming weak enough to cause the condom to break on its own. They can also see that my DNA and that of an unknown man are on the condom.[28]

In other words: with a simple DNA test, it could be determined that the unknown man is Julian and that all unknown DNA in the investigation is from Julian. This would prove he lied in his first and only hearing. This would prove that what he said about the condom being used throughout intercourse and not breaking is incorrect. But since he didn't do any test that the Swedish judiciary can use, the stain on the sheet could, in theory, have come from another man.

March 14, 2011

I'm offered a job at Kista community college. They want me to start the day after tomorrow. I'm so happy! I really want this.

March 19, 2011

I'm reading the statistics on reports of sexual abuse from 2010. In August, there was a clear increase compared to previous years, and the increase seems to be continuing. This warms my heart. The debate about whether to report abuse and the media visibility of the crime seems to have encouraged other victims. The rate of reporting has also increased among boys who her if she doesn't want it. It is because Julian did this to me that he's suspected of a crime, nothing else.

March 2, 2011

In an interview with the British magazine *Private Eye*, Julian accuses the *Guardian*—especially its editor-in-chief for investigative journalism David Leigh—of leading a conspiracy against WikiLeaks. He also mentions some other journalists and points out that they are Jews. When the journalist says that one of them is not Jewish, Julian replies that he is "sort of Jewish".[27]

March 7, 2011

Claes comes with me for another police hearing. This time, it's about Julian's DNA traces in my bed, namely the stain left on the sheet in connection with the abuse. Julian hasn't had the opportunity to ejaculate in my bed any other time than that, so the stain is important evidence. It shows that Julian's story that a whole condom was used is not true. The stain shows that the sperm was not collected but inseminated.

The state's forensic laboratory has now also been able to confirm that the condom was damaged by the small tip at the front, the sperm container, being torn off. The legal technicians have examined the dividing surface and scratches and write in an expert opinion that the evidence is of grade +2, which means that "the possibility of obtaining these results if any other hypothesis is true, is considered to be small."

To reach this conclusion, they have tried to tear

against what I experienced as being the bigger crime; involuntarily being exposed to the risk of fertilization or infection.

What I think or feel about that, what I was most offended or humiliated by, is not legally relevant. The assessment by the media or the Internet haters doesn't matter in front of the law either. The text of the law alone is decisive for the legal decision-making process. Maybe it's time for the law to be updated; maybe it's needed to strengthen the protection against involuntary conception and infection. Sometimes, legislative amendments are needed to ensure laws match our society's morality. But there are also several facts in this case that cannot be legally regulated, problems that need to be tackled with different means than through legislation.

For example, Julian burping in my face felt worse than him trying to pry my legs apart; it smelled horrible, and I felt humiliated. The fact that he didn't flush when he went to the toilet was more disgusting than him touching my breasts or pressing his naked genitals against my clothed body, even though I didn't want to. His way of treating me like his housekeeper was more upsetting than him holding me with force against my will. But it isn't a crime to burp in another person's face, to neglect to flush the toilet as a guest, or to leave dishes on the table for women to take care of—and it shouldn't be. Being a jerk is not illegal (in most cases). However, it *is* illegal to forcefully pry a woman's legs apart with the aim of penetrating her and touching her breasts; press one's naked lower abdomen against her body—clothed or not—or hold or taking advantage of this other person "due to unconsciousness, sleep, intoxication or other effects of drugs, illness, physical injuries, mental disturbances or others circumstances that puts the other person in a helpless state."[25] In addition, a number of other sexual offenses are also classified under the term "sexual constraint." In the global debate, Swedish legislation is portrayed as extreme; that Sweden has an exceptionally broad definition of what rape is. But Schultz shows in his article that this, in fact, is not the case. He writes:

> *In French law, rape is any type of penetration that takes place by force, coercion, threat, or surprise. New Zealand defines rape as when person A has sexual contact with person B and penetration is carried out without person B's consent or without reasonable grounds to believe that person B has consented to the contact. Russian law defines rape as heterosexual vaginal intercourse by force or by taking advantage of a victim who is in a helpless state. In the United States, the laws vary slightly across state borders, but in some states, there is also a law that covers "rape by deception"—there it is therefore rape to have tricked someone into having sex.*[26]

The criminal classifications could've been different depending on the country in which the abuse towards Maria and me was assessed in court. But overall, the Swedish sexual crime legislation does not differ significantly from other countries. Swedish legislation, however, like many others, is written to protect against involuntary contact with genitals, not to protect not. In Riddle's verdict, he delivers sharp criticism on this matter. He writes that Hurtig's testimony that Assange was available for interrogation consciously misled the court. Assange was evidently making himself unavailable for the hearing in Sweden. (Later, Hurtig received a warning from the Swedish Bar Association for this deception.)

March 1, 2011

I'm unaware of any other instances where someone has consciously destroyed a condom. But today, Mårten Schultz comments on this subject in a long, interesting article in the magazine *Neo*. He explains the Swedish legislation on sexual offenses:

Since the discussion about Assange has been characterized by a special interest in condoms, it should be added that it, according to my understanding, is not rape to have sex without a condom with a voluntary partner who demands using one. It is also not rape, to remove or destroy a condom during the act. (However, it may be a less serious crime, sexual harassment.)[24]

For the first time, I'm also confronted with the term *stealthing*; to have sex with someone without a condom in spite of a prior agreement to use one. I didn't know it even was a thing, but apparently, it is, and I assume the concept can also be used for the deliberate destruction of a condom.

According to Swedish legislation, rape is defined as a person forcing sexual intercourse or similar sexual contact with another person through violence, threat,

February 24, 2011

City of Westminster Magistrates' Court judge Howard Riddle announces his decision. He approves Sweden's arrest warrant and decides Julian will be extradited to Sweden for further investigations. Mårten Schultz, professor of civil law at Uppsala University, comments on the verdict as "a balanced and—of course—elegant and sharp reasoning." He concludes that the decision "picks the sometimes downright ridiculous criticism of the Swedish legal system that Julian's English defense has put forward completely to pieces."

Julian's attorney Björn Hurtig also took part in the process. He claimed in court that Julian had been available for questioning but had not received a summons from the prosecutor. This was thoroughly refuted in the verdict. Julian had voiced, via Björn Hurtig, he would be questioned again on September 28. The prosecutor Marianne Ny—who took office September 1 and began trying to get in touch with Julian the following day—made every effort to advance the interrogation. Yet Julian refused, which made Hurting withstand September 28. Ny accepted this and waited until the agreed date. Yet on September 27, one day before the scheduled interrogation, Julian escaped from Sweden and the legal process.

In the British court, it was Ny's word against Hurtig's, but Ny showed the actual text messages she sent to Julian's defense attorney. Riddle then demanded that Hurtig show his messages. It was evident that the messages had reached Hurtig—they were saved in his phone. Ny was telling the truth, and Hurtig was

February 12, 2011

I receive an email with a photo attached. I have the crosshairs of a telescopic sight on my forehead, and the text says I'm going to be executed, guilty of treason. With the help of friends, I manage to find evidence of his identity and location, and I have half an investigation of files when I report him to the police. The sender is a Dutchman who apparently has personal connections with Julian. Initially, the police don't want to accept my report since it's a foreigner and because the threat happed online and "anonymously." But I insist, and they finally accept it.

February 17, 2011

I receive a letter stating that a police investigation will not be initiated. It feels completely pointless to file complaints if even obvious death threats from a known sender won't be examined.

February 18, 2011

I pack my stuff at Petra's and Pontus' place. Finally, I get to go home! My bodyguards, two police officers, Anna and Peter, think it's reasonable for me to move back into my apartment. But of course, I have their cell phone numbers, so I can call at any time if I suspect my security situation is under threat. None of the neighbors have reported any strange people on the staircase for a while, and I miss my apartment enough that it's worth the risk.

February 7, 2011

"Go fuck yourself you worthless bitch, everyone in the world hates you go kill yourself, there's nowhere to hide from the people."

The message comes from a student at the Royal Institute of Technology in Stockholm, who has been bullying me on Twitter almost every day. He is suffering, as so many anti-feminists over the past months, in pity for all "real rape victims." While others leave me alone after a few comments, he goes on and on, completely open under his real name. As if harassing me is a human right that he doesn't even need the protection of anonymity to exercise. I report him, but the case is dropped by the police without investigation, just like all my reports of hatred, threats, molestation, harassment, and insult.

There's a court hearing in London about the extradition of Julian according to a European arrest warrant.

I feel abandoned and sad. It seems like I'm only appreciated in very limited online channels, inside my own filter bubble. I wonder if life is really worth living. If the whole of mankind only wishes bad things for you when their hate is so much stronger than love, what's the point? If life is slowly and increasingly emptied of love, recognition, and respect, just because you told the truth about abuse, what kind of place is the world, really? Is it really a place worth staying? Is it worth fighting for this humankind to be allowed to be a part of it?

farmers who are kept off their land by the settlers' barbed wire and guns. I play with a three-year-old girl who already knows at least seven different terms for military vehicles and go shopping in a Christian Palestinian souvenir shop threatened by bankruptcy after having been cut off from the tourist route at Rachel's grave by a seven-meter-high wall.

February 1, 2011

David Leigh and Luke Harding publish their book, *WikiLeaks: Julian Assange's war on secrecy*. In it, they analyze Julian's defense strategies pretty much the same way as me. They define three characteristic strategies: Plan A, Plan B, and Plan C. The first, the Pentagon explication, or Plan A, states that Maria and I reported Julian for rape as a part of a CIA conspiracy. As fewer and fewer believed this plot, Julian and his team traced everything back to a feminist conspiracy instead, Leigh and Harding explain. According to this strategy, the so-called Plan B claims there's a secret intention to circumcise men's rights and subject them to the power of women, and in this, I'm said to have a key role. The third strategy follows the claim that the accusations are a component of a conspiracy between states to punish Julian. In this plot, I'm no longer portrayed as an active driving force but rather as a person who was played by the Swedish police and prosecutors, a passive pawn in a game played by the United States with aid from Sweden and Great Britain. Leigh and Harding describe this strategy as Plan C, and it seems to exist simultaneously alongside Plan B.

obviously illegal to impose your sperm into women without their consent. And whether he was infected or not doesn't seem to be a question the police will handle. Julian doesn't even seem to have gotten any questions about this during the hearing he attended on August 30.

January 26, 2011

I'm packing one more time to fly to Palestine. I'd love to go to the little West Bank village I'm thinking of as my home, and I've planned a visit. But today, I find out that the head of the accompanying program on-site forbids me. The security situation has normalized, but she thinks my presence could inflict damage on the program.

January 27, 2011

I choose to go to Palestine anyway. I fly from Stockholm to Tel Aviv and drive from the Airport directly to my friend, Sara, who works for the charity organization Diakonia in Jerusalem.

January 28, 2011

I travel alone on the West Bank, independent from the accompanying program. I'll refrain from visiting Yanoun, but Ramallah, Qualqiliya, and Nablus are on my itinerary. I deliberately do *not* ask permission to visit a few of the other Swedish accompaniers in Jayyous and Bethlehem. I go with them to monitor checkpoints, eat sandwiches with young Israeli conscripts, and chat with settlers and Palestinian harm, quite the opposite. There are concerns about why I said anything at all. According to the motto, 'Of course, the thing happened, but was it really necessary to report it?' After all, this had enormous consequences for our association."

The officer also asks why I didn't report it immediately. The forced insemination and risk of infection—the actions that, in my opinion, constituted the real assault—don't seem to be an unambiguous crime. It may be a case of molestation, but not for sure, legally speaking. I answer:

"[I] felt it was abusive, but not as something illegal. Not that I really had something substantial to accuse him for, no real crime to report."

(...)

The officer continues:

"So, in summary, what happened to [Maria] was an assault, and the way you were treated was more a behavior you thought could prove that?"

"Yes."

"Okay. Yes."

"At this time, I still didn't think that what he had done to me was illegal, but it was the same strange behavior."

"You still didn't think you'd been subjected to unlawful treatment at that point?"

"Well, yes, the risk of infection I actually thought was criminal. That he deliberately exposed me to this risk. (...) That's why I only told the police about him tearing the condom in the first hearing. And not that he also pinioned me and all that."[23] In the country Julian calls the Saudi Arabia of feminism, it is still not

January 25, 2011

I'm called to a new hearing. The police need to ask me about the latest media utterances from Julian and his defense. Among other things, the police have questions about the other reasons I'd potentially have for filing a criminal complaint, other than Julian's illegal behavior towards me:

"What consequences has your complaint against Julian Assange had for you and your organization?"

"Well, we are not WikiLeaks, and we do not have any influence over the actions of the organization, their handling of sources, and so on. But the basic ideas that I work with are that we need truth and transparency to bring peace to the world and that people need to know what is going on with the export of arms and many other issues. This is crucial in order for people to protest. That is what's important for us. So, for my association, this means a very unlucky shift of focus. Media no longer wants to talk to us about truth, transparency, and openness, but rather asks questions like 'What kind of person is Anna Ardin?' and 'Does she often make things up about men?' or 'Does she hate men?'"

"Mmm."

"I don't think you should get away if you've committed a crime just because you're a celebrity… However, nobody within my organization wants to discredit WikiLeaks or Julian personally. After all, we are part of the movement that he is fronting right now.

(…)

"No, I haven't been pressured into doing him any

was never transferred, and Julian has been fiercely criticized for this. The material Manning leaked is the largest source of income for WikiLeaks. The revelations this material made led to WikiLeaks' increased fame and meant they received many donations. WikiLeaks also renders income through collaborations with the media. It's deeply immoral for WikiLeaks not to honor their promise of financial support. Today, the *Guardian* reports that WikiLeaks reduced the sum even further, but finally, approximately fifteen thousand dollars (nine thousand five hundred British pounds) was finally paid.[22]

January 17, 2011

I've written several angry blog posts without publishing them. I intend to summarize them one day and make a book out of them. Through these posts, I meet a large publisher who wants to publish my story as quickly as possible. However, I want to wait for the trial; I want the legal process to come first. Apparently, the same publisher has also signed a contract with Julian to publish his book. They want to sign a contract with me, too, but I'm terrified this could be used against me.

I also don't want to write a story that will sell well just to make money from it—I want to write what's important. The publisher and I cannot come to an agreement.

January 8, 2011

EvaMaria, the girl renting my apartment, throws a party and invites me. What a wonderful feeling it is to come home. I have been longing for it infinitely. My apartment is one of the really important pieces of the puzzle making up my life, of which there are currently too many pieces missing.

"Would you like to stay?" she asks.

"Oh, that's really kind of you. Thanks. But to be honest, I don't dare yet."

In the end, I leave the party and my home with a big bag full of my belongings.

January 9, 2011

I'm incredibly sad and feel homeless. I'm going back to work, but I'll soon be unemployed. Who will ever want to hire me?
　　I'm aching to see Andreas, and I hate it. I need to give him back his guidebook about Spain that I borrowed. I sneak into his stairwell with a pounding heart and manage to put the book in the mailbox unnoticed.
　　My neck hurts so bad.

January 13, 2011

In December, WikiLeaks promised to pay twenty thousand dollars for Manning's defense instead of the initially promised fifty thousand. However, the money tint. She also perms it. I'm now a curly brunette. It's strange to hardly recognize yourself in the mirror, but it looks quite good!

January 5, 2011

I have a meeting with Pia, the other lawyer at the Borgström law firm, who's handling my case alongside Claes, and we go over the previous police hearing. I have another one at ten o'clock. They present new data that Julian's defense has brought up in the process and ask more questions:

"What did you get out of filing a criminal complaint?"

I think of all I've lost, my job, my home, my security. I also think about all the threats, all the hate, and not least, that it now costs others to defend me now that I'm a low-status person. After a moment of thought, I answer:

"Nothing."[21]

January 7, 2011

We celebrate Ester's first birthday, the daughter of my good friend Ida. We talk about the case, which I regret as soon as I open my mouth. I wish that my other topics of conversation were more interesting than this case. And I wish I'd never gone to the police. I want to crawl out of my own skin and disappear.

January 1st, 2011

I get coffee in bed after a nice New Year's Eve celebration with my Gotland friend, Kajsa, and her family yesterday. It feels like I'm well taken care of, and I think things might be okay in the end after all.

January 2, 2011

My cousins come and get me to go attend an eight-course dinner at my eccentric artist aunt's place in the countryside. I'd rather not talk about the case at all, but it's hard when everyone's been thinking so much about it. I feel like a parrot repeating itself. Gradually, I forget whom I've told what. At the same time, I realize I'm going through a process. The more I talk about it, the easier it is for me to release myself from the story. It feels like putting it in a bowl, being able to look at it but not having to host it anymore. Slowly but surely, I manage to separate myself from the assault and from the online hostilities. I am regaining the contours of my own identity, a completely different person than the disgusting person made up by the Internet mob.

January 4, 2011

It's time to leave my safe space on the island and go back home to Stockholm to work. Back to the journalists' hunting grounds. Petra and her partner Pontus have offered to let me stay in their big apartment in Kungsholmen in Stockholm's city center.

My mother is a hairdresser and dyes my hair dark brown again, but with real color instead of a cheap

2011

equal rights. Right-wing populist parties, xenophobic parties, and parties denying climate change are growing in Europe, and their leadership positions are occupied predominantly by men. These men and their Internet armies in anonymous forums, blogs, and Internet magazines are increasingly spreading the idea that men are more oppressed than women. But as their support for Julian grows, they are also taking pieces of his credibility away. I don't have the funds to defend myself against his staff; however, despite all the PR consultants and lawyers funded by WikiLeaks, I have the impression that public trust in Julian is falling. The strategy to destroy my reputation to bolster Julian's no longer seems to work.

December 31, 2010

Someone with a Swedish phone number hopes I'll get run over by a bus and die, bleeding in the gutter. This is the last SMS of the year. Thank you, God, that 2010 is finally over.

must prevent, investigate, and punish gender-based violence against women—including preventing rape and other sexual abuse. They must ensure crime victims receive support, assistance, and rehabilitation. States must also work to change the social attitudes that pave the path for discrimination against women.[20]

Women in Sweden receive slightly more equal salaries for equivalent work here than in many other countries. There is a greater percentage of women engaged in politics than in many other places, women might be abused a little less, and men perhaps have slightly less leeway to mistreat women and avoid judgment for it, but it isn't anything more than that. Even in Sweden, women are disadvantaged in most measurable categories in comparison to men. Feminism has not gone too far. On the contrary, it has by no means achieved its goal of gender equality. Feminism must go further.

December 27, 2010

The anti-feminists are cheering. It seems like all the misogynists, fascists, and right-wing populists are on Christmas vacation and therefore have a lot of time to repeat Julian's "perfect formulation" that Sweden is the Saudi Arabia of feminism. And Julian, via WikiLeaks' Twitter account (that I'm convinced he still handles himself), is thanking and liking. As long as the support is uncritical, no one from WikiLeaks protests, no matter how brutal the violations against women.

Julian has also earned new fans among people who do not support WikiLeaks' agenda on peace and

In a world where the oppression of women is so often considered normal, where men's sexual abuse so often is diminished, victims ridiculed, and abuse allowed to continue, perhaps it is extreme to claim the right not to be maltreated the way I was by Julian. But it still doesn't have anything to do with conspiracies. It has to do with legal certainty and victims' rights to get violations tried in court.

If there is anything I understand through my involvement in the feminist movement, it would be this: Feminism has not gone too far. In Sweden, we haven't reached equality, and the feminist oppression of men simply doesn't exist. The fact that Sweden is on top in international equality comparisons is no more than proof that we're a little less unequal here than in other countries. For example, Amnesty International believes that Sweden still has a lot to do in order to denounce and judge gender-based violence. A form of violence affecting all genders, but that affects women more often and more severely than men, and where men almost always are the perpetrators. Most crimes within this category are never reported, and only a small proportion of complaints are tried in court; the majority of police investigations into reported rapes against a person over 15 years old are dismissed with the claim there isn't sufficient evidence to prove a crime.

According to international laws and human rights, states are obliged to do everything in their power to combat all forms of gender-based violence, ensuring that existing laws provide adequate protection. They

December 26, 2010

Julian is interviewed. He has apparently heard about the photo I posted on Facebook of him lying on my sofa fully clothed. He thinks it's a "trophy photo," meaning a nude photo of him in my bed. His fans become furious at me for "behaving like this." He also says Sweden has degenerated into the "Saudi Arabia of Feminism." Meaning Sweden has deprived men of all democratic and civic rights in the same way Saudi Arabia has done to women. Again, he is trying to invalidate the accusations by claiming that it's actually about something other than his behavior. He means, for example, that it's about hatred towards men and in a hornet's nest of revolutionary feminism. He literally says, "I fell into a hornet's nest of revolutionary feminism."

This is a new defense strategy from Julian and his team that might replace the previous Pentagon strategy that now only a few people believe. This strategy seems to aim at planting a story in which I'm part of a secret plan to frame him with criminal charges to limit the rights of men and to subjugate them under the power of women. Wanting to stop men from being able to inseminate women against their will is now being described as something revolutionary. Personally, I think this is a minimum requirement for anybody claiming they want gender equality, but it's still all that's needed to convince some that feminism has gone too far.

In practice, the statement "feminism has gone too far" seems to mean that "any feminism has always gone far."

working to increase equality. Sometimes these gray zones are exactly that—gray. However, it's important to recognize that sometimes the borders are clearly visible, the laws unambiguous, and the evidence crystal clear. In this instance, it's not gray at all but black and white.

I would like to bring the way we talk about sex, assaults, and rapes to a more reasonable level without all the misaligned bossiness. At the same time, we must be able to be very distinct on the principle of every human being's right to their own body and our right to set our own limits. Regardless of what type of sexual offense we are subjected to, the offenses should be associated with a legal penalty. I want the sexual abuse of power to come to an end at last.

December 24, 2010

I spend Christmas at my parents' home. Other than Somar, nearly nobody knows I'm here. My life is a disaster; I'm still on leave from work, my apartment is sublet, and I miss Andreas. I'm unemployed, homeless, and lonely. It's Christmas eve, and I get a call from a hidden number.

"Hi?" says an unknown male voice, who sounds quite surprised that I pick up the phone. "Hi? Is this Anna Ardin?"

"Yes," I reply.

"You are so fucking disgusting," he says. "How does it feel to be the most hated woman in the world?"

I hang up and turn off the phone. *Merry Christmas*, I say to myself.

something else from their partner, regardless of whether they receive it. One partner may remember what happened for a long time, and the other may forget about it immediately afterward.

The legislation could be better at protecting the people it's supposed to protect. However, the righteousness and ardent hate speech against victims and perpetrators harms and prevents the necessary conversation the public needs to have.

Situations of rape and other forms of abuse are normally quite similar to "normal sex." Abuse is when an act crosses someone's boundaries, regardless of circumstances. Aspects of these boundaries are defined legally. However, the same behavior can be either illegal or permissible depending on whether the one who is exposed agrees or not. For example, being penetrated while sleeping. Similarly, it can also be OK to take things without asking for permission if there is a mutual understanding that the behavior is acceptable. This is, then, not a case of theft. At the same time, things that are legal can still be offensive; legal sexual acts more about dominance than romance can have more to do with the exercise of power than equal sex.

It's important to go to the police even without reading up on the law and to understand that it isn't a slap in the face to other maltreated people. I simply do not accept this accusation.

To address the problem of sexual abuse, we need to be able to allow cases to be examined by the courts, not least those in the gray zones. We also need to prevent abuse by talking about it and constantly about bag-snatching is pissing on people who have been injured during a burglary in their own homes? Would they refer to people being scammed for a million dollars and never getting restoration as an argument for fraud victims of a few thousand to keep quiet? I really don't think so.

Neither do I think talking about gray zones devalues the concepts or damages the possibilities of reaching conviction in the clear cases or the coarser crimes. On the contrary, I think that it can strengthen the whole spectra of crime victims. Both someone who knows for sure that they have been raped and me, who just knew something was wrong but could not immediately put words on it, can be helped by an open discussion that is liberated from taboos. Talking about it gives us the language to strengthen those who have been abused and everyone who is at risk of abuse. It is not leaching to talk about it, as the former Member of Parliament claims. To ask the question of whether what we have experienced was rape—in a legal or moral sense—is a road towards understanding, not mockery.

I think there is often no clear demarcation between consensual sex and violent dominance. When we humans have sex, there is almost always some element of dominance, even when nothing describable as encroachment occurs. One sex partner is on top; one provides the rhythm, and one responds a little late or not at all to the signals of the other about what they want or don't want to do. One "owes" the other an orgasm; one needs sex for the sake of confirmation, and the other wants sex because they believe they will get

> *leach on the concept of rape!!!! For all women who have experienced rape, it is mocking that some women don't know whether they have been raped. When Claes Borgström says that you do not always know what a rape is, then you hit at all of us who have experienced a real rape. Claes Borgström only wants to become famous, but you are doing this at the expense of all real rape victims—you are making fun out of us!*[19]

She—like so many others—has a distorted picture of what happened in my apartment, what words I used to describe it, and the headings the police used in the report. She judges me from this picture. Of course, hearing her say I'm doing a disservice to all the women of the world and that I have damaged women's rights globally saddens me. But the point is still interesting since it is symptomatic. There are so many who believe this, and they are very upset. As they say, there are coarser crimes than the one I was subject to—crimes with more violence within the sexual abuse category—I interpret their claims as the abuse against me not being rough enough to be reported at all.

Wouldn't this position be perceived as very strange if we were talking about other crimes, such as theft instead of sexual offenses? Would Camilla Lindberg, Naomi Wolf, or the student from Halmstad University say that I was hitting robbery victims in the face if I reported a smaller theft? Would they claim that we ought to look through our fingers with shoplifting out of respect for victims of brutal robbery? Do they really think that someone who tells us

December 23, 2010

"You piss on every woman who has been raped for real. Shame on you."

With this text message, a young student of international relations from the University of Halmstad summarizes yesterday's debate on Swedish TV and many of the comments on blogs and in newspapers following it quite well. To report something perceivable as being in a gray zone is considered to diminish what "real rape victims" have experienced. The gray zone is apparently something very controversial. And keeping the term "rape" out of the conversation has become a political stand in the public debate surrounding my case. The shades of grey between hero and monster, between Madonna and whore, that every single one of us human beings find ourselves in is reduced to a glaring white or pitch black by the discourse. All nuances disappear, and with them, the truths that were once there.

A woman named Camilla Lindberg also took part in yesterday's debate on Swedish television. She is a former Member of Parliament from the Liberal Party who is known for rejecting expanded surveillance laws against her own party. She develops her thoughts on my case on her blog.

> *I have been raped and I can guarantee that if you have been raped, then you know what a rape is. Do not devalue the concept of rape, rape is terrible and may not be confused with sex that felt so and so (...) When you call a broken condom rape, it is like a slap in the face to all of us who have been raped for real. Do not*

December 22, 2010

Despite the rekindled hate, Somar and I pack our bags, check out of the hotel in Barcelona, and travel home to our respective parents in Gotland.

In an interview with the *Times*, Julian says that a black prison guard handed over a note saying: "I only have two heroes in the world, Dr. King and you." Julian also believes that this "is representative of 50 percent of people".[17] That sounds quite pretentious, but he's got a point. For some reason, many people seem to have a slightly distorted image of Julian, which feels nice in a way. The shame of being starstruck and having missed his flaws becomes a little easier to bear when I know I share this mistake with others. *Guardian* columnist Catherine Bennett described Julian's dazzling effect on his admirers, men as well as women, a few days ago:

[Julian Assange's] chief British benefactor, the former army officer Vaughan Smith, has shown that the Assange effect goes way beyond standard manipulation of the groupie reflex. Smith's atmospheric account of the night before his hero turned himself in might easily have been set in the Tower of London on the eve of a royal execution. "I feel that I am intruding," Smith writes, "but Julian smiles at me. He does that: brings you in and makes you feel you are important to him when most of us would feel too preoccupied to do such a thing.[18]

nonsense.

Julian's online defenders, nevertheless, do not let go of this idea. A man I have never heard of sends an email to my employers, presidents of different organizations I am a member of, and even my manager:

> *Anna Ardin is a skilled but ice-cold psychopath who deals with intelligence agencies in troubled spots like Cuba, Buenos Aires, and Washington. In my eyes, she's a traitor and a security risk. After all, I have taken note of her; this is my overall judgment. I now fight to distribute this since Swedish media so far refuse to write about her activity as an agent and her probable collaboration with the CIA.*

WikiLeaks' reputation seems to be free-falling from a significant advocate for freedom of speech to a dogmatic organization dedicated to defending an individual man and his rights.

In the evening, SVT's *Debatt* is broadcast on Swedish television without my involvement. The title has indeed been changed, but the discussion is still dominated by the question of guilt. Men reading excerpts from investigative files and women who "were raped for real" testify that what happened to Maria and me is actually not rape. A few from #prataomdet attempt to nuance the conversation and talk about abuse, but they get effectively silenced. The flood of messages sent to me after the program suggest I was convicted, and Julian acquitted. After a couple of days' rest, the hate has now taken new speed.

Of course, if Julian Assange accepts his extradition, travels to this liberal hellhole, and answers the relevant questions, something approaching the facts might be established. Why doesn't he just do it? He could clear his name.[16]

December 20, 2010

The producer of the program *Debatt* on Swedish television (SVT) gets in touch with me and wants me to take part in a panel discussion on the subject "is Julian Assange guilty?" This idea is probably as close to a people's tribunal as you can get. But I don't want to be judged or assessed by self-proclaimed experts and so-called "witnesses" with absolutely no first-hand insights about me, Julian, or what happened between us—those who have invalidated the whole legal system.

I don't want to meet the Internet haters who have been screaming themselves hoarse that I am a liar or have made huge collages of small clues, insulting me and detailing grotesque invented allegations. I tell SVT that I don't want to give the bullies that kind of space for their speculations and that it's completely unreasonable to treat the matter of guilt in this way. The producer promises to change the subject.

December 21, 2010

Finally, in an interview with the BBC, Julian admits that both the CIA and the Pentagon traces are implausible. It took four long months, but at last, he withdraws this accusation. It comes now, after months of experiencing others dismissing this story as today. The police now assess that I can travel home and celebrate Christmas with my family!

December 19, 2010

Julian and his attorney, Mark Stephens, describe the accusations against him in the media as "Dark forces at work." Stephens also speaks of a "honey trap," which spurs Julian's defenders online to dismiss the assaults as an invention of the CIA.

I simultaneously experience more support for my cause. Even international journalists increasingly start to see through Julian. Catherine Bennett writes in the *Guardian* that:

The WikiLeaks founder's reluctance to face his accusers sits badly with his avowed role as champion of freedom. And to keep delaying the moment of truth, for this champion of fearless disclosure and total openness, could soon begin to look pretty dishonest, as well as inconsistent.

Was it the plan, back at dark forces HQ, that Assange's name should now be so potent among legions of influential, normally judicious supporters, as to place him above the law? To listen to them, the creation of WikiLeaks and an allegation of sexual impropriety are two utterly irreconcilable concepts: there is no way the person who did the former could have to answer for the latter.

Any interest in establishing the truth through the Swedish legal process, as opposed to claim and counterclaim in the media, instantly translates as disloyalty to Assange, the world's greatest champion of the truth.

perpetrator. This is something we need to talk about in order to have a language in place in cases where it really matters. When someone has been injured, when lives and careers are at stake.[15]

Other large media and local press publish a long series of chronicles referring to Johanna and their initiative, #prataomdet. Various authors describe personal experiences of assault and other unpleasant memories within sexual gray areas. The testimonials lead to the creation of the website prataomdet.se. It feels like a crucial turning point in my life. What happened to me is finally moving into a bigger context, and the reports seem to me like a huge mobilization of support and understanding. Although the purpose of the campaign is to draw attention far beyond the fates of individuals, I experience it as if the Swedish public now seriously—and for the first time—believes me more than they believe Julian. Today, our cases are no longer described only as two individual bagatelles threatening freedom of speech and transparency. Now it's also about every human being's inviolable right to their body—even if the abuser was a famous, popular, or important person.

It's exactly those gray areas that Johanna Koljonen is talking about that are central in my case. Is it punishable to deceive someone by not using a (functional) condom, despite a pre-agreement to use one? The #prataomdet campaign has taken the edge off the screaming hatred that persecuted me during the autumn. There are almost no hate comments

He would.

What was revolving in my head? Banalities. I did not want to be a nuisance. The damage had already been done. I had already shown pleasure, and it felt childish to interrupt. And gratitude that he, at that very moment, when he was moving towards my body, in my body, called me wonderful. Somewhere, in a haze of sexual choices from the night before that I participated in and enjoyed but did not really stand for, there was also the feeling that my right to draw boundaries was somehow forfeited. I had been too willing. It would have been too much fun to be her, the girl who uncomplicatedly enjoys sex.

I kept going until it was finished. I made coffee and followed him to the subway through my suburb and knew we would never have sex again. I didn't feel like an abuse victim. I was not angry at him, just a little at myself while I kissed goodbye and noted in my mental to-do list that I needed to be tested for STDs. The discomfort I felt in relation to this man was so vague in its contours that I needed ten years distance to distinguish its form: a piece of shit. This lovely guy had behaved like a piece of shit. [...]

In sexual abuse situations, the victim is often helpless. I was not. I could probably have broken the situation with a single word. But I did not want to be annoying. [...] I did not feel like a victim, but I would have been entitled to it. The guy I slept with certainly did not feel like a

December 18, 2010

Today, Johanna Koljonen writes an article in the *Dagens Nyheter* newspaper. She is direct and to the point. Even if her case is completely different from mine in many ways, and the perpetrator acted differently than how Julian did, there are many parallels:

> *When I was younger and with much lower self-esteem I was once invited to dinner by a man perhaps fifteen years older from my own industry. Early during the evening, he told me that he intended to seduce me. I thought that seemed like a fantastic idea. We got ungovernably drunk on more expensive wine than I had ever afforded and then we had lots of wonderful sex. But I am not an idiot: we used condoms, of course, at my request.*

> *Did he negotiate the condom? Did he try to escape? I wish I could remember, but I don't. I have reasoned with cajoling men so often that the instances are blurred.*

> *The next morning, I woke up to tender caresses in his arms, hungover and quite happy. Or rather like this: I woke up with him inside me. That's where the memory of the morning begins, with penetration as a fact. I wanted to have more sex but could not concentrate because of a throbbing anxiety. Does he have a condom? He does have condom, right? I did not dare to ask. Our agreement was so very clear: condoms in every hole, otherwise there will be nothing. He wouldn't...?*

more worried about his ability to get into my computer. At the age of 21, Julian, aka Mendax, was arrested for hacking into NASA and convicted of cybercrime.

The court decides to release him on bail of £370,000 British pounds. English celebrities like John Pilger, Jemima Khan, Ken Loach, Bianca Jagger, and a few others vouch for him. He receives an ankle monitor and a duty to report to the local police station. After his release, he salutes with the victory V as if he had already been acquitted. The journalist Vaughan Smith offers him accommodation on his estate in British Norfolk. Julian gets to dine with silver cutlery, walk around in an oilskin jacket, and regains access to the Internet.

In Spain, Somar and I are starting to live everyday lives. Our tourist ambitions are subsided, and we don't have too much money left. This morning, we sit silently next to each other in our beds with our computers as we suddenly realize that it's already 9:55 a.m. We have to hurry if we want breakfast, it closes in five minutes. The breakfast is included in the hotel fee that the police paid, so we try to eat late and properly to last until dinner. We manage to get down just in time today and remain seated while the dishes are cleared away. Somar tells me about a young greengrocer that she had just read about who burnt himself to death in protest against the regime in Tunisia. We talk about how we can support the democratic movements in the Middle East.

It feels like everybody is now talking about assaults and gray zones, and it's done in a way that isn't about distorted facts or attempts to prove Maria's or my stories wrong. Rather, it feels like we now have a window of opportunity to move forward with society's views on victims and perpetrators. Something infinitely broader and more important than two individual assaults on women by a spectacular man. It feels like a candle lighting up in the dark. A positive new opening.

At the same time, Julian's detention hearing takes place in the City of Westminster Magistrates' Court in London. The British Judge, Duncan Ouseley, made the following question during the hearing: "If he is so eager to clear his name, what prevents him from voluntarily returning to Sweden?" Julian's lawyer answers shortly that it's his client's right to appeal. It is only a matter of principles. According to which principle, I don't know, but perhaps the principle of Julian's Rights is a priority before the rights of others.

Later that evening, Julian makes a statement to the *New York Times*: "I have enough anger to last me 100 years." Apparently, he's furious at the judiciary system for trying to determine whether he is guilty of sexual offenses. I told the Swedish newspaper *Aftonbladet* some time ago that I wasn't afraid of Julian, but now it appears dangerous to be his enemy. I remember him telling me that he had been into squatting for a while, where his role was to climb into apartments from the roof. This now causes me nightmares. What if he gets into my apartment? When I'm awake, however, I'm seriousness, including a mathematics test (result: *Math Wiz*); which character from Shakespeare are you? (Result: Hamlet), how good are you at guessing who is a virgin? (Result: 61 percent), and "the Asperger's Syndrome Test" Simon Baron-Cohens Autism Spectrum Quotient (result: 39 out of 50). He has stated liberal-left views and subtracted some years from his true age. The system comes to the conclusion that we match each other 88 percent. Yet, he seeks no girlfriend but an affair and "to make babies." On the question: "What am I doing with my life?" Harry answers: "Directing a consuming, dangerous human rights project which is, as you might expect, male dominated. Variously professionally involved in international journalism/books, documentaries, cryptography, intelligence agencies, civil rights, political activism, white collar crime, and the internet."[14]

Where women are problems in Julian's eyes, men at least appear to be solutions. And to his white-collar crimes, one or another sexual offense may now have been added. Male-dominated crimes, as you might expect.

December 16, 2010

The hashtag #tackanna was thrown in the trash already at the idea stage, and instead, the campaign was called #prataomdet ("talk about it"). Many people involved in the debate draw parallels to our cases and reactions to the news about them, but what's more important is that more and more men and women reflect on their own and others' experiences and limits.

and interested writers can get in touch with her. "Just a thought," she writes. People start to volunteer to write and publish stories of bad sexual experiences. Then, Johanna realizes that a hashtag is needed to make the texts searchable. "I personally find #tackanna ("thank you anna") quite nice, yet it sounds like taking a stand in the question on guilt in the court case. I like #Jagärannaardin ("IamAnnaArdin") too, but perhaps it holds the same problem?"

I follow the conversation, but I don't want the campaign to be all about me or be limited by personal stakes. Besides, I don't want—under any circumstances—to get any more media attention. Johanna hears about my position through a friend we have in common, and she immediately apologizes, saying she didn't know what she was thinking when she published my name. But that she did it is actually rather irrelevant. It seems much more important to me that more and more people are refusing to speculate about the question of guilt. It makes me hopeful that the debate about Maria's case and my case can, perhaps, start being about principles.

December 15, 2010

I get a tip that Julian has a profile on OK Cupid, a dating site I've also used. His pseudonym reads Harry Harrison, and it's easy to find. If he had access to the Internet in the pre-trial detention, he definitely would've deleted his profile as soon as it was discovered before it went viral. But now, I can rummage around among everything he's written. He's completed 45 different tests of varying degrees of that someone like me, who has analyzed sex offenses professionally, has the guts to report myself as a victim. He presupposes, like so many before him, that I made it all up just to prove that apparently, feminists can't be abused. Many of the online comments on my case so far revolve around this very topic; how strange it is to first talk publicly about sexual abuse and then claim to have been abused yourself. But I find it completely logical. The probability is, of course, a lot higher that we who are engaged in the subject and know something about the mechanisms will report when we are abused.

At home, in Sweden, today is the day of the Lucia festival celebrations. Here in Spain, we try to do sports. We do water aerobics with a young male instructor who knows all the elderly ladies, at least ten of them, with their colorful bathing caps, by their first names. "Good, Flora, you're doing great!" he shouts to a woman in her 90s. She's delighted and giggles back. All is well, and nobody recognizes me.

December 14, 2010

Due to the accusations against Julian, the Finnish Swedish journalist Johanna Koljonen initiates a conversation on Twitter about sexual gray areas. Towards the evening, she concludes that the way to be able to discuss cases like this publicly is to have a far more nuanced picture of what's really happening in such situations. She considers that personal testimonies on this question could be powerful and suggests that every major daily newspaper publish such a text every day. She writes that culture editorials ignore any comments from now on. All I want is to hibernate and be woken up again in 2015 when it's all over.

December 12, 2010

Somar has recently met a new guy, and she talks with him on the phone every day. Today, she spends a few hours with her cell phone to her ear in the corridor, but for the rest of the day she's available; she's here for me just as before. She seems happy, and that feels good. While she's on the phone, I go through today's harvest of hate e-mails. But as it turns out, it isn't only hate today. One e-mail stands out. It's from someone claiming she represents a group called the *Witches of Berlin*. She writes that the attention surrounding the case of Julian Assange got them to organize a demonstration for girls' and women's rights not to be abused. They have also collected 38 euros to support me. She asks how she can transfer the money.

This is one of the nicest things anyone has ever done for me. A group of completely unknown girls think of me, and they have done what they can. It's heartwarming, and for a moment, everything feels more bearable. I reply to them that they should transfer the money to a women's shelter because I think the work there is extremely important. Believing a woman's story can save lives.

December 13, 2010

Today I receive an e-mail from a man. He finds it absolutely unacceptable and downright "disgusting" get good help with my self-loathing:

> *"What is the mental disorder she has called? I don't mean that nasty feminist shit, I mean the real diagnosis..."*

> *"Chewed fingernails. Nerve problem? I get some really bad psycho vibes from this chick."*

> *"When these unruly feminists can't handle even a batch of cum, I guess they have to stick to their dildo friends. What's so difficult about that? After all the ladies I've had sex with, I've come to the following conclusion: the more "feminist" they are, the more often I get to hear really fucking kinky stuff. They want to be fucked really hard and get so "exploited." That's my experience anyway. Guess that in bed contrasts from your own everyday life turn you on."*

They say my time is up, that they want to brutally beat me, that assaulting me is a good thing to do. I am already convicted in these peoples' private courts. It feels like there is no more air for me to breathe.

But none of what I read in the threads is new. There are no perspectives added that I haven't seen before. And all the answers I mentally formulate are repetitions. What I respond or how I react is completely irrelevant. Reading these outpourings on social media is no longer about keeping track of the haters' attacks; it's pure auto-aggression. I decide to words or understand all the academic theories to be a genuine feminist; a little sisterhood often goes a long way.

So many people are willing to sacrifice us—and women's rights in general—to protect Julian and WikiLeaks. Wolf illustrates that clearly. All due credit to feminism in theory, but ultimately, it's the feminists in practice, those who take a stand for people affected by patriarchal power structures, who change the world.

December 11, 2010

It's Saturday night in Barcelona, and I want to go out to dance. Somar accompanies me and we have several drinks. I'm desperate for positive attention and confirmation. I make out with a Catalan separatist activist, and we exchange phone numbers. Shortly afterward, I meet another guy and make out with him. We leave together. I leave Somar alone at the venue, and I pour my heart out to this stranger. I trust him with various, probably completely incoherent, truths about who I am and what I'm doing in Spain. He becomes noticeably uncomfortable, and we have nowhere to go. He leaves, and I will never hear from him again.

I'm sitting alone on a stone wall next to a garage on the outskirts of Barcelona, with the remains of a spilled drink on my new coat. I have rings of smeared mascara around my eyes, as unevenly dark as my already washed-out hair. It's half-past four in the morning. I'm a pathetic friend and a bad person. I read some hate speech about myself in online forums and likely to be convicted. There are definitely factors here that are in my favor, e.g., that I am a well-educated Swedish citizen. My perpetrator also violates norms and is different from other people in several ways, so he's perceived as odd. Therefore, discussion of the injustices in the system is appropriate. But it is never an insult to take someone's testimony seriously. No one, no matter how high or low their position in society, has the right to get away with sexual crime. The problem is that some sex offenders are spared because of their position, not that others are convicted.

While sex crimes are viewed as both the worst and the foulest of all crimes, they are something that can be excused, explained away, and minimized with the very weakest little argument—as long as the perpetrator is part of society's "in crowd."

Wolf does not appear to consider Maria and me good enough feminists. She writes that we are using "feminist-inspired rhetoric and law to assuage what appears to be personal injured feelings."

The fundamental definition of feminism is acknowledging gender-related inequalities exist, acknowledging how women are often the losers in this gender hierarchy, and wanting to do something about it. Being a feminist very simply means wanting everyone, regardless of their gender, to have the same rights. For me, that goes without saying. It isn't extreme feminism or pretend feminism to demand that Julian be brought to justice, even if his defenders claim that. Nor do you need to know all the fancy

Because nobody cares about prosecuting rape under normal circumstances, it is somehow an insult to rape survivors to prosecute Assange for it now.[12] *[...] for all the tens of thousands of women who have been kidnapped and raped, raped at gunpoint, gang-raped, raped with sharp objects, beaten and raped, raped as children, raped by acquaintances—who are still awaiting the least whisper of justice—the highly unusual reaction of Sweden and Britain to this situation is a slap in the face.*[13]

I am being accused, yet again by someone who is well-read, of slapping the victims of "real" rape in the face. Out of respect for rape survivors, Julian Assange should not be accused. Out of respect for victims of sex crimes, Sweden should *not* prosecute an accused sex offender. Slandering victims and minimizing accusations are part of the very rape culture that Wolf opposes. Her position in the debate will be important to all the people who want to invalidate my testimony and lower our credibility. Because in sexual assault cases, the decisions are so often about credibility. It affects whether the report is initiated, whether the charges are prosecuted, and it affects the likelihood that the legal proceedings will result in a conviction.

When it's one person's word against the other's, the status of the parties involved become important in a way that is unparalleled with other types of crimes. It's clear in the media and in popular culture that social status is a key factor in adjudicating sexual crimes. A woman who is homeless, a prostitute, or maybe even taking drugs rarely wins in court against a gentleman. Similarly, dark-skinned offenders are more supporting Julian. The acclaimed feminist author Naomi Wolf—one of the leading figures in the fight for women's rights—has been upset for a long time at how victims are discredited and that their reports are not accepted, that men go free, and that their abuse and assaults are not taken seriously. She has talked about her many years of studying rape around the world. She confirms how people who report the crimes are shut down, how the cases that do go to trial rarely lead to convictions, and where one of the main arguments is that no one wants to "ruin the life" of a man who has "made a mistake." Wolf says victims are blamed and rejected because, in practice, rape is considered too difficult to deal with. She indicates that that's why people blame the person who speaks up— or why the crimes are trivialized.

Her descriptions of the cultural mechanisms surrounding rape are important. But then, suddenly, Naomi Wolf does exactly what she herself describes as the problem. She trivializes the assaults against Maria and me. Possibly because she doesn't want Julian Assange's life to be ruined "because he made a mistake." She writes a piece in which she completely ridicules us. Her reasoning is based on the idea that "two women had consensual sex and that a condom broke,"[11] and that we are upset that he began "dating another woman while still being in a relationship with the first." She dismisses the whole assault against me as a "dispute about a condom" and writes in the Huffington Post:

flannelgraph and a couple of strange, sticky photos, Beck slinks around his studio, claiming to "expose" one nutty conspiracy theory after another. Like a humorous circus magician, he pulls various unexpected cards out of his jacket sleeve. He repeatedly pauses for dramatic effect, changes the pitch of his voice, and talks complete nonsense as he does his next trick, like pulling out the UN logo or a caricature of me which he slaps onto his flannelgraph.

In the end, he comes to the conclusion that Muslims, socialists, feminists, and the UN are behind the allegations against Julian. I laugh, hard. It's impossible not to laugh. Completely impossible not to view it as anything other than satire. When I interpret it as a comedy show, the clip becomes a prop. An illustration of exactly how crazy my haters are and how little they actually care about the truth.

Julian probably doesn't sympathize with Glenn Beck at all, but he benefits from the type of conspiracy theories Glenn Beck advances. Julian's defense attorney, human rights lawyer and feminist Jennifer Robinson, says, "We are seeing increasingly on the Internet research into the backgrounds of both women that raises real questions about their credibility and the credibility of their claims."[10] So, she is citing the smears as evidence that we are not credible.

Glenn Beck sees this as an issue where women's rights threaten men, but there also seems to be some anxiety among feminists that women's rights are being harmed by the backlash they believe I'm causing by reporting a hero to the police. More feminists start exactly how it felt during the assault, and that's precisely why I didn't do what so many contributors think I should have done—run away screaming. I have heard that absurd metaphor many times. As if I were standing in line with tickets to a roller coaster and wasn't allowed to change my mind. As if no child ever got scared and backed away as their turn approached. As if no one ever changed their minds maybe only seconds before it was time to climb on and buckle themselves in.

I picture Glenn Beck. He's bought tickets to the biggest roller coaster he's ever seen, and then he realizes that it has serious—potentially life-threatening—safety risks: loose rails, broken seatbelts, and the staff are drunk. Then, his own voice blares out of the loudspeakers: "IF YOU BUY THE TICKETS, YOU RIDE THE RIDE." I also picture myself turning off the public address system and matter-of-factly explaining to him and everyone else in the line that "no, of course you shouldn't go on the ride." Just get out of line and ask for your money back.

This is how it should be in sexual situations, too. Regardless of your reason, you are always entitled to withdraw consent. No promises, neither spoken nor unspoken, are valid if you no longer feel like it. Your body is your own, and no one has any right to force you to continue to have sex if you don't want to. You never need to go on the ride, even if you bought the tickets. A roller coaster should be fun; otherwise, you might as well not go.

The whole Fox clip is about freeing Julian from suspicion by casting it on Maria and me. Using a

The seven steps to legal revenge I linked to actually outright dissuade people from making bad plans, such as lying about assault.

Despite the seven steps not even fitting to the mob's story, they use the headline. My crime is the fact that I once used the word "revenge."

Before I testified to the police, Julian made me suffer by violating my body in a way that is probably illegal. I never had the slightest plan to violate his body or cause him physical pain. The civilized consequence of assault is a matter for the legal system to deal with.

December 10, 2010

Talk show host Glenn Beck on Fox News does a segment reporting on the timeline of the Assange case. Obviously, he brings up the seven-step template as proof of motive but reports only on step number seven, "ensure that your victim suffers." He also goes through my CV. My work as a gender equality officer in the student union in Uppsala is viewed as compromising, as is the fact that the organization I work for is called the Brotherhood Movement. It should have been translated as *fraternity* as in the motto it comes from—*liberté, égalité, fraternité* (liberty, equality, fraternity)—not as *brotherhood*, which evokes an anti-Muslim trope and terrorism. He swears that he doesn't support Assange on the free speech issue or in his journalistic work, but rather that his support for Julian has to do only with the sexual assault. Another type of brotherhood.

Glenn Beck explains things to his viewers and me: "If you buy the tickets, you ride the ride." That's

The mob claims that I invented the accusations against Julian to get revenge for some form of hurt feelings. That is ridiculous. Julian came inside me against my will and, since then, has actively tried to sway public opinion to make people believe that there were motives behind the police report other than his guilt. I want him to at least try to understand what he did. I want him to take responsibility, acknowledge what happened, apologize, and never assault anyone again. But there's nothing in what he subjected me to that I think is unforgivable. If he took responsibility and asked for my forgiveness, I could give it to him. I know sexual assault is often presented as something unforgivable, but I simply don't think that. So, revenge isn't appropriate. My testimony about the assault is a consequence of Julian's actions. Revenge that would be proportionate to the original deed would not only be extremely inappropriate, but it would also be a crime.

Few people believe that it's easy to get someone convicted of sexual assault. Reporting Julian Assange for something that might be assault has a low likelihood of success; it requires enormous input from me, and the satisfaction for me is minimal. If the police report per se was revenge, that would rank extremely low on the list I published. Since I have worked with these issues for a long time, I'm no stranger to the concept of victim blaming. When it comes to sexual assault, the person who reports it to the police often experiences smears.

that revenge will not only match the deed in size but also in nature. A good revenge is linked to what has been done against you. For example, if you want revenge on someone who cheated or who dumped you, you should use a punishment with dating/sex/fidelity involved.

STEP 4 Do a brainstorm of appropriate measures for the category of revenge you're after. To continue the example above, you can sabotage your victim's current relationship, such as getting his new partner to be unfaithful or ensure that he gets a madman after him. Use your imagination!

STEP 5 Figure out how you can systematically take revenge. Send your victim a series of letters and photographs that make your victim's new partner believe that you are still together, which is better than telling just one big lie on one single occasion.

STEP 6 Rank your systematic revenge schemes from low to high in terms of likely success, required input from you, and degree of satisfaction when you succeed. The ideal, of course, is a revenge as strong as possible, but this requires a lot of hard work and effort for it to turn out exactly as you want it to.

STEP 7 Get to work. And remember what your goals are while you are operating, *ensure that your victim will suffer the same way as he made you suffer.*

describes "7 Steps to Legal Revenge."

Thousands of people are shocked at this "manual," and it is taken as proof—by both private individuals and large media firms—that the allegations against Julian are false.

My post contains a stupid link that I uploaded one day when I was sad and angry at Andreas. It was a way for me to share the insight I gained that it is almost always better to leave someone than to get revenge. Now the post is being interpreted completely differently. As if it's about bloody revenge and is my personal manifesto, my life's work, my ideological values, and the starting point for all my actions in life.

I wonder if everyone kicking up the frenzy has read what the steps actually say. I tried to contact the author to ask for permission to publish it but couldn't find who they were.

Unfortunately, the original page on the internet has also been taken down, perhaps due to all the fuss, but I found it via Wayback Machine. Here's the wording:

> STEP 1 Consider very carefully if you really must take revenge. *It is almost always better to forgive than to avenge.*
>
> STEP 2 Think about why you want revenge. You need to be clear about who to take revenge on, as well as why. *Revenge is never directed against only one person, but also the actions of the person.*
>
> STEP 3 The principle of proportionality. *Remember*

to tear my sails, but tonight it doesn't get to me. I treat Somar to a sangria, and we toast the fact that we're alive.

December 9, 2010

At breakfast at the hotel, I see the man I've regularly noticed as he has eaten only white bread with tomato and garlic several mornings in a row. He's also reading today's newspaper; Julian is on the front page, and I shiver. I sit in a corner facing the wall and try to make myself smaller to limit how many people can see me. Messages pour in for me in every medium all the time, and I don't think there's a newspaper in the world that's not reporting on the case. I send Johannes a text:

Johannes, what am I going to do? This is completely out of hand! You know that this isn't a conspiracy, you know his view of women and behavior towards them. Can you explain some of that to someone? He's going to take WikiLeaks down with him in the case, that's so wrong! / Anna

Johannes doesn't respond, but a little later, an anonymous person from WikiLeaks in Sweden tells the newspapers and says that what is in the media now was not staged by anyone and that it's not about WikiLeaks but rather a matter between Julian and the women.

One of the most important pieces of "evidence" that the online mob has against me is the blog entry I posted in January 2010, where I linked to a page that terrified, that someone will recognize me and tip off the newspapers, I ask the police officer to do the check-in under her name. She helps me quickly exit the police car with its protective tinted windows and find my room so that I don't need to stay in the lobby for too long. My friend Somar arrives a few hours later.

I will be hidden in a country that the Swedish police cooperate well with, and I have been hoping it will be a place where I know the language. The police choose Barcelona, Spain, and I will leave tomorrow. They arrange for the travel and the hotel. For a while, it feels almost luxurious.

In the pitch black of predawn the next day, the police fetch us again. They escort us out the back way, and they drive around the outside of the airport building all the way to the gate with special authorization. The police estimate that the threat against me is so serious they do not want to risk anyone recognizing me at the airport, where it might spread and let the world know where I am. We board the plane, and then we lift off.

When we land in Barcelona, the very first thing I do is go to a hair salon. I ask them to dye my hair dark. I buy a spring coat and check into our hotel with a reservation held under my alias, Carolina Blomgren.

We can't cook at the hotel, and we're on unpaid leave, so we realize before we even get to the pizzeria on the street corner that this trip is going to cost us quite a bit in restaurant bills. That worries us, but when we view it from a refugee perspective, suddenly, it feels ridiculous. There is a media storm, and it tries starting to spread, the idea that I'm just a fictional character. A blog entry from my time at the Swedish Embassy in Buenos Aires in 2005 about how I see similarities between the Social Democrats in Sweden and Argentinian Peronists becomes national news in Argentina, and the non-Peronists are mobilized against me. Everyone finds ways to get at me.

If Julian were just tried in court, maybe I could go on with my life. I want the courts to investigate the matter. However, the issue is only being dealt with in the media and online, like a kangaroo court that is completely devoid of law or order. So many people seem to want to capture, drag, bribe, force, and threaten me into participating in the tribunal, which now seems to be taking place on Julian's terms.

How could I win that? I'm a nothing; a volunteer, a lone grassroot without a weapon like fame or friendships with journalists and presidents; a made-up character with a broken heart without the slightest hint of star qualities. The court needs to evaluate the evidence, not the media tribunal. That's my only chance. And it seems like that will happen now. Julian turned himself in to the police, and things seem to be closing in on a decision. At the same time, the storm intensifies into a hurricane, howling that I have myself to blame for the frenzy since I consistently refused to tell my side of the story. They say that I want to keep people in the dark about it. (Quite a bad strategy for being an attention-seeking whore if you ask me.)

Two bodyguards from the Stockholm police come and pick me up at Andreas' place and drive me to a hotel in Upplands Väsby. Terrified, completely

December 8, 2010

I'm offered money to share my story with a big German newspaper that mentions the "possibility of a five-figure sum in Euros." I send part of the query to Maria in a text to show her how absurd it all is, absolutely unreal. I think they contacted the wrong person by mistake, and I don't respond. It feels like every move could give me away, allow the predators to spot me and eat me up. No amount of money in the world could make me talk to anyone or hand them more fuel for that bonfire. I ask Claes to fend off the most persistent journalists.

I sit at Andreas' kitchen table and look at all the emails, text messages, missed phone calls, and tweets. I hear from friends and neighbors that people come to their homes and that people have stood around at various locations waiting for them, and I feel completely paralyzed.

The various online groups find their own reasons to disapprove of how I acted. The feminists are angry with my failure to warn Maria about Julian. The anti-feminists are upset about my dedication to feminist causes; anyone who's pro-Castro is mad at my demands to release Cuba's political prisoners; and with pro-U.S. people, it's my defense of Cuba's social rights, ride-sharing system, and strong cultural sector that is highlighted and found unacceptable. Among Muslims, suspicion is spread about my relationship with the U.S.; among Islamophobes, my commitment to the rights of Muslims; and among the public, a suspicion that maybe I don't really exist at all is

If you had to choose between letting someone escape punishment for what he had done to you and being derided, threatened, having every last detail of your private life aired publicly, having to answer to your relatives who were also being exposed, being distrusted even by the authors who are on your own bookshelf, not being able to do your job, being forced to hide in various locations, having journalists in your stairwell and bodyguards when you're at meetings (that happen to have been announced publicly), would you have filed the police report? I ask myself that, and today, the answer is crystal clear. If I'd had that choice, yes. But I didn't.

In hindsight, despite all the times I wished I hadn't done it, I still would have filed the report today. But I will never ask anyone else to report a man whose social status is higher than her own. I would support her if she chose to do that, cheer her on if she is brave enough to do it, definitely, but never try to convince her to proceed just because it's the morally right thing to do. Never. Because I know that what comes afterward is worse. You might be able to obtain redress for the assault, but not for the character assassination that he, his friends, people he has paid, and whoever else wants to bask in his glory will do to you. Despite that, it has still been worth it to me. If I can contribute—even just a little—to the patriarchy someday falling, it's worth it. Maybe they are right when they call me crazy. It seems like a little bit of crazy is needed to change the world for the better.

neither my relatives nor the law supports the oppression against me. I'm grateful that the men online don't have that much power in my life and that their parties didn't create the laws that govern my rights. And I hope that they never will. Because I see how they organize themselves into parties, and I see which parties the worst of them are in.

A lawyer from another country gets in touch with Claes. A young woman had contacted her about Julian assaulting her in a way that was similar to what he did to us. She didn't want to report him, but she wanted to testify in our trial. She wanted to remain completely anonymous, though. Claes contacted me to discuss how he should respond to her.

"It's not possible to be an anonymous witness in Sweden," Claes says.

"No, OK, then you just have to explain that to her," I say, but obviously it would be valuable if she could testify.

"Yes, I'll tell her that."

"But you also need to be really clear that it's literally life-threateningly dangerous. Her name will leak out, and the online mob will find her."

"Yes, she needs to be aware of the risks if she does it."

The woman withdraws.

I call Somar, one of my best friends, and explain.
I want her to come with me, but I also know that it's a really big request to ask someone to take so much time off from work all of a sudden. But I don't even need to ask.

"Do you want me to come?"
"Oh, yes, if you can?"
"*Of course!*" she says without a second's hesitation. She just needs to check with her boss. She calls me back a little while later.

"That went well," she says. "I just said that I have a friend who was being threatened. He was super understanding. I think he assumed that it was somehow honor-system related, and I guess you could say it is," she laughs.

In the Swedish Prison and Probation Service's summary about honor-related violence and oppression, I read that "honor culture is a concept for cultural patterns that restrict people's freedoms and rights." That "honor-related oppression is when honor culture is wielded against people who do not live up to the honor culture's values." That it is "a social system in which strict control is exercised" over "primarily girls' and women's sexuality." When I read what the anonymous men write to me and discuss in their forums, it is hard to miss that they want to control my sexuality and that they think I am violating their culture's values. It's not family-related, and I'm grateful to live in a context, a place, and time where

"This woman is so incredibly vindictive and actually must be a little crazy. Pretty obviously a psychopath with a grandiose, narcissistic self-image. Unusually ruthless and obsessed with getting ahead at any price. To behave so extremely shoddily just for revenge and even publish online how to get revenge on 'men.' Talk about being racist against men!"

"She is not the person her superficial acquaintances think she is, and she doesn't live up to either a Christian or a feminist ideal. I'm fucking disgusted. She is so fucking disgusting, I hope you read this Anna, you are so fucking disgusting."

"YOU ARE A DISGUSTING EXCUSE FOR A WOMAN!"

"She's an attention-seeking whore."

I receive more threats and worse ones, more concrete than before. The police's personal security group makes the assessment that my security situation is serious and is getting worse. They recommend that I should be hidden abroad for a while—for two weeks to begin with. It's cheaper and safer than bodyguards. Obviously, because of the threats, but also to protect me from the British media especially. The situation is completely unbearable. I'm humiliated, demeaned, and hunted, and I agree to let them transport me to a secret location, but I have to be allowed to take someone with me. The police approve my request, and keep sinking!! That woman is both crazy and a danger to the public. Holy crap, she should be locked up! Pardon my language, but it was a fucking shock to me! That she has the guts to walk around strutting her stuff about how she supports WikiLeaks when she is singlehandedly trying to destroy both free speech and the whole free internet!"

"The island of Gotland created her so let them deal with all the trouble she causes. I hope she never gets an entry visa to the mainland again. I'd rather see 100 guest workers come—Turks, Greeks, Yugoslavs—than a single extreme feminist Gotlander like her."

"Aw, hell, isn't there anyone with enough of a dick to grab hold of this and shut the case down? Anna FUCKING Ardin, what a goddamned bitch!!!"

"Anna Ardin—lone fool or political pawn? The elevator definitely doesn't go all the way to the top floor on that one, so I'm voting for 'lone fool.'"

"I wonder how the rest of the world's attitude toward Swedish women has changed thanks to this WikiLeaks-groupie-radical-feminist-whore that is Anna Ardin? It would be cool if you folks who live abroad could let us know what you think about this?"

"If you ask me, she's exactly like any old Swedish woman: rabid fucking politically correct radical feminist and Marxist who doesn't hesitate to put a person in jail if you damage her inflated ego when it becomes clear that she's a whore."

first sex partners (older, fatherly socialist men, who turned out to be corrupt and have a weakness for young cunt and alcohol). She wishes she were a lesbian but unfortunately, it's the repulsive penis that entices her. She has a serious narcissistic borderline personality disorder. I assume she's feeling really bad now that she's starting to understand how wrong her opinions and actions both are."

"You've got it all wrong. All her previous partners were younger than her. Most of them were right-wing around the liberals, extreme liberals, or deeply conservative."

"Interesting!!! So, she has been drawn to people who are her ideological opposites, typical borderline personality to sleep with someone who feeds their self-loathing."

"A disgusting groupie whore."

"What's the sexual history of the stupid feminist Anna Ardin? How many fuck partners has she had besides Assange and which ones? How many Gambians has she fucked? How many Muslims has she fucked? How many STDs does she have/has she had? Did she get HIV in Gambia, and was that why she didn't want to fuck without a condom (my own speculations here)?"

"Anna Ardin seems to suffer from a desire to get revenge on men."

"That goddamn sour-cunt is just too much. She doesn't have the tiniest scrap of shame in her whole body. Ugh! Unbelievable... some people never hit bottom; they just

just as bad as in August, I was wrong—as it turned out, not just in Yanoun, but all over the world—it was much worse. You could tell that Julian was significantly more famous now and had much stronger support. Thousands of people are supporting him with posters and online hate. The same media-frenzy tribunal that exonerates him convicts me. It feels like absolutely everything that can be found out about me is being used against me. By describing me in the discussion as active and aware, the man who violated me is reduced to a passive victim. Even though I am trying to steer well clear of the trolls, they catch up to me and make up tall tales, occasionally with but usually without the slightest grain of truth, respect, or goodwill:

"I know her, let me tell you."

"Exciting, tell us everything you know about her sex life. What does she like in bed, etc.?"

"What's her agenda in making a name for herself as a woman who will basically sleep with anyone? How many people had this woman slept with before she offered her body to Julian Assange? Had she planned it, to lure him to her, so that she could then report him to the police and make a name for herself as a willing woman for men with 'power'?"

"Gee! She's not shy about showing her perverted soul right out in the open, here's my little amateur diagnosis of her based on this little revenge list: Her father was notoriously unfaithful to her mother, and Anna had bad luck with her

the subway station, some distance away. I leave my suitcase outside his door and start walking. And reflecting. A breakfast meeting? Why would he schedule a breakfast meeting before eight o'clock in the morning after a night when he hardly slept at all? Suddenly I realize that he's tricking me. He's in his apartment but wants me out of there. Why? My heart is pounding, and I start running back. He's not alone.

Naturally, when I get back to his apartment, he's not off at a breakfast meeting. He's home. He says he sent the woman away and I should come in. I don't know what she knows, but I'm on the verge of a breakdown. In the end I swallow my humiliation. I don't know where else to go.

Julian actually does go to the police. He turns himself in and is arrested and awaiting further processing. The media firestorm happens. At least 15 journalists go to tiny Yanoun. Of course, many of them are from Tel Aviv, but also from other cities around the Middle East and from the European tabloids. I am baselessly described as a Jew-hater and a rabid defender of Israel's violations of international law. Suspected, accused, and convicted by angry people on all sides.

There are demonstrators outside the prison in London where Julian is being held. One holds a poster that says, "I want your babies." If Julian's motive was conception, there seem to be some good opportunities for that without needing to use force.
    When I guessed that the media attention would be

If the program's leadership recommends that I stay home, I don't see how I have any choice. I say goodbye to Mats, and with the help of the airport staff, I manage to retrieve my luggage while my plane takes off without me. I sit down on a bench in the terminal, in shock and alone with my big suitcase. My puzzle is once again completely broken. I have no job, nowhere to live, a media firestorm looming, and on top of all that, there's an anonymous gang of misogynists who, in various ways and via all channels, keep telling me that they're going to rape me and kill me. Life has been more fun.

Andreas is the person I'm closest to. He might only have gotten a little sleep, so I don't want to bother him by calling. Instead, I take the bus and then the subway and walk to his apartment unannounced. The same apartment that I had at one point suggested we buy together after all those years I spent living in apartments that were only his. I punch in the door code and drag my suitcase up all those stairs. Then I ring the bell. *As a surprise*, I think. We were going to try again, after all, even though it turns out we didn't get to take a break. But no one answers the door.

I call his cell phone, but no one answers.

I try again: the phone, the door, the phone again.

Finally, I receive a text message. He's at a breakfast meeting but doesn't want to say where. He says we should meet at a café on the opposite side of times before, we both think that it will work out. It feels as if the puzzle pieces of my life are falling back into place.

December 7, 2010

My phone alarm wakes us up at five, and Andreas calls two taxis. One that takes me to the airport and one that takes him back to his place to go back to sleep.

I meet my friend Mats, a Christian Democrat who is going to Hebron, at the airport.

We check in our bags and get coffee at the gate.

I notice a recognizable figure on one of the TV screens. It's Julian. I shush Mats and listen to the story. Julian has announced that he intends to turn himself in to the police today. Today of all days. After having avoided questioning for months, he will now go to the police in England, which, sure enough, is where he is. This news is on Al-Jazeera, which means that the Middle East is talking about it. It's only just after six, and Karin, the Swedish coordinator for the accompaniment program, is asleep when I call her.

"Whoa, that's not good," she says when I tell her.

I believe the media commotion will be just as big as when the news first broke. I believe that I will be hounded by the press, TV, and radio just like last August—and that I will be just as hated. I picture how both Israelis and Palestinians might consider me an enemy, and Karin agrees with my conclusion.

"The violence is closer to the surface on the West Bank, and if it becomes chaotic, then we don't have the resources to protect you," she says.

December 6, 2010

Every day, a variety of newspapers write about WikiLeaks. Regardless of whether it's interviews or analyses, people spin onward from the topic of WikiLeaks and bring up assault accusations, eventually linking it to me. But the media circus has definitely settled down since the story first broke in August. My blog isn't receiving more hate comments than I can handle, and I feel like I can start living a relatively normal life again. For some reason, Julian seems to want to prolong this process as much as possible, but it's the status quo. I just want to put it behind me now and move on. And that is exactly what I'm going to do. I leave tomorrow!

Andreas comes over and helps me finish the last of my packing. We are at it until the wee hours, and the few hours we do sleep, I do so in his arms. He's sad that I'm going away.

"But it's good that we'll have a real break for a few months," I say.

"Yes, time to think. And when you come home, then we'll try again," he replies. "I love you."

"I love you, too."

Even though I wrote on my blog that I had thought about revenge after our long and humiliating breakup, and even though he has broken his promises many bringing him up, she gave him very strong values, that he is intelligent and sensitive and that he fights for good against evil.

I think that she knows him well, she is credible, and all her statements are probably correct. But the thing is, he's *also* suspected of sex crimes. His character is not illegal, but some of his actions may still well have been immoral and abusive. The perpetrator's and victim's characters should not be relevant, and yet time and again, the person they are is allowed to stand in the way of what a case is really about.

December 5, 2010

I am packing for my trip to Palestine and cleaning my apartment. I'm going to sublet it for three months. I carry a bunch of stuff up to store in the attic to make room for the tenant. I see that Julian is doing his thing. WikiLeaks releases more material about the U.S.'s relationships with other countries.

From the U.S. Embassy in Sweden, it leaks that the ambassador wrote to President Bush that our conservative Foreign Minister Carl Bildt is a "medium-sized dog with a big-dog attitude" and that he has "limited political skills." Before one of Bildt's trips to the U.S., George Bush was advised to flatter him by playing on his desire to operate at a high level and pretending to be impressed by his international achievements. Certainly, I find this entertaining as a Social Democrat and someone who has long considered Bildt to be vastly overrated, but I am not sure how it's a key pro-peace or free speech issue.

training sessions in everything from first aid to Middle Eastern history to language courses in basic Arabic and Hebrew, I feel prepared. I'm really looking forward to living the theory in practice.

I feel that I need to "come out" to the program's administration. I pull one of the leaders aside during a weekend training session and tell her that I was one of the people Julian Assange assaulted and that this needs to be included in the risk analysis. I also explain that I had thought that the matter would be cleared up before my departure, but since he was evading arrest, there was a risk of a new media frenzy at any point. She was a little shocked but thanked me for telling her.

November 28, 2010

Two hundred and fifty thousand American embassy documents leaked to WikiLeaks are published by the *Guardian* and other outlets. They reveal widespread corruption in Middle Eastern regimes and what the American diplomats really think about their placements.

November 30, 2010

Julian appeals the Svea Court of Appeal's arrest warrant decision to the highest court, the Swedish Supreme Court.

December 2, 2010

Julian's mother, Christine, steps into the media tribunal as a witness of character. She says that in

November 22, 2010

Julian appeals the District Court's detention order to the Svea Court of Appeal. I devote myself to working, looking for a new job, and purging my channels of the steady stream of hate that continues to come in.

November 24, 2010

The Svea Court of Appeal refuses the appeal and decides that the arrest warrant for Julian should remain in place, on suspicion of illegal coercion, rape, and two cases of sexual molestation with the highest degree of suspicion during arrest and detention, "probable cause." The international request and the European Arrest Warrant are upheld in accordance with the District Court's decision.

I don't know which molestation charge was deleted, but I'm guessing that it was his refusal to leave my apartment. Both the violence and the forcible insemination were presented and classified as crimes, and probably also that he pressed his genitals against me while I slept.

I don't care all that much about it because today, I learned where in the West Bank I am going to move next week—the village of Yanoun, with a population of 90 people. A village beleaguered by aggressive Israeli settlers where I will serve as an international presence to prevent animals from being killed and wells poisoned, as has happened in the past. I call the village "my new home" in a post on my restarted blog as part of the outward-facing communication that is required for the accompaniment mission. After

Someone announces that he'll be participating in a seminar in London, so it seems likely that that's where he is.

The investigation cannot move forward if Julian cannot be interviewed, so prosecutor Marianne Ny orders his detention in his absence, suspected with probable rape, three cases of sexual molestation, and illegal coercion. Stockholm District Court decides to detain him in accordance with Marianne Ny's application for a detention order. To execute the detention order, he is sought internationally, and the prosecutor issues what is called a *European Arrest Warrant*.

November 20, 2010

My HIV test is negative. I laugh and cry in relief. My relief, however, is quickly replaced by anger. This has been ridiculous. The risk of becoming infected, even if the person who forcibly inseminates you is actually infected, is very small. The fact that I have not been infected says nothing about Julian's health status. He still needs to be tested to know anything about that. I have had three nasty months that he could have spared me if he had wanted to.

He has called my police report a dirty trick. But going to the police and sharing my experiences was no trick. I would do it again. And I wouldn't wait until the police decided to file a report. I would demand that they'd do it.

November 13, 2010

The three months are finally up. I go and get a blood test. I'll get the results in a week.

November 16, 2010

A woman emails me. She refers to #freeassange and writes:

"The truth will come out in the end."
"I really hope so!" I reply.

That's what the whole thing is about for me—the truth. I long for a trial where evidence and witness testimony are presented. Where one by one, we can go through all the misinterpretations and conspiracy theories about whom I know, coups supposedly planned by the police, which sarcastic text messages I sent, or how my behavior was "wrong" and thus didn't match the prejudices about how real rape victims behave. To be able to go through the technical evidence and the witness testimony point by point. I know that our chances of winning are good if only the evidence can be presented. I sincerely hope this woman is right, and that the truth really will come out in the end.

November 18, 2010

No one knows where Julian is, but WikiLeaks continues to release material, including material about the United States and its ties to other countries.

often in the debates about peace, free speech, and transparency that are being held hostage in a global apologia for sexual assault.

After being transferred from Iraq to the brig in Quantico, Virginia, Manning was reportedly held in solitary confinement for 23 hours a day without even access to clothing, which classifies as torture according to Amnesty International and other groups. Manning was also reportedly subjected to abusive treatment daily.

Money that comes in for WikiLeaks is used for Assange's defense and expenses, not for Manning's. That stresses me out. Swedish author Jan Guillou puts words to my thoughts in a column in *Aftonbladet*:

It should be reasonable for Manning to defend himself by saying that he contributed to revealing American war crimes and that democratic principles therefore excuse his leakage of information. The intention cannot be for the American armed forces to be able to keep their crimes secret and deceive their employers, the American people. Great legal principles are in play, and Bradley Manning needs the best lawyers that can be procured. And in the American legal system, that means money is needed. Despite its promises, WikiLeaks has not provided that. Instead, Julian Assange is now retaining three English lawyers to help him avoid coming to Sweden for questioning.[9]

According to Manning's support network, WikiLeaks has now also promised to chip in fifty-thousand dollars.

October 22, 2010

WikiLeaks releases *The Iraq War Logs*. It reveals details having to do with civilian casualties, torture, and extrajudicial executions among other things. The person who risked everything to leak this to WikiLeaks is an intelligence analyst by the name of Manning, who views the leak as a part of "the truth of 21st-century asymmetric warfare." Manning is thus one of the great heroes of our modern history. Manning was accused as early as June of having leaked probably the most important thing that has ever been leaked during an ongoing war: *The Afghan War Diary*. These archival documents gave us irrefutable evidence of exactly how repulsive war really is. And these specific documents were the reason we had wanted to invite Julian to Sweden.

One of the 22 offenses Manning was charged with was "aiding the enemy by indirect means," which can carry the death penalty in the United States. There have been no reports of anyone being injured as a result of this leaked information, and no one besides Manning has been accused of any crime due to what came out in these leaks. The people who committed war crimes in the Collateral Murder video have not stood trial.

Manning, the 105-pound soldier who questioned the war crimes, was born December 17, 1987, in Crescent, Oklahoma, and sent to Iraq in 2009 to conduct intelligence work at an army base outside of Baghdad. At this army base, Manning had access to top-secret databases.

Despite this, Manning has been forgotten far too

with a variety of arguments still claiming he was framed—for completely different and much more important reasons than the sexual crimes that this is actually about.

If it really is espionage and not the sex crime charges that he is afraid of being held accountable for, I wonder why he fled Sweden—a country that does not extradite people to the United States if they are suspected of political crimes—to go to a country that is one of the United States' closest allies. Why does he think he will be apprehended and sent to the United States if he sets foot in a Swedish police station when he has already been in a Swedish police station for questioning—without being apprehended?

Julian is obviously a key figure in WikiLeaks, but he is not alone. He wasn't the only one creating and running WikiLeaks. There are many people who wanted it to happen and who worked for it. Julian is destroying the WikiLeaks he played such an important role in creating.

Moreover, his supporters let him do that by defending him for everything without discernment.

I am convinced that what he is most afraid of right now is being held accountable for sex crimes. He doesn't want either the court or the media to start poking around into why he breaks condoms against his sex partners' wishes. And out of principle, he is not planning on letting anyone else put limits on how he behaves.

October 18, 2010

Johannes gets in touch again:
"Hi, I just talked to him and passed on what you asked me to. Things aren't looking that good. I think he's going to make a circus out of the whole thing…"

"I don't understand what he thinks he can gain from that. For the sake of WikiLeaks, he should pull himself together, but as far I'm concerned, I don't think it matters that much for me personally. Thanks, A"

The prosecutor thinks Julian should be questioned further, both for the suspected crimes against Maria and several other unclarities in my case, but time and again, they fail to get him to present himself. Pia, my lawyer, along with Claes at Borgström's law firm, is surprised that Julian is staying away. She says that she was pretty sure this would be a quick case, but now we will have to wait.

The Swedish Migration Agency rejects Julian's application for a work and residency permit.

I find out that I have been accepted into the accompaniment program and will spend three months in Israel and Palestine starting in December. Unfortunately, my father wasn't accepted.

October 19, 2010

Julian chooses to continue using WikiLeaks' good reputation to whitewash his own. He claims in the press that he is afraid to appear for further questioning, that he thinks he is being persecuted, and

September 27, 2010

Julian Assange is detained again in absentia.

October 15, 2010

I found out that they were not able to question Julian as they had planned. The new prosecutor has been trying since she took office at the beginning of September, but he stays away and refuses to show up. I want to communicate with him in some way since we have a shared interest in not harming WikiLeaks with a drawn-out trial and continued media coverage about the wrong things. But Julian seems to have changed his phone number, and I don't get any response at either of the email addresses I have. But maybe Johannes or Donald can help, I think. I start by sending Johannes a text:

> *"Hi, Julian didn't appear for questioning today, if he continues to stay away from the request & requirement to present himself, then an international arrest warrant will probably be issued this week. So, if you are in touch with him, could you implore him to contact the police immediately so this [can be done] as quietly as possible? Thanks."*

> *"I'll do my best. Hope you're OK."*

> *"OK, thanks. Things are so-so, but it's going to be all right."*

determined that I will be a controversial person, possibly forever. In a best-case scenario, a victim. Ultimately, this also means that even people who don't officially think I did anything wrong still unofficially exact a portion of the punishment.

September 19, 2010

The Social Democrats lose the election. The Sweden Democrats, the party founded in 1988 by veterans of Nazism, militant racism, and fascism—including a volunteer from Nazi Germany's Waffen-SS and with the fascist torch as its symbol—gains seats in the Riksdag for the first time with its almost six percent of the vote. I leave the election night coverage in tears and agony.

September 22, 2010

It's settled that I'm going to be fired from my job. Formally, it's because of a lack of money following the election loss. I receive one month's extra salary as compensation. I will work until the end of March, but before then, I need to withdraw the six weeks of vacation time I have saved. I'm fine with that. My father and I have chatted about working as volunteers with an organization abroad after he retires, and we see this as a good opportunity. We apply to be observers in the World Council of Churches Ecumenical Accompaniment Program in Palestine and Israel.

Feminist Initiative, and the Muslim Brotherhood. The trolls even claim that I am testifying against Julian out of loyalty to a relative in the military.

September 16, 2010

I wrote an op-ed piece about not wasting a progressive vote on a small party that won't make it into the Riksdag. And I hear back from one of Sweden's biggest newspapers that they will pull a piece by the Christian Democrats' party leader to run my piece instead. That's a big deal to me. Given that there is an all-out battle between the parties over every millimeter of media space, I have secured a channel that reaches close to a third of the voters every day.

I am summoned to the Social Democrats' media relations office, and it's not to celebrate.

The representative is pleasant and proper, but it isn't even a conversation. I am simply informed that the article can't be published under my name. There are only days to go before the election, and support for Julian Assange is considered a left-wing issue. Therefore, they can't risk the Social Democratic Party being linked to what is perceived to be a betrayal of him—me. They simply cannot be linked to me.

It's not hard to understand why, and I have no objections. The media firestorm was brutal, and they can't risk sacrificing voters. It makes me sad, but I understand. I make sure that my friend Kristina gets credit for it instead, but at the same time, I feel a nagging sense of abandonment. This is about the terrible media logic that dictates that each person can only be known for one thing at a time, and it has been high-risk regions.

But there's nothing I can do about that other than go over it again and again and panic in advance. If Julian doesn't get tested, I will be forced to wait at least three months before I can find out. It's been two weeks.

September 8, 2010

"I know in my heart that you are telling the truth" writes the woman from yesterday in our continuing email exchange. She describes exactly the same feeling I had when Maria told me her story. We know on the basis of shared experiences. She worked closely with Julian, and it is no coincidence that she believes us wholeheartedly.

September 9, 2010

The media attention has settled down, and I'm putting pretty much all my waking hours into campaigning in the lead-up to the parliamentary elections, knocking on doors in Tensta, Fittja, Upplands Väsby, and Södermalm. But I hear from several fellow party members that it is inexpedient for me to staff any of the public info-spots. I am a very unpopular person, and it might harm the party if someone recognizes me when I try to represent them more publicly.

September 12, 2010

Many people keep blogging about me and the case. There are conspiracy theories that I have ties to the CIA, the Pentagon, the FBI, ZOG, the UN, the

such. But specifically in this sexual situation, he was sort of really different to me. That, yes, well, it was as if he was very determined that he would decide the precise terms."
"Hmm."
"And I've never experienced that before."
"OK."
"[I was] upset [or, I mean that it was] an upsetting experience, the kind of experience that makes you see yourself in a different perspective." [8]

September 7, 2010

A woman formerly involved in WikiLeaks writes me an email.

> *Dear Anna. Just wanted to draw your attention to the fact that J used to live in Kenya and travelled a lot in Asia, especially in Vietnam. Both countries have rather high aids ratio.*

My concern about HIV has not been a topic in the media as far as I've seen, so I'm guessing that it's her personal experience of his risky sexual behavior that causes her to feel worried for me. It is sweet of her to get in touch; I grasp the sisterhood in the letter. At the same time, it stresses me out. Of course, I have thought about it. Some days that's about the only thing I think about in all the tumult. Did he deliberately put me at risk? Am I going to die? He's obviously obsessed with having unprotected sex, has extremely little judgment about who and how many people he sleeps with, and everything suggests he's been carrying on this way for a good while—even in blog posts increase. They publish and mock my attempts to reply or get in touch. They start demanding that I do things according to their agenda and pressure me for information based on incorrect starting points. They're like predators whose hunt intensifies when they smell fear and weakness. I don't dare respond this time. The powerlessness feels overwhelming.

At the same time, a thought begins to take root, that maybe speaking out about what happened is contagious. And maybe this is precisely why it's so important to so many people to silence women who bear witness—all to keep more people from speaking up.

September 4, 2010

One of my friends read online that someone is offering five thousand dollars to whoever kills me. I thank them for telling me but ask again not to receive this type of information.

September 6, 2010

Today I'm called in for further supplemental questioning. I receive more questions about the course of events, about other people, and about my motives for acting as I did.

One of the things I describe during the questioning is my experience of how Julian treated me:

> "*For most of the time [that he was staying at my place], he treated me as the person he treated me before we ate dinner and*

believe in him. They think people like him know more about what happened in my apartment that night than the judicial system does. And the signal that blogger sends doesn't warn people against lying; he effectively warns against testifying about sexual assault. This is nothing new. It's a strong signal that permeates society. No one who's in doubt as to whether they should tell truths like mine has missed it. No, what's happening to me is not what happens to women who lie during questioning. What's happening to me is what happens to so many who tell the truth about sexual crimes.

I want to respond that even if someone is famous, rich, popular, and influential, it still does not put him above the law. That was precisely why I had stood up for WikiLeaks.

When you see something very wrong happen, even if it's happening inside your own organization, it needs to be discussed. There are more, probably many more, women with the same experiences as me, but there is silence. I want to explain to the blogger that the price of speaking out is too high. That I understand it's easy to believe what they believe, but that it's wrong. I want to say I'm sorry and hurt and that I think if they could only understand I'm a human being, they'd come to their senses and understand I'm not a fictional character created by a staff of conspirators in some office for secret agents. I've tried repeatedly, and in a few isolated cases, it worked. There are men who thank me for writing and do apologize. But most of the time, my vulnerability makes it even worse. Their hateful remarks and nasty press release. Where "all events" means that he tried to penetrate me without a condom, forcibly inseminated me, held me down, and that he refused to leave my apartment and made unwelcome sexual advances. These crimes are viewed as less serious than rape, which he is suspected of in Maria's case. The statute of limitations for my case is five years, and for Maria's case, ten years.

September 3, 2010

Someone named Jacob writes, *"I never thought that I would say this, but that woman deserves to be raped for real."* Someone else is upset and emails me: *"You're exploiting the judicial system for personal gain in a shameless way and deserve to be named and exposed for that."* An American blogger I don't know but who is clearly well-read and seemingly serious explains why it's wrong to name and shame people online. He writes that not even guilty criminals deserve to be bullied, that in most cases, outsiders don't know too much, and that we should not act on this. He seems sensible but thinks that none of this has to do with me, like Jacob, this man sees himself as a different type of person than those who spew hate online. Then, he pivots and concludes that, in my case, it's necessary to send a strong signal, a "bigger message," about what happens to women who "lie about being raped." He posts my personal identity number, my telephone number, and my address. To illustrate his opinion, he also posts a picture of my door.

All the people who come to the door he shows, all the people who chase me and harass me every day,

I start working again. The reporter from *Expressen* who wrote the first article and who had previously been a Facebook contact of mine is sitting in the lobby, waiting for me. A little over a year ago, he started one of his many tirades against a female, left-wing politician. He did the same thing then, waiting by her workplace's exit. When she didn't leave, he simply took pictures of someone who looked like her, and the unknown woman's stressed facial expression resulted in new headlines.

I know that this is common in other countries, particularly in the U.K., and several British journalists have pursued me that way. But this man is the only Swedish journalist who repeatedly behaves in this extreme and intrusive way toward me, like a stalker. I peer at him from outside the building. I have been out for lunch. He does not seem to have left his post for fear of missing a scoop—whatever it might be. So, I return to my office through an entrance he isn't aware of. In some ways, it's an advantage to have a workplace like the Social Democratic Party headquarters, one that's used to media mayhem.

September 1, 2010

A third prosecutor, chief prosecutor Marianne Ny, takes over the case from Finné. She makes the same assessment as the police and the first prosecutor and increases the suspicions again. Maria's case is reopened.

The preliminary investigation concerning molestation in my case is expanded to include "all events in the report," the prosecutor writes in her sometimes, but not in any way that was significant. No, not anything that would be abnormal."[7]

He also otherwise confirms my version of the sequence of events; apart from that he claims we had sex multiple times and denies that he used force. He also says he didn't break the condom—he thinks it never broke at all.

August 31, 2010

WikiLeaks' critics are using the assault as a weapon against the organization. At the same time, several people who have worked with WikiLeaks say that Julian should take a break from being its representative to avoid criticism of his personal behavior spilling over onto WikiLeaks. They think the two issues shouldn't be mixed. Julian, on the other hand, seems to *want* them to be mixed up. His approach is that the police report was motivated by politics and not sexual offenses. He chooses to use the movement and its whole purpose to protect himself. But the legal case is not about WikiLeaks. It's about Julian's inability to respect other people's integrity when it stands in the way of his own desires. It's about a suspicion that he does not conduct his sex life within the bounds of the law, and it's about the fact that he cannot be allowed to continue mistreating women. It's also about truth having an intrinsic value. That we, especially in the acute crisis our planet finds itself in, can never build a fair and equitable world without truth as a cornerstone.

be turned against me. What I learn here is not my beauty score but rather the importance they attach to my appearance; they want to measure women's worth by their looks so badly.

They want to define me as an object, chattel, rather than a subject with agency, a person in my own right. This is the patriarchy, the gender power structure we live in. I hate the patriarchy.

I feel like screaming in these men's faces and asking them to shut up. But I don't want to confirm their image of me—or of women who demand women's rights in general—as hysterical, so instead, I think like this:

There's a dilemma in what they claim. On the one hand, there's an expectation that I will be pretty, approachable, and appear before male gazes rather than hide. And on the other hand, I have myself to blame for my accessibility, in this case via a high-resolution photo. It's a double punishment, a domination technique. The patriarchy has many of them.

August 30, 2010

Julian is currently only suspected of molesting me; in other words, for intentionally breaking the condom. Today he's questioned about this for fifty-four minutes. I'm not allowed to see the contents of his questioning, but I do get to read sections of it in *Expressen*.

To a direct question, Julian admits, according to *Expressen*, that I rejected his sexual advances: "Yes, makes heterosexual men assault them.

Or exactly the same thing from someone with slightly better manners:

"*You chose to be photographed in a way that shows cleavage, tried to accentuate your womanliness, and obviously take no interest in protecting yourself from the male gaze, so you shouldn't be surprised at what happened.*"

Analyses based on my appearance become commonplace, about my hair, my nose, my fingernails, and questions of whether it's possible to be a feminist and be so attractive at the same time. The very first comment I saw in the discussions when my name was revealed, and someone dug up that specific photo was simply "*pretty.*" For a brief time, that comment sat there, sort of as a little something in my favor. Other people think I'm ugly. Some can't decide whether I'm repulsive or attractive:

"*That disgusting toad is extremely dangerous. I definitely think a horny, drunk, upper-class brat from posh Östermalm who got boozed up at Riche would bite since she's not super well known.*"

"*Damn! That person really ought to spend more time exercising and fix up her body and maybe cut back a little on the tweeting? I mean, only 31 and already the chassis is so run down...*"

"*Her appearance isn't repulsive, but maybe her soul is.*"

They can't agree on whether I'm ugly or not but my beauty and ugliness both become things that can out of concern that someone might recognize my voice. Worried that someone will kill me the way they say they're going to. So, when I have to go out, I just try to make my way from point A to B quickly and silently.

August 29, 2010

A relative sends me an email from Mexico. She'd bought something fragile in a store that the salesperson wrapped in newspaper. There was a big picture of my face on the paper. A colleague lets me know that a Norwegian paper published the same picture. My old host family from when I was an exchange student in Uruguay sees it on TV. The *New York Times* takes it down from their site when I contact them and assert copyright. A magazine in India features it prominently.

The picture had been taken a few years earlier while I was having my make-up done before appearing on Swedish Television morning show. I'm wearing a jacket and a slightly low-cut knit top and looking into the camera. I have used the picture as my byline for op-ed pieces I've written and as my profile photo on my blog. It worked for me as a woman and a commentator. Professional, tidy, and with a relatively neutral facial expression. No one has ever even hinted in a comment before about the picture being sexual. It has been viewed as a normal picture.

But something happened when I became a target.

"With those boobs, you can't accuse Julian of having done anything wrong. He was just following his instincts," someone writes as if the mere sight of women automatically

not possible to defend myself. Friends inform me of terrible things they've read about me in various forums and comment threads; they send screenshots, quotes, and summaries. Again and again, I thank them for trying to help me and tell them I don't want them to send me that type of information, but again and again, they send me new information with good intentions. The hatred is like waves. It carries away the beach of my soul into the ocean, grain by grain, and my barrier to keep the waves from coming ashore is broken down both by nice people who want to help and mean ones who do it on purpose. Like the "Sweden first" men who atted me today when they were talking on Twitter about making a living pinata out of me. A thoroughly Swedish version of stoning someone, with a Mexican touch.

I can't escape the threats. I erode.

The fact that there is so much text about me, that I have lived a life online, and that I, my views, and my pictures are searchable makes it much easier to attack me—both electronically and mentally. But it's not just that. I'm afraid of violence in real life, too, of being recognized as I move about in the world.

Every journalist who tries to find me feels like a potential threat. How would I know if a person approaching me was a hater straight from the comments section? An outraged hardliner who has stepped out of the screen to make good on his threats? I have become silent in town. The more I hear, the more dangerous it feels, so I have stopped talking to people in public spaces, stopped having coffee with people, and stopped speaking on the phone in public investigation into whether Maria was raped. He thinks we might be able to get Julian convicted of rape in my case as well since Julian rubbed his genitals against my body while holding me against my will. His view of the details is that from a legal point of view, I was raped too. But I don't want to expand the scope. It's still the risk of him knowingly spreading infection that I want tried; how it's categorized doesn't matter to me. Besides, I'm not up for taking any more shit for what words I use, or don't use, to describe the crime. From a purely legal perspective, however, it appears that there is indeed a basis for calling me a rape victim.

August 28, 2010

One out of the twelve weeks has passed before I can get tested for HIV. I think about it several times a day. I still want Julian to be tested. Sometimes I feel death agony.

Sometimes I picture a life where I throw up every day because of anti-retroviral drugs, which Maria attests is a side effect of the medication she was prescribed. My thoughts keep revolving about how I will need to reconceive my life, that I might not have many years left if I can't cope with the medication, either. Andreas is with his new girlfriend, and I sit alone with all my thoughts about how hard it will be to have a family.

Every day I get threats and messages saying I'm a whore, tons of them. I've password-protected my blog, made my Twitter private, and stopped writing for newspapers completely. Occupying any public space makes me a target, so I try to avoid that. But it's *to your friend because you want attention."*

The email is from a stranger, but the topic is familiar. The fact that I had accepted a friend request on Facebook a long time ago from one of the journalists who wrote that first article about the case—and the fact that I had worked for *Gotlands Tidningar*, a newspaper with the same abbreviation, GT, as *Göteborgs Tidningar*, one of *Expressen*'s regional editions—were considered proof I had planned the media frenzy. If the person who sent me the email could see my face as I read what it says, that would have sufficed for them to understand that I am not at all pleased, that I'm not enjoying the attention, and that I'm not the one who leaked—even though it's kind of ironic that leaks are the worst accusation that can be leveled at someone testifying against Julian Assange. If anything, it seems that the prosecutor quickly realized that Julian wasn't planning to cooperate, and that made her issue an arrest warrant for him. Julian's assessment of Sweden as one of the world's most transparent countries is true. An arrest warrant here is on public record, and that is precisely what led to the media finding out. Maybe the police should have realized this could happen and shouldn't have been so sure we would remain protected. On the other hand, a warning about the risks probably wouldn't have affected our testimonies.

August 27, 2010

Claes Borgström requests a judicial review of the prosecutor's decision to dismiss the preliminary that appear on the site. A group of activists pitch in on my side and help us contact them all. They contact automakers, clothing stores, online gambling companies, window manufacturers, and travel firms, referencing the strong criticism regarding a lack of media ethics that *Journalisten*, the Swedish Union of Journalists' publication, has directed at Newzglobe. It turns out none of them want to support the public shaming of crime victims and media ethics breaches. Even non-profits who received free advertising didn't want to appear there anymore. Or at least almost none. Silja Line (a ferry company with a history of handling their own big problems with sexual abuse controversially) respond that they don't have any problem with the site. Their advertising agent, on the other hand, receives queries from so many of their other clients that they terminate the relationship anyway. And so *Newzglobe* loses its most important source of income. The site is going completely ad-free.

Their marketing manager contacts one of the activists and is very upset. She says that the site would have been happy to take down the articles if he had contacted the paper instead of the advertisers. I help him make a long list of all the unsuccessful attempts to sway the editor-in-chief. The marketing manager doesn't respond.

No other Swedish papers publish my name, and in a few months, the editor-in-chief in question is fired.

August 26, 2010

"Are you satisfied now that the story is off to the races after you tipped Expressen *off about the police report? You leaked this*

the right of women to be believed when they speak up about sexual offenses.

Newzglobe is harshly rebuked on several fronts and accused of violating media ethics.

Lisa Magnusson writes in *Aftonbladet*:

> *It is even more striking when a news site decides to disclose the name, photo, and other information of a woman who has reported a crime. I would actually like to call that downright ill-advised. The editor-in-chief who was first to go public with Julian Assange's identity defends the publication by saying that there is a public interest in knowing when a public figure is suspected of rape. And yet there absolutely isn't. There is interest among the public, but that is something completely different. When newspapers name the individuals involved, that is instead about punishing, shaming, and stigmatizing people to give others malicious delight.*[6]

When the *Newzglobe* editor-in-chief still doesn't want to take down the stolen photos, my name, or the threatening comments, my friend Ida starts a campaign against them based on the principle of "hit them where it hurts."

"If they don't listen to media ethics and only care about clicks and money, then that's where we need to strike to make them listen," she says and explains her idea. It's a matter of contacting all their advertisers to get ahold of their media agencies to ask if they really want to finance this stuff. I think it could work.

Together we make a list of over forty advertisers

August 24, 2010

I get in touch with Olof again, wondering if he has time today instead. He seemed so excited and was clearly interested, and I want to pretend that life is still normal. He doesn't answer, but I happen to run into him on the street by chance. He's completely cold toward me.

"You said that you didn't sleep with him," he says.

"Yeah, I didn't want people to know about it. I regretted it, and I didn't think it was any of your business or the right time when you asked."

"You lied to me, didn't you? You lied," he says. There's a smile on his lips, but his eyes look angry.

I guess he's angry because I didn't immediately tell him the intimate details that he can now read online.

"I'm not okay with that," he continues before leaving. He has obviously read about the case, gotten cold feet, and absolutely does not want to see me anymore.

August 25, 2010

Public prosecutor Eva Finné formally decides to dismiss the preliminary investigation into Maria's rape and several other alleged offenses. As I had guessed, she stands by her early response. Julian is still suspected of a crime(s) against me, but the public debate is out of control. The online army takes the dismissal as proof that *everything* was a lie. They scornfully wave another person's case in my face, and it's impossible to avoid seeing what's being written. At the same time, a defense begins mobilizing for me for

I need to find a good lawyer. Someone who values women's rights, a feminist, someone who can handle a case with a lot of media attention. After some consideration, it feels very logical when the former Equality Ombudsman Claes Borgström occurs to me. Of course, there are big potential drawbacks regarding the media's potential response to someone also associated with the Social Democrats becoming my counsel. Plus, Claes runs his firm with the former Social Democratic Justice Minister, who isn't popular with WikiLeaks' supporters.

Our network "Social Democrats against Big Brother" and I have criticized him for his policy to increase the public surveillance of citizens. Claes' connections with the former Justice Minister will probably be turned against me. But the pros outweigh the cons, so I send an email and ask if he will take this on. He responds right away and doesn't hesitate to say yes.

I bring up my worries about the risks of negative attention, but Claes dismisses them.

His opinion is that this is a case, and the most important thing is what happened. We need to completely ignore irrelevant aspects like the election or the media circus.

Maria also trusts Claes, and together, we submit a request to have him appointed as our counsel.

Olof, the cute guy I was able to stay with when I needed to flee from my apartment, gets in touch and cancels the date we'd scheduled.

curious way of convincing each other they understand the entire situation after reading some documents or seeing a few deleted tweets.

It feels like I'm stuck between two walls. Like there's constant pressure from all directions and nowhere to go. The air hasn't really made it down into my lungs for several days. The hatred is like a swarm of wasps working together to hurt me with thousands of little stings.

I get sick, really sick, from stress. I'm shaking with fear and powerlessness. I collapse onto the floor. I throw up. It's so terribly distressing not to have control of your own body.

It feels like a crazy overreaction, but evidently, this can happen when you are harassed. When a person gets more hate than love, it eventually becomes deadly. I'm falling apart.

I really need someone to help me both with the law and the media. But how can I afford that? Neither the police nor the judicial system can say whether I'm entitled to compensation for a complainant's counsel.

Then Thomas, the ombudsman for the local Stockholm organization within the Social Democratic Party, sees how hard the firestorm is hitting me—not just me as a Social Democrat but as a private individual. He promises me they'll pay for the financial risk if my request for counsel is denied. This is such a relief. In purely practical terms, this means that I can get help right now before my request for counsel has been submitted, let alone approved. But most of all, it feels like an expression of solidarity, a feeling that I am not completely alone.

already been pre-judged, and it doesn't matter what I say. There's nothing I can do to improve the situation.

People—the overwhelming majority of whom appear to be men—write, shout, photoshop, and even animate various degrading opinions, insulting language, or threats of assault, bodily harm, and death. Women, even the ones who are furious at those who mock crime victims, calling them complicit in the crime, still defend Julian and deride me. Mothers and grandmothers chime in with a chorus of accusations, lies, and conspiracies. Men, even those who believe the death penalty should apply to rape, think that I should be raped.

Naming and shaming Julian goes hand in hand with naming and shaming me. The frenzy is directed at both of us. *Newzglobe* is, of course, only one of a slew of media outlets around the world chasing after clickbait details precisely because Julian Assange is Julian Assange, just as they did with Silvio Berlusconi, Dominique Strauss-Kahn, Roman Polanski, and other powerful and well-known men who were accused on probable grounds or convicted of sexual crimes. It's exactly the same as when famous actors are arrested with drugs or when politicians cheat with their taxes. Famous people are much more interesting to read about than regular people, like a mutual acquaintance to us all. But there also seems to be a particular logic when it comes to sex crimes that cannot be explained merely by celebrity-status.

Sexual crimes, in particular, seem to rally people, using their own honor, words, and judgment as arguments to settle the question of guilt. People have a

Last spring, when the party lists were drawn up prior to the election, I ended up on a list for the city council in my district without actually wanting to, well below an electable position, twelfth place, on a list where we usually get two people in. This apparently makes me a "public figure," and the editor-in-chief at *Newzglobe* says in an email that the crime I endured is in the public interest. The same thing he claimed as his defense for having published Julian's name.

No, I'm not on sick leave, even though I'm not feeling well at all. I haven't withdrawn any insurance benefits, but the paper won't print a correction. The editor thinks the publication is in order. It is well disseminated, and I guess it's resulting in good ad revenues.

I send a text to one of the reporters and ask how it feels to encourage a mob. He responds:

"I tried to contact you and get a comment, your story, before it was published. You made the choice then not to answer at all."

He thinks I made my own choice to be bullied online. Nevertheless, he is far from the only one who tried to get me to talk by threatening to publish false information or who punished me for not making myself available for an interview. But it's not to be ungenerous or out of disinterest or snobbery that I'm not making myself available. Quite the contrary, I have been trying to serve the public interest. Even though I only said the absolute most basic things to *Aftonbladet* and weighed every word, it did not turn out well. I've with sharp objects to extracting my teeth. What's happening now is the same but with volume turned up to maximum.

"People in the terminal stage of fatal cancer have to work, but this fucking whore gets to live it up on our tax money," someone writes. *"She's mentally ill, and I mean that in a purely medical sense. This is confirmed. But her illness isn't so serious that she can't work. It's a tragic case. Unfortunately, innocent people suffer when she goes after them after she freaks out for some reason that, to other people, is completely inexplicable,"* another writes.

It's difficult to do my job as a press secretary when I'm of global interest as a private individual and now offer relatively minimal and provincial angles on the news I am trying to communicate. I'm not sure whether I could get any other job. I have 100, 110, and 150 missed calls per day and need to focus full-time on *not* talking to journalists. It's barely possible to exist at all. I feel like a rabbit during hunting season, a refugee in my own city. The threats and hatred force their way into every aspect of my daily life. I've grown too afraid to be in my own home. I occasionally need to go to my apartment to pick things up, but various friends let me stay with them and help me stay underground.

Someone took my trash that I had forgotten in the stairwell. I hope that it's some nice neighbor who helped by throwing it in the garbage room, even though forgotten trash is usually left to sit there. People stand waiting for me in the lobby at work, and online, hundreds of people say that they want me to be locked up, die, or be raped.

if I'm contagious, and distancing themselves or even betraying me is a way of protecting themselves.

Lots of newspapers chase me, especially the British ones. But Sweden's *Newzglobe* is the worst. They steal and publish pictures of me and allow lots of threatening comments through. They portray me as a criminal, as guilty, as someone who should be ashamed. A couple of reporters from the newspaper are extremely insistent in calling, emailing, and texting, demanding that I talk to them. They add me on all social media platforms and search for me on every conceivable channel. Yesterday, they threatened to publish more if I didn't talk. I didn't talk to them. Today they have published even more.

The election campaign is in its final phase, and there has been a lot of talk about seriously ill people's unemployment benefits running out, and they're being forced back to work or into poverty. The Flashback and *Newzglobe*'s comment sections—as well as countless threads on Facebook, Twitter, and other social media—link me to this debate and claim I'm committing fraud. They've now learned that I've been away from my job for two days, and claim I am getting money I am not entitled to. An enormous amount of hatred is directed at me for this; enormous.

I've received emails threatening me with violence and messages about what a whore I am since long before these woman-haters ever heard of Julian Assange. Once, someone surfing for porn found my blog instead and got upset. He called me at 2:30 in the morning, threatening me with everything from rape truth—simply decides to say something he knows isn't true to avoid taking responsibility for his own actions. And to protect himself, he uses the WikiLeaks organization as a shield. Julian starts contributing to the frenzied tribunal with more than one statement. When he begins introducing new theories, elevating and allowing himself to be elevated by those who are threatening me and using WikiLeaks' Twitter account as a coordination hub, it feels increasingly directed.

WikiLeaks' supporters listen. Thousands of people around the world cooperate with Julian to assassinate Maria's character and mine.

And with that, he commences a different type of assault than the one I accused him of in the first place.

August 23, 2010

An established media channel publishes my name: "Social Democratic leader confirms that Ardin filed report," reads the headline in the online newspaper, *Newzglobe*, which becomes the first Swedish media outlet to reveal my name. And, sure enough, a Social Democrat I work closely with chose to serve as a source. I text him the link and ask:

"What are you doing? Why?"
"But they already knew."
"You know very well that they can't confirm that with Flashback as the source. Why are you selling me out?"

Few people choose to risk anything for my sake now. Many turn their backs on me.

Being associated with me is something bad. It's as

world... *but apparently my world and those rabid feminists' world differ quite a bit. What luck that I have never drawn a losing feminist lottery ticket like JA did."*

The police investigation into my case is also continuing. The police ask for technical evidence.

I have been gone for a few days and haven't had a chance to take out my trash or wash the sheets since Julian stayed with me. The technical evidence is still there, among the trash and laundry. I sneak into my apartment through the attic and find what the police are asking for. The condom and the sheet.

I take out the trash and put it in the stairwell. But when I leave, I take the same attic route out and forget the bag of trash outside my door.

I had hoped my statement to *Aftonbladet* would have a calming effect, but the opposite happens. It's like throwing fuel on the bonfire they built to burn me with. Every single word is intentionally misunderstood and turned against me. I decide that from now on, I won't say another word about the crime outside of the legal and police proceedings. I want this to be tried impartially. The online frenzy starts to play out in the press too, and I don't want to take part. Julian chooses to take part. He tells *Aftonbladet* that he has no idea who his accusers are, but he claims he knows it has to do with world politics and not sexual practices. He repeats that he believes it's the Pentagon using dirty tricks to sink WikiLeaks.

Julian—the man considered by so many people right now to be the world's foremost defender of *false reports of assault. Sorry loser :lol:"*

"*Haven't read the whole thread, but if I understand correctly, both of them wanted to have consensual sex. He didn't want to use a condom, but she did want to. She decided to have sex anyway and then he ejaculated in her mouth or on her back/stomach. Now she wants to make this into a rape or at least sexual molestation. WTF, that would make me into a serial rapist and probably most of the men in Sweden, too. A little off topic but, fuck, are Crazy Horse Anna, Mona Muslim, Hashish-Bodström, and Rape-Victim-Wannabe Anna Ardin really the best the Social Democrats have to offer…"*

"*That Anna Ardin woman makes rape into the new career move among these rabid ladies who try to make people believe that they are defending other women's vulnerable situations. In my eyes, Anna Ardin is simply a slut. She lay down on her back voluntarily, or engaged in a little doggy style, which resulted in Anna being so rough in her sex with Julian that the condom broke! Says more about how Anna Ardin has sex with men than about Julian's relations with attention-seeking women! We know that Anna Ardin is happy to spread her legs, but we don't know yet what the cost is for the man she sleeps with!"*

"*And Anna Ardin thinks that for this he should be punished so that he, as an international figure, is accused of rape and WikiLeaks' reputation is at stake… because he came in a girl's face while they were having consensual sex?!?! The level of stupidity of Anna Ardin isn't small at all, is it?? The only punishment Julian Assange deserves is quite simply that he doesn't get any more sex with this girl… it's that simple in my*

Sunday, August 22, 2010

The online trolls' investigation continues. It is harassment. Following it in real-time means I'm harming myself but also that gradually, little by little, I'm becoming numb and placing everything outside of myself. It's as if this isn't about me at all. These groups that pride themselves on their independent thinking and their defense of free speech are so strikingly lockstep:

"A childhood friend of mine who reports knowing this Anna Ardin really well since they have worked on various projects together has some info. This Ardin was giving Assange a blow job, unclear whether that was the only thing that was done or if that was the conclusion, and she told him that she didn't want him to come in her mouth. He ejaculated in her mouth anyway. The stuff about the condom is some police matter that came up when the question was supposedly, 'if Assange had a condom, would you have completed the oral sex?' to which supposedly the answer there was yes, but the thing was that she didn't want to have his semen in her mouth. So, no rape but only molestation. I guess that angle doesn't feel completely unbelievable, and my friend was really pleased to have these details."

"Doubts prevail about whether she was really fudge-packed. But Julian Assange sprayed semen on Anna Ardin's body :) Anna Ardin's whole part in the affair is about a few centiliters of sperm that ended up, like, a little wrong :) Then Anna Ardin lost it and reported Julian Assange. A lovely story to say the least, and with that Anna Ardin's chances of becoming a high-ranking social democrat VIP came to an end. Now the name Anna Ardin is synonymous with sperm, derailed feminism, and

she's on their side. Finné then dismisses some of the suspicions that the first prosecutor had about my case and all the suspected crimes against Maria. She also tones down the classification of the remaining suspicions somewhat but establishes—just as the police and the on<call prosecutor did—that Assange is still suspected of crimes against me.

Many people express the importance of publicly identifying Maria and me so that it's possible to investigate whether we're credible. There's also a flood of guesswork about what actually happened—although the vast majority of people assume that it was nothing worth going to the police about. Early in some of the numerous threads, someone writes that the whole thing boils down to: "she wasn't into anal sex." After a few more hours, the rumor that I was raped anally during consensual vaginal sex becomes a truth.

I'm glad that didn't happen, but it's scary how consensus seems to prevail on Flashback, Reddit, and other online fora that a scenario like that is insignificant. Something women should accept. Something to laugh at. Something men like Julian are somehow entitled to. It is not. It is rape.

More and more guesses become truths, and together they create a sequence of events that is not at all realistic. But the fact that the stories about me don't add up isn't interpreted as a sign that they aren't correct; they are interpreted as a sign that I am crazy.

Julian doesn't match people's preconceived profile of a "real rapist," which the press wants to squeeze him into. He is being shamed and hunted based on completely incorrect assumptions, and I want to prevent that. I hope and believe that my statement will help to show a different picture of me, him, and what this is about, a more accurate picture.

The Flashback Forum connects the case to me at 5:58 p.m.: "Does anyone know how old Anna Ardin is?" A while later there are links to my blog, Twitter, Facebook, home address, CV, which organizations I belong to, my political affiliations, that I have a sister, what I was like when I was in school, and so on. I start receiving messages that people know it was me, that I should be ashamed, and that I'm lying. There are threats. I have started to get haters.

The case is transferred to permanent prosecutor Eva Finné at the Stockholm City Public Prosecution Office. She takes over from the on-call prosecutor and makes a statement to the press on her way to the office, "There is no reason to think that he has committed any rape." Then she says that she will familiarize herself with the case. She is obviously stressed and does not seem to have any media training. The first thing I learned was to keep quiet until I am thoroughly acquainted with what the noise is about. Finné does not appear to have taken that class.

When she says it's not about rape, she's expressing her opinion, perhaps instinctively, that there are no grounds to detain him. Even though Finné didn't say anything about my case, the growing group of anonymous online trolls interprets this to mean that

that other people started about Julian as a dangerous perpetrator—I decide to make a statement. I contact one of the people who emailed me: Jan Helin, editor-in-chief of *Aftonbladet*.

We talk for a long time. He thinks I should talk to one of his reporters, but he agrees that I should be allowed to write what I want to say. With Andreas's help, I write a brief statement that is quoted in the paper:

In light of the ongoing police investigation, the woman in her 30s does not want to share more details at the current time, but she has provided the police with a very detailed account. The second woman has also provided detailed witness testimony to the police.

"I immediately believed her information because I myself had an experience that was similar to her story," the woman tells Aftonbladet. *[...]*

"It is completely wrong that we were afraid of Assange," the woman says. "He's not violent and I do not feel threatened by him." [...]

"The other woman wanted to report a rape. I gave my account as evidence for her account and to support her. We fully stand by the information," the woman tells Aftonbladet. *[...] The woman in her 30s flatly dismisses the conspiracy theories that are flooding the internet right now.*

"Of course, the allegations against Assange were not orchestrated by the Pentagon or anyone else. The responsibility for what happened to me and the other woman lies with a man with a skewed view of women and trouble taking no for an answer."[5]

posts on Twitter that could reveal this affiliation, two posts that hadn't been retweeted by anyone, and that only people I know had interacted with. One was asking whether anyone was having a crayfish party they could invite Julian to, and the other was about the magical August night when the crayfish party took place.

The police call me as planned for proper questioning.

Within an hour or so, the word is out among journalists that I'm one of the ones who filed a report. Then, it feels like everything takes off all at once.

As the Swedish and British press ramp up to full staffing and as more people find out that I am one of the alleged victims, my phone rings with increasing intensity. *Expressen* calls 48 times, *TV4* 46 times. They call my employers, my friends, and my parents. Finally, it is only a matter of time before they come to my home and knock on the door.

In a small window between all the furious phone calls I decline, I manage to dial a number myself, Andreas.

Andreas has a friend whose apartment will be empty for a few days, and we can borrow it to hide me. I leave my apartment through the attic. I go out the back way, exiting down a different stairwell, probably only minutes before the first journalists arrive looking for me at home. Neighbors report that strangers who couldn't reach me by phone are looking for me in the stairwell.

To counteract the frenzy—the crazy rumors Julian triggered about the Pentagon and the nutty rumors that this could not become public until there was a public record as part of a potential trial, but it seems to have already spread the very same day we were at the police station. I realize that more journalists will be getting in touch very soon.

Julian's name and our allegations were apparently in the paper only moments after we visited the police station yesterday evening. Emanuel Karlsten comments on the news in *Expressen*:

> *Of course, no one is guilty before a verdict is reached. Just as no one is innocent. That fact will divide the songs of praise that have thus far been sung in unison about Julian Assange. Because although WikiLeaks is the work of far more than one man, Julian Assange is the only face we have been given to identify with the revolutionary organization, an organization for which there is no historical comparison. I also assume that because of the report there will be a flurry of conspiracy theories that the CIA has finally succeeded in infiltrating the Swedish authorities.*[4]

That is exactly what becomes Julian's first defense strategy as well. At 9:15 a.m., he Tweets from the WikiLeaks account that they had been warned of "dirty tricks" and that this was the first. He latches onto those who defend him with conspiracy theories, and they latch onto his Tweets in turn.

Media frenzies usually last for a few days, but I think this one might last longer. I start trying to hide the fact that I have had contact with Julian in my personal life. Maybe I can avoid the mob coming to understand that this involves me. I delete the two happened to me. Apparently, that's not the case. There's no longer any possibility of rewinding unless I stop telling the truth.

We talk for a short time before Maria passes the phone to the police officer who questioned her. It turns out to be a woman who I met at the pride festival last year. We're both part of the same network of social democratic bloggers, but I didn't know then that she was also a police officer. She expresses her regret for what we've been through and wants me to come in. I tell her it can wait until Monday.

"But I won't be the one doing the questioning on Monday," she says.

"OK, good," I reply. "It's better for it to be with someone I don't know." I hop onto my train and go.

I run into Andreas at the party, totally caught off-guard. My grief and my broken heart for him are easier to handle when we don't see each other, but now he's standing here open-hearted, and I have so much to say. I know he will understand and support me, and I have missed him so incredibly much. We talk the whole evening. Then, we go home, each to our own new lives.

Saturday, August 21, 2010

My phone wakes me up at 6:10 in the morning. It's the newspaper *Dagens Nyheter* calling me in my role as Julian's press contact, and they want to talk about the criminal allegations against him. At first, I go completely cold, almost paralyzed, then my cheeks heat up, and I feel like I need to act very quickly. I just don't have any idea how. The police had promised reassure me and explain that nothing can become public until a trial, if there is one, and that their preparing the report does not entail any risk of a media frenzy against me, Maria, Julian, or WikiLeaks. If there's no trial, it will never be revealed.

I'm in the police station for a very short time; then I ride my bike back to my office.

I'm going to a party at Marta's place in Uppsala later. As I'm standing on the railway platform, Maria calls me. The police want to question me tonight, even though it's almost seven.

"No, no," I say. "I'm catching a train right now. I don't want to be questioned now. I don't know if I want to proceed with this."

But Maria explains that it falls under public prosecution, and therefore there's already a case. Both sexual molestations—as they put as the header for what I had been subjected to—and rape, as they put as the header for what Maria had been subjected to—fall under public prosecution. That means a report is created regardless of the victim's consent or permission. We can confirm our interviews—which were written down but not recorded—are correct, but we're otherwise not expected to sign anything as I'd thought we would be.

In addition, the public prosecutor has already had time to issue a warrant since they cannot get ahold of Julian.

I am surprised and stressed. I had not done any risk analysis, and I had thought I still had a choice to back out if I didn't want to proceed. I thought I would get to say no to further questioning about what advice on what actions she can take and what options there are to force him to get tested. She wants me to go.

I'm still at work and feel strongly that I don't want to. I don't have time! Plus, I absolutely don't want to explain any of this to my coworkers. But I pushed her to go to the police and have not allowed her to suspect my doubt. Maybe I even convinced her with my promise that I would go with her. I said what I said, and I know what I think, in theory. I hear myself say, "Yes, I'll come!" We decide to meet at Klara Police Station in downtown Stockholm since it's less than ten minutes by bike from my workplace.

It's not like I have to file a report. There's still time to think it over a little more. After all, we're just going to check with the police and see how they assess the cases and the possibilities of proceeding. I think if I get this over with quickly, no one will notice anything strange. I'll just go there and explain how I know she's telling the truth.

Maria is waiting for me outside the station. We give each other a hug and walk in together.

The police officer I meet listens to my account and says seriously:

"He screwed up. That's not OK. What you're describing is assault, criminal assault, and we're probably going to have to file a report about this."

In the report drawn up, the police assess that I'm the victim of a crime. [3] When Maria recounts what happened to her, the police make the assessment that she was also the victim of a crime. I express my concern that the case might affect WikiLeaks, but they confirm Julian's behavior toward Maria. Her story is so similar to mine that it feels obvious to me that it's true, not because of some kind of female intuition but my definitive, unpleasant experiences with a certain man and his conduct. I feel that it is my duty to support her, that I need to go to the police not just out of principle, but for a sister—one with whom I have only a very passing acquaintance, but still.

No man has a moral right to force or cheat his bodily fluids into anyone. If he's infected, then it's likely he knows this or has reason to suspect it. I know that HIV transmission can be prevented when people who are infected take the right medication, but I haven't seen any medication despite the entire contents of his travel bag being spread throughout my home. Knowingly exposing someone to a risk of infection is illegal. I tell Maria all of this. Julian needs to take the responsibility that he refuses to admit is his.

"I think you should go to the police, and yes, I'll go with you. Naturally, I will also tell my story."

I say *naturally* as if it was that, but deep down inside, it doesn't feel the least bit natural. It's for Maria's sake, for the sake of other women, because they have a right to their own bodies. But in my case, my body feels significantly less important.

A few hours later, Maria calls again. She is on her way from the hospital to the police station, accompanied by her father. She wants to ask the police for their assessment of what she was subjected to and ask for

"Sex offences are a weapon of the patriarchy and a declaration of war against gender equality," I wrote in my notebook several years ago alongside a quote from philosopher Susan Griffin: "As the symbolic expression of the white male hierarchy, rape is the quintessential act of our civilization."

I have thought a lot about rape as a symbol of the abuses people commit against nature, the structures that allow these violations to go on, and how rapes and the spread of infection are used as weapons of war. I have been shocked at the prevailing lack of punishment for the vast majority of sex offenders. I haven't just analyzed the problems but also the solutions—how can politics and the women's movement work toward better laws? And maybe most of all: how can we work to ensure that the laws so many people have sacrificed so much to put in place are followed? Some of the answers have to do with a need for the police and courts to take sexual crimes seriously. Reporting is one way of demanding that. Daring to report is an act of resistance against the hierarchy that Griffin discusses. That's why I wanted to tell every single victim of a sex crime not to back down and that they have a right to their own body.

Maria ought to go to the police. But the thought that I should too still has not occurred to me. I suppose I never really considered I might wind up in this situation myself. *And I am not in that situation now, either*, I think. What Julian did is hardly "maintaining hierarchies" of an international significance, is it? It was unpleasant, but that's how it is sometimes... At the same time, I know that I am a witness who can

Donald calls Julian, but it doesn't help. Julian refuses. He calls me again instead and keeps yelling.

"This is blackmail. I'm going to report you to the police," he shouts. "This is a threat. That's illegal. I'm going to put you away for threatening me. You're going to get caught!"

Again and again, he asks if we've gone to the police and if we're going to go to the police, but I've already seen through his façade. I have solved the riddle, and I have a clear picture of what happened: he assaulted me and perhaps even endangered my life, and now we're in a situation where he's considering reporting me to the police because I'm not accepting that.

Yes, I think to myself. *Whatever. Report me to the police, and then we'll see what's more illegal, telling the police the truth or assaulting people.*

It's important to make reports for things to change. I said exactly this so many times during my years at university, in student politics, and later in Avantgarde, Rebella, and Laboremus. In my classes and at the student union, I put a lot of time into discussing assault, the significance and consequences of filing reports, and various aspects of women's sexual and reproductive rights. I published magazines on feminist research, organized big conferences about sexual harassment, and translated the first part of Nina Björk's book *Under det rosa täcket* (Under the Pink Duvet)—a basic introduction to feminism—into Spanish.

yourself. You noticed that I thought it was nice you were gone and that I wanted you to move out for the whole week. For God's sake, I helped you figure out how to get over there when you were planning to go see her."

He cuts me off and says, "Well, no matter what, now is not the time. I really don't have time for this kind of thing."

We end our call. In his eyes, he is too important, and we are unimportant.

I call Donald again instead. Maybe he can convince Julian to get tested? I emphasize that it can be done without a police report, without fuss, then it can be over and done quickly. And I explain that if the risk of a blood infection can be avoided, then I don't think Maria will file a report. This is an attempt to underline that the test is Julian's way out, his opportunity to take responsibility. This applies to both assaults, but I don't say anything about myself. I haven't "slept with Assange." It's not something I want to take responsibility for to Donald, and preferably not to anyone else, either.

I don't understand, of course, what will happen if Julian complies with our wishes. We don't know each other, Maria and I, and I have no idea what she's planning to do. But I'm guessing that the situation is much more acute for her than for me. She seems to be in an extremely bad state.

Maria asks me for advice. I say that I think she should go to the police, thinking that she can make a police report but not sign it, not proceed with it, just to persuade him to go and get himself tested.

of infection completely against our will. You need to take responsibility for that."

"You should know that I'm not that kind of guy." I laugh bluntly.

"Oh my God, Julian. If anyone should know that that's the kind of guy you are, it's me!"

He gets upset and raises his voice again.

"I am a white Australian. Australian men don't have HIV."

"The fact that you believe your ethnicity protects you from infection does not make me the slightest bit calmer. But seriously, I don't give a damn about your prejudices about HIV. You need to get tested. I want to know, too."

"Yes, if you want to get yourself tested, then go get yourself tested," he tells me.

"It takes three months before I can know anything. I have no desire to walk around for three months worrying about maybe being infected. Shape the fuck up. It'll take an hour, tops."

"I got tested three months ago, so it's okay. No risk."

"Why did you get tested if you don't believe that white Australian men can be infected?"

"You're jealous," he says. "Right? You're just doing this because you're jealous. You're mad because I went over to Maria's place. You're doing this to punish me."

"Ha ha, just stop! You don't even believe that

who I am!"

Maybe his yelling is intended to make me insecure, but it has exactly the opposite effect. He shrinks in my eyes, and I feel calmer. Telling the police is not a threat but an alternative if he can't behave more reasonably and resolve this with us. Neither Julian nor I hang up, and he calms down and changes his conversation strategy.

"You have to understand that I'm under a lot of pressure," he says again.

From what I understand from him, we were there to help him relax, and we should continue to volunteer, not for him, but for the sake of the greater good. Not for Julian, but for WikiLeaks, even though it was Julian who violated us and not WikiLeaks. Forcing him to get tested is apparently like forcing all of WikiLeaks to take a break, like trying to impede the dissemination of secret documents, like supporting corrupt men in power. He references everything other than what actually happened—that he had unprotected sex with us against our wishes and that we want him to take responsibility for that. He refuses to get tested.

"I just won't do it."

"You broke the condom," I say.

"No, I did not. Condoms can break, you know."

"Yes, they can, but if so, how could you not notice that?" He changes the subject.

"I am responsible for lots of people's lives. You can't do this to me."

"As I see it, you're the one who can't do this to us. What you did was not legal. You subjected us to a risk ends here. He's gone another way; whatever he does or doesn't do is none of my business. I will receive neither glory nor discomfort, and that is such a beautiful thing.

But it isn't over. Julian makes sure that it doesn't end.

When I get to work, Maria calls me again and that says she talked to Julian for a long time. She tried to get him to come to the hospital but failed.

No, he cannot reasonably know that he's healthy—at least not in Maria's case. After all, he had unprotected sex with me just a few days before and knew nothing about my health. He'd probably had sex with the other woman Donald mentioned only a few days earlier too. It's obviously risky behavior, and he's exposed us to risk without our consent. Maria and I agree that he at least needs to take an HIV test.

We talk more about his dangerous behavior, about what he did to both of us, and afterward, I call Julian myself. I tell him that I agree with Maria, and he needs to go to the hospital. He gets annoyed.

"There's no reason for me to do that."

Again, I need to take a deep breath before I respond, "Julian, you know that this is about me, too. You need to go there and get yourself tested. I'm scared."

That's an understatement. I'm terrified. He loses his temper. He becomes furious and yells into the phone:

"I am under extreme pressure! I'm way too busy for this kind of thing. I don't take any instructions from you at all. Who do you think you are? You know in their emergency room for women who've been raped. They used a rape kit and started antiretroviral therapy to prevent HIV. The antiretrovirals can prevent the virus from replicating if they're started within three days of exposure. When I went to the clinic on Monday, too many days had already passed for that to have any effect. Either I'm infected, or I'm not.

I promise her I'll talk to Julian to try and persuade him to go to the hospital and have the necessary tests done, but first, he needs to leave my apartment. That feels like the most important thing in my life right now—to get him off my sofa.

My call with Maria gives me the final push to get him out. While I gather up his socks and the other things he has spread throughout my home, he continues to sit on the sofa and work. I stuff everything into his brown travel bag and set it out in the stairwell. I put on my shoes.

"Now," I say. "I'm going now. You have to go now."

He finally stands up, closes his computer, and puts on his shoes. My shoulders sink as I sigh, and down on the street, he gives me a kiss on the cheek, thanks me for letting him stay with me, and we each go our own way.

I do not want to call Julian now that I have finally gotten rid of him, so I call Donald and ask him for help in getting Julian to contact Maria immediately.

After this, it feels like the story's finally over. As long as I haven't contracted any incurable disease, it but I interrupt his sentence and reply:

"No. No, you won't. You will give it to me now. I'm going to Uppsala tonight, and I need it now."

I stand at my front door, but he's still sitting on my sofa and continues typing on his computer.

Maria calls.

Julian doesn't understand Swedish, but I go out onto the balcony to talk to her anyway. She's obviously scared and upset.

"What do you mean he's a pig?" is her first question.

I explain that he's filthy, makes a mess, refuses to move out, and needs help tackling his own basic needs. She says that Julian, against her will, penetrated her without a condom—while she was sleeping!—continued when she woke up, and then came inside her.

In other words, he did to her exactly the same thing he did to me and inseminated her against her will. But what she speaks of falls more clearly into the category of assault. Penetrating someone who's asleep is rape under Swedish law.

I take a deep breath and tell her what happened to me, that I recognize the behavior she's describing. She says she recognizes that what I'm saying is true, that his behavior toward me doesn't seem to be unique, and I realize what I was subjected to really was an assault. It's like a difficult riddle, where the call with Maria provides key clues. The situation he put me in a week ago Friday wasn't OK. I also feel like I have a responsibility to Maria.

She says that she is at the hospital in Stockholm,

Julian. We have no romantic relationship."

Then I close the door and go.

First, I call Joel, a close friend who lives nearby. Luckily, he's home, so I go there.

From there, I get ahold of Olof, the guy with the Schnapps.

"My home has been occupied by a disgusting guest," I say.

"You're welcome to come over here and stay the night." When I get there, I explain further.

"I would never have guessed that when I saw Julian at the seminar," he says.

We lie there talking half the night. Sex isn't even on the table; I have become celibate.

Friday, August 20, 2010

A week has passed since Julian took up residence in my apartment. In various places online, it now says that it's possible to reach him by calling me. I'm one of the few people who have his actual cell phone number and can contact him directly, which is why Maria, the volunteer from the seminar, texts me that she wants to get in touch with him. *"I am relying on your discretion,"* she says as she asks for help in getting in touch.

I immediately think, *Shit.* I have a strong feeling that I know what this is about. I reply to her: *"He is in my apartment. You can call me. He's a pig in so many ways."*

Then I go home to ask Julian to move out. This time there will be no pretending that he doesn't understand.

"I'll put the key in the mailb—" he starts to say,

from work, I can't get my key in the lock. My spare key is still in the lock from the inside. *Fuck*, I think, *he's still here.* I don't even want to enter.

I go in.

It smells strongly of an unwashed body, of urine, of dried sweat, and there are poops floating in the toilet. Again, he hasn't flushed. He also doesn't appear to have eaten all day. I didn't make anything. His things are spread out all over the place, and he's sitting in exactly the same spot on the sofa as this morning.

"You were supposed to go and leave the key in the mailbox. Why are you still here?"

"I like it here," he says.

He smiles and tilts his head as if it's a good thing that he's still here. With his open bite and tousled hair, he looks like a little boy. Today I can't see it as cute or charming.

"Sure," I say. "Of course. A place where you can get full service and someone to wash up after you."

He seems completely indifferent to my chastising him. I have trouble understanding why I didn't see any of his bad sides that first night when they're so obvious now.

I put on my jacket and shoes.

"Are you going on a date?" Julian asks.

"Yes, I'm going on a date."

I flee my own home, not knowing where to go. I just need to get out of here. Just before my door closes all the way again, without looking up from his computer, Julian says:

"But we have a romantic relationship."

I open the door again, look at him, and say, "No,

ever see each other again. He pulls me down onto the sofa and starts touching me. I become angry and raise my voice, break free, and walk over to the door. I'm looking for my keys.

"Oh, come have a seat here," he says, wanting me to come back to the sofa. "Cut it out. I just gave you a hug."

I have a strong feeling that he won't release me next time.

"Put the key in the mailbox when you go," I tell him as I hurry out the door.

When I come home, he's still there.

He's very engrossed in something important, and I change and go to bed to sleep. A while later, I suddenly wake up and Julian's lying in my bed. He's taken off his pants and underwear and is pushing his erect penis against my butt. *What the fuck?* I think. I become angry and clench my teeth but don't say anything. I just get up, pull my nightgown down, and lie on the mattress on the floor. Luckily, he doesn't follow but just goes to sleep in my bed.

Much later, I learned that this was the day he applied for a residence permit in Sweden, and he did not seem to have any plane ticket, neither to France nor Iceland.

Thursday, August 19, 2010

I go to work early, and Julian promises—yet again—that he will leave my key in my mailbox. He's really moving out today.

At around 9:00 p.m., when I finally come home

ever experienced. It smells acidic and rotten, and I feel incredibly humiliated. I guess it was unintentional, but he doesn't make the slightest sign of saying he's sorry.

I feel sick. I will remember this smell for a long time and feel like I want to throw up just at the thought.

A journalist from *Medierna* on Radio P1 wants to do an interview with Julian. I ask Julian if it's OK to book it, and he says yes. One reason he mentioned for wanting to stay in my apartment is that it's a safe place since no one knows he's staying here. So, I make a choice not to book the journalist at a nearby café but rather invite him to my apartment.

"What? Is he going to come here?" Julian is upset. "Why should he know where I'm staying?"

"It doesn't matter, does it? I mean, you're moving out today," I say, hoping my plan will work.

"But I might come back."
"No, I don't think so."

Donald said that Julian is going to France today. Julian tells me he's going to Iceland.

I try to get him to hand me my key because getting him to leave it in the mailbox hasn't worked. But he says he has something really important to finish up quickly, so he needs to sit on the sofa and work.

"You need to move out today."

"Yes, of course. I have my plane ticket, you know," he says. "Okay then. But give me a goodbye hug."

I walk over to give him a hug and hope we won't

woman he had never met before. They left the dinner hand in hand, headed for her hotel room, I'm guessing."

"Well, I'm not going to sleep with him anyway. I can guarantee you that," I say, meaning, of course, that I won't sleep with him *again* because it was a horrible experience. But I'm ashamed to tell it like it is. Just as very hot spices can disguise expired food, meeting a celebrity can make people blind to warning signs that normally would've been obvious. Fame is like chili.

I think about how exceptionally easy we humans find it to ignore risks and shortcomings and to only see the positive in someone; how easily we make people into heroes and let them get away with the kind of things that make us call others villains. We so often and so willingly buy into myths about completely ordinary people being demigods.

It begins to dawn on me that a hero can also be a villain and that what Julian did to me may very well be illegal. I managed to avoid being penetrated without a condom, but he forced his semen into me regardless. I still don't fully understand why. What motive would there be for using a condom with a hole in the tip anyway? Maybe to get me pregnant? Or for the feeling of dominating me? Or to deliberately infect me with something?

Wednesday, August 18, 2010

In the morning, before work, Julian sits down next to me on the bed and puts his chin on my shoulder as if he's going to kiss me on the cheek. Instead, he burps in my face. It's one of the most disgusting things I've

Who has received this money or who has the right to decide how it is used is unclear. Julian or WikiLeaks? I'm starting to understand what I didn't grasp before he came here and what being the founder of WikiLeaks means. "Mr. WikiLeaks" summarizes it very well.

Julian stays up the whole night working on something. He doesn't bother me, but it's starting to become quite uncomfortable. He knows that I want him to move out, and he has promised to. Yet, even so, he has come back and made himself at home without apologizing, without attempting to explain why he can't move out, as if it goes without saying he's entitled to hold onto my key. Someone is unlawfully occupying my home, and this is a completely new situation to me. I don't know what to do about something like this.

    I ask Johannes if he can help me, but he seems aware of his friend's strategy for finding places to stay and doesn't have any tools to help. Donald, on the other hand, seems less accustomed to Julian occupying other people's homes. So, I call him instead.

"Donald, what should I do? I can't stand it."

He doesn't have any answers either, but as we continue to talk, very briefly, about how Julian seems to prefer to stay with women, Donald says:
    "Julian is the only man I've met who makes a pass at one hundred percent of all the women he meets. The other day, he hooked up with an American

I respond, *"He's not here, was planning to sleep with the cashmere girl every night, maybe he accomplished that last night?"*

"Bad taste! Do you have her number?"

"Not sure if he has taste at all (honestly), but she was cute, wasn't she? No, unfortunately not, works at [a museum] and email address, that's all I know."

Julian returns that evening. He still has the key. I feel sorry for him; he has nowhere to go. The feeling I had at the restaurant that first night, as though he needs someone to take care of him, returns. He needs me. He's a handful, but he isn't a bad person; he just has a few problems—as we all do. It's equally true that I feel I was subjected to an assault. The truth is not found in a definite form here; there are multiple truths. Double emotions, black and white at the same time, emotions in gray areas. I make my decision based on his having showered. I decide once again not to make a scene but to let him stay one last night.

Someone has given him Tove Klackenberg's book *Påtaglig risk att skada*. He giggles and holds up a note he received along with the book:

Dear Mr. WikiLeaks.
I think you will find the quotes on page 65, 79, 87, 97, 131, 137, 165, 181, and 201 to be quite of august.

There are large banknotes on the specified pages, and it's obvious that both the donor and Julian believe that Julian is Mr. WikiLeaks. Neither of them seems to care about the difference between him and WikiLeaks.

After a brief meeting, I see the president of Reporters Without Borders walk out of the room and briefly ask him about how it went, but he just shakes his head. When he leaves the office, I ask Julian the same thing.

"I left him shaking in his boots," Julian responds with a smile of superiority.

It was a meeting with an important organization aiming to establish cooperation, but Julian is obviously satisfied with having succeeded in frightening its representative.

Who can actually demand accountability if Julian ruins WikiLeaks? There does not seem to be any board or auditor, or management with the mandate to dispatch someone else in those contexts where Julian is ineffective. Is WikiLeaks even an organization? Or is it rather a personal brand, impossible for anyone but Julian to control?

When I return home very late after work, Julian still has a bunch of stuff in my apartment, but he isn't here. He's somewhere else, and I don't contact him to find out where. It's a big relief to get my home back.

Tuesday, August 17, 2010

Johannes texts me, *"Good morning. Can you remind J that we have a meeting at noon at the Swedish Union of Journalists. Incidentally, I suspect he's sleeping and unfortunately, I don't have time to pick him up today…"*

appointment for eight days' time, which is when I can do a test for chlamydia and gonorrhea; they think syphilis and HIV are also relevant, but for that, I need to wait three months.

Julian is going to chat with *Aftonbladet*'s readers a little later, and we decide he should do it in my office at the Social Democratic Party's headquarters. We run into former prime minister Göran Persson in the elevator. I'd tried to say hello to him before and didn't get a response, but with Julian next to me, he wants to shake hands. In his somewhat drawling Central-Swedish-accented English, he says, "Mr. Assange, you should know that there is tremendous support for your work in Sweden."

Julian is popular at all levels. At the same time, his façade is beginning to crumble.

As I get to know him, I see more and more of his personal shortcomings and how they negatively impact the WikiLeaks organization. One example is the meeting with the president of Reporters Without Borders, an organization that, along with the Swedish Union of Journalists and Amnesty, is very close to WikiLeaks on issues of freedom of expression and transparency. But Reporters Without Borders have also criticized some of WikiLeaks' actions, such as that they don't protect their sources well enough and that their public releases don't account for privacy issues. We manage to arrange the meeting on short notice, and they are interested in cooperating; they especially want to support WikiLeaks in trying to resolve what criticism has pointed out.

the saying "to play with fire." 2. Threaten to reveal his odor to Expressen. 3. If nothing else works—put his computer in the shower.

Haha, ok, sure, but couldn't you just ask some cute Pirate babe to make it a condition before she takes him home or point it out to him herself or something? At least I forcibly washed his clothes...

I discuss Julian's personal conduct, hygiene problems, and similar issues very frankly with both Johannes and Donald. All three of us must repeatedly treat Julian as the child he acts. Both Johannes and Donald have been like parents to Julian these days. They keep his schedule, give him rides, and remind him of both personal and professional things. I am clearly a part of the team now. A lot of our contact goes toward trying to organize Julian's life, but I'm starting to feel like I don't have the time or energy to be responsible for this man's nutritional intake and hygiene or serve as his answering machine anymore.

I seek out a sexual health clinic and talk to a couple of different midwives. I tell them what happened—that I was exposed to a risk of infection against my will—but I feel foolish when I mention details about why it feels so uncomfortable. They seem to think that it's none of their business to assess or comment on my activities, and I accept that. Sometimes sex doesn't feel fun; obviously, that's totally normal.

I want to get tested for STDs, but that's not possible. Enough time hasn't passed yet. I make an contact with have and mixes WikiLeaks up with Wikipedia, thanking him for this important grassroots-driven information source. Julian is pleased even with the misdirected appreciation. The mood surrounding us helps me to deny and minimize all he's done over the last couple of days. If he can mean so much to so many people, then his thoughtless lack of responsibility and ill-concealed contempt for women's rights becomes tolerable. Maybe even less likely.

We eat dinner with the Pirates, and I discuss some press inquiries with party leader Anna Troberg. We take a picture, then go home.

Julian plans to go to Enköping but gets stuck on his computer. He stays in my apartment yet again but doesn't sleep in my bed. I don't know if he sleeps at all; I don't think he does.

Monday, August 16, 2010

His hair is incredibly greasy, his TV makeup is still on, and his shirt sticks to his back.

"I'm doing a load of laundry, Julian. Give me your clothes. They're filthy. And while I'm down in the laundry room, you need to shower," I say.

He nods. When I come back up, he's in fresh clothes, but the makeup is still on. I text Johannes:

Hi, I've told him three times now that he needs to shower. He smells awful. I can't stand it! You're his best Swedish friend. Can you come up with some way to solve the problem? Thanks, Anna

Ha ha ha! Alternative 1. Pour lighter fluid on him and explain